Watershed
in
Europe

———

Watershed in Europe

Dismantling the East-West Military Confrontation

Jonathan Dean

Union of Concerned Scientists

Lexington Books

D.C. Heath and Company/Lexington, Massachusetts/Toronto

Library of Congress Cataloging-in-Publication Data

Dean, Jonathan.
Watershed in Europe.

Includes index.
1. Europe—National security. 2. North Atlantic
Treaty Organization.   3. Warsaw Treaty Organization.
4. Arms control.   5. Nuclear arms control—Europe.
I. Title.
UA646.D42 1987   355′.03304   85–45021
ISBN 0–669–11120–1 (alk. paper)
ISBN 0–669–11121–X (pbk. : alk paper)

Published simultaneously in Canada
Printed in the United States of America
Casebound International Standard Book Number: 0–669–11120–1
Paperbound International Standard Book Number: 0–669–11121–X
Library of Congress Catalog Card Number: 85–45021

The paper used in this publication meets the minimum requirements of
American National Standard for Information Sciences—Permanence
of Paper for Printed Library Materials, ANSI Z39.48–1984.

ISBN 0-669-11121-X

86 87 88 89 90 8 7 6 5 4 3 2 1

To my father, Kenneth Dean,
and to my wife, Theodora,
two of the rare people who have
known how to distill cheerful love
from every adversity and, with it,
to make life happier
for all whom they meet

Contents

Figures and Tables

Preface

It is impossible to overlook the problem that is the subject of this book: the NATO–Warsaw Pact military confrontation, the largest peacetime military concentration in human history. It comprises the greatest destructive potential ever assembled, including, according to NATO figures, over 10 million men in active-duty military forces, over 200 ground force divisions, 40,000 heavy tanks, 10,000 combat aircraft, and over 2,600 naval vessels in the seas bordering Europe. In addition, about 15,000 nuclear warheads for tactical and intermediate-range delivery systems are deployed in Europe, including the western Soviet Union, not to mention the strategic warheads targeted at this same area by both superpowers.

This huge force concentration consumes at least two-thirds of the total yearly expenditure for armed forces of all the countries of the globe, now running at about $1 trillion annually. It accounts for well over half of the military budget of the United States and at least 60 percent of the Soviet budget. Conflict generated by this confrontation or spreading to it from another area could be the source of all-out nuclear war between the United States and the Soviet Union, which could mean the end of our species. This conglomerate of military forces is so large and so lethal that it also entails a high potential for conflict through human or technical error, misperception, or miscalculation. Like the U.S.-Soviet nuclear standoff, the East-West confrontation in Europe lowers over the world political landscape like an immense volcano that could become active at any time.

This book tries to forecast the future of the NATO–Warsaw Pact confrontation over the next twenty years. It differs from many other treatments of this subject in several respects. It does not suggest that disaster will overwhelm the United States and its European allies in the absence of far-reaching steps to augment NATO military forces or radically reform NATO's military strategy. Instead it suggests that existing NATO strategy is suited to NATO's military and political situation and that NATO forces, though they have known defects, are adequate to deal with the most frequently cited contingencies or are within close range of becoming so. Nor does it suggest that catastrophe may strike in the absence of far-reaching steps to reduce NATO and Warsaw Pact armed forces through arms control. Despite built-in risks that should be lowered and despite continuing escalating competition in some especially dangerous types of weapons, the military situation in Europe is relatively stable.

The analysis presented here suggests that the peak of the East-West military confrontation in Europe has probably passed—that the watershed of the book's title has been reached—and that there is a possibility over the next twenty years of the gradual decline or attrition of the confrontation under the combined impact of arms control, political measures, and budgetary shortages. The main contingency for which the NATO alliance was established—to deter or repel deliberate Soviet attack aimed at the conquest of Western Europe—has become increasingly remote, so remote that it is now negligible.

This conclusion, however, does not in any sense justify a further conclusion that there is no longer any risk of war in Europe. Conflict could break out under several other contingencies. War unleashed by remote contingencies is no less catastrophic for those concerned—all of us—than war starting from more probable causes. Strong NATO forces are still needed. Moreover, even if the principal conclusion is correct in the general sense, it is not reflected in the force structure of the two alliances. The upward pull of adding more effective armaments to both alliances is stronger at present than pressures making for reduction of the confrontation. Even if downward pressures come to predominate, they will be stronger in the West than in the East, posing a problem of great difficulty to Western leaders.

Any conclusion that the possibility of Soviet aggression in Europe for the sake of conquest is no longer an active one is controversial and will be debated among experts. Yet the conclusion needs to be stated, discussed, and further examined. If it is correct, it means that the original function which the NATO alliance was established to perform is no longer necessary. This development increases the requirement for farsighted leadership of the alliance to a level far more exacting than in the period of the buildup of the military confrontation.

The book expresses only my own views. It has been written from the vantage point of a forty-year experience as a close observer of the East-West confrontation in Europe and a sometime direct participant in many of its aspects—the buildup of NATO forces in the 1950s and a decade of negotiation with Soviet officials in the 1970s. I am personally committed to negotiation as a means of helping to temper and dampen the confrontation. But I have tried as rigorously as possible to take a dispassionate and commonsense look at both the nature and dangers of the confrontation and the practical prospects of reducing it through arms control and negotiation.

This analysis has left me with the conclusion that the European confrontation and the rival military alliances that organize it will be with us for many decades to come. But there is no requirement for the confrontation to be at the present level of size, cost, and risk. To the contrary, now that the high point of the confrontation has been passed, the task is to move deliberately but also cautiously toward dismantling it to the extent possible.

It is the custom in books on this subject matter to urge NATO governments to act rapidly to improve the situation. The most urgent suggestion I make to these governments is to do nothing— and to spend a lot of time thinking about the dimensions of the new task facing them.

First and foremost, Western leaders will have to think in serious, not merely tentative, terms about how best to go about dismantling the confrontation in Europe while maintaining security and stability. Second, Western leaders will have to meet the downward pressures of their public opinion with new explanations of the need for defense that take into account changes in public perceptions of the Soviet threat and in the objective nature of the threat. Third, and directly related to the first difficulty, they will have to cope with a situation that entails an even greater possibility of aggravated friction between the United States and its European allies than we have seen in the past decade of controversy and drifting apart. Finally, they will have to cope with the fact that the problem of how to engage the Soviet Union in more effective reciprocal steps to lower the level of confrontation has been resolved only partially and that it may not be soluble to a much greater degree.

I want to thank the Union of Concerned Scientists for making it possible for me to devote my time and thought to this book. In addition, I want to thank Nancy Maxwell of the Cambridge office for her steadfast and discerning editorial work; without it, the book would not have been written. And I thank Barbara Disckind and Wendy Smith for their gallantry, patience, and skill in transcribing scrawled notes and illegible hieroglyphics.

About the Author

Former Ambassador **Jonathan Dean,** now Arms Control Advisor of the Union of Concerned Scientists, writes from the vantage point of many years spent as a close observer and sometime direct participant in various aspects of East-West security, arms control, and U.S.-European relations. In the 1950s, Ambassador Dean served in Bonn as liaison officer between the U.S. High Commission and the newly formed Federal German government and assisted in establishing the German armed forces. In 1968, following appointments in Prague, Katanga, the National War College, and the State Department, he returned to the American Embassy in Bonn for a tour as political counselor and deputy U.S. representative in the negotiations leading to the Four-Power Agreement on Berlin. He then served as deputy head of the U.S. delegation to the NATO–Warsaw Pact force reduction negotiations in Vienna from the beginning of these talks in 1973, and as the head of the delegation from 1978 to 1981. From 1982 to 1984, he worked on European security and arms control issues at the Carnegie Endowment for International Peace. Ambassador Dean is a frequent contributor to such publications as *Foreign Policy, International Security,* and the *Bulletin of the Atomic Scientists.*

Part I
Problems of NATO Defense

1

The End of the Western
Defense Consensus

From 1981 to 1983, Western Europe was rocked—and the United States shocked—by large and widespread public demonstrations against deployment of new U.S. intermediate-range nuclear forces (INF) on the territory of its European allies. The NATO Council had decided in December 1979 to deploy 108 Pershing II ballistic missiles in the Federal Republic of Germany and 464 ground-launched cruise missiles in Federal Germany, Britain, Italy, Belgium, and the Netherlands—all in an effort to lend more credibility to the U.S. nuclear deterrent against Soviet attack on Western Europe. Ultimately, millions of citizens participated in demonstrations in nearly every Western European country against deployment of the very weapons intended to defend them. It was an unprecedented protest against a major decision of the NATO alliance. Public opinion polls showed that the huge public demonstrations were not merely an impressively successful propaganda effort by left-wing radicals. A considerable majority in each of the countries that were to receive the new U.S. missiles opposed their introduction.[1] The INF controversy both reflected and intensified a long-term change in underlying values and attitudes of European political and public opinion on defense and arms control, a shift that is one of the major elements constituting a watershed in the East-West confrontation.

Although the crisis over INF deployment has been the most visible and far-reaching controversy over NATO's defense strategy in the 1980s, it has not been the only one. A related aspect of

NATO's defense strategy has provoked controversy among defense experts: the question of NATO's commitment to possible first use of tactical or intermediate-range nuclear weapons to counter a Warsaw Pact conventional attack that threatened to overwhelm Western Europe. In 1982, several prominent observers called for the United States and NATO to consider relinquishing this first-use strategy. Those raising the issue included Federal German Christian Democratic leader Kurt Biedenkopf, several respected British authorities on defense, conservative American commentator Irving Kristol, and four former U.S. officials of unusual eminence— McGeorge Bundy, George Kennan, Robert McNamara, and Gerard Smith. NATO's official response has been unambiguously negative, but the subject remains active. Most opposition parties in Western Europe now support a no-first-use policy, and the Soviet Union has pressed at the United Nations and at the Stockholm Conference on Disarmament in Europe for an international agreement that would commit its signers to a no-first-use policy.

Controversy over President Reagan's March 1983 announcement of a major U.S. program for space-based defense against Soviet ballistic missiles, the Strategic Defense Initiative (SDI), spread immediately across the Atlantic. European leaders, after their strenuous efforts to shore up the U.S. nuclear deterrent in the face of the heavy public resistance to INF deployment, were quick to react to this apparent U.S. desire to withdraw behind a shield protecting only the United States. They foresaw possible subsequent development of missile defenses by the Soviet Union, leaving between the two superpowers a Europe stripped of effective U.S. nuclear protection. Cabinet ministers of major NATO allies criticized "Star Wars" as a threat to the NATO alliance with high risk of further fueling the arms race between the superpowers.

And finally, the recurring question of U.S. troop commitments in Europe has again raised its head in the 1980s. In 1983, the U.S. Senate froze the level of U.S. forces in Europe, and in 1984, it threatened withdrawal of some of these forces unless European NATO governments decreased their reliance on U.S. nuclear weapons through improving their conventional forces.

Underlying these debates and disputes is the question of the role of nuclear deterrence in the defense of Western Europe and the more general question of what is the best defense strategy for Western Europe. Although most of their themes are not at all new, the form taken by the controversies of the first half of the 1980s—over the deployment of new U.S. missiles in Europe and the first-use strategy that these missiles might someday carry out, over a U.S. shield against Soviet missiles, and also over U.S. troop commitments in Europe—does provide unmistakable evidence that the firm Western defense consensus of the postwar years is seriously unraveling and, with it, the cohesion between Western Europe and the United States in the NATO alliance.

Evolution of NATO's Defense Strategy in Brief

The object of Western defense measures—as it has been from the end of World War II—is to prevent the extension of dominant Soviet influence over Western Europe through the use of Soviet armed forces, whether by conquest or by intimidation. For the United States, this aim is paramount among all foreign policy interests, next to defense of U.S. home territory, for achievement by the Soviet Union of controlling influence over the huge human and material resources of Western Europe would tip the world balance of power decisively in its favor. For the European members of NATO, the issue is one of survival. The first and most direct need has been for NATO forces capable of frustrating outright attack by Warsaw Pact forces. But it is not necessary to posit any immediate Soviet intention of attack on Europe to be concerned about this issue; the sheer military power and proximity of the Soviet Union and its past record of using military force to extend and maintain its influence are grounds for continuing worry. The practical day-to-day problem for NATO is to insulate the decisions of Western European political leaders from worries about adverse Soviet reactions and from possible Soviet pressures.

Within five years after the end of World War II, the Soviet takeover of Eastern Europe, their blockade of Berlin, and the outbreak of the Korean War, where both the Soviet Union and China provided material support to the North Koreans and Chinese troops participated in the fighting, convinced many in Western Europe and the United States that Soviet armed forces would advance into

Western Europe whenever a favorable opportunity presented itself. At that time, many—particularly the Germans, who had been driven back from the gates of Moscow by Soviet counterattack and were still reeling from the devastation of their armed forces at the hands of the Red Army—considered Soviet aggression imminent. As seen in the West, the Soviet Union was the greatest land military power in history, its forces held together by a militant ideology and assisted by increasingly well-equipped armies of East European allies. NATO was established in 1949 to try to deal with this threat.

But from NATO's inception, and ever since, the military balance has seemed hopelessly in favor of the Warsaw Pact. In the early 1950s, the NATO governments rapidly decided that they could not match the ninety-five divisions the Pact then could field in Eastern Europe. Instead of trying to match estimated Warsaw Pact strength man for man, tank for tank, aircraft for aircraft, the NATO coalition for thirty years has placed primary reliance on U.S. superiority in nuclear weapons, with conventional forces playing a lesser role. The reasons for this decision were many, including distrust of excessively large West German forces and the sensitivity of West Germans to the idea of prolonged conventional warfare on their soil. But in large part, the decision reflected the belief of the NATO allies that the Warsaw Pact's conventional advantages were so great that NATO would find conventional parity too expensive in economic and political terms, especially given the weakened postwar state of the European countries. During the period of clear U.S. nuclear superiority, the U.S. strategy for deterring Soviet attack against the United States was the threat of massive nuclear retaliation against the Soviet Union. The extension of this retaliatory threat to cover Soviet attack on NATO Europe came to be called extended deterrence. During the same period, the Soviet Union has had a policy, evidenced by its own pattern of nuclear deployments and public statements, of threatening to launch nuclear weapons against Western Europe in the event either of war with the United States or of attack by NATO forces on Eastern Europe and the Soviet Union. Taken together, these two policies made war in Europe the most plausible cause of all-out nuclear war between the two superpowers.[2]

By 1954, the United States had committed itself to protect its

NATO allies through a tripwire strategy, under which conventional forces would provide a shield to establish that a Soviet attack was actually taking place while the United States would deliver a counterblow of massive retaliation against the Soviet Union itself. Formally, the strategy was incorporated in a decision paper adopted by NATO's Military Committee known as MC-14/2. At the outset of the 1950s, the United States had the capacity to strike the Soviet homeland using B-29 and B-50 bombers deployed in the United Kingdom. By the late 1950s, a network of forward bases for U.S. Strategic Air Command B-47s and B-52s had been established in Spain, Morocco, Libya, and Saudi Arabia and also in Guam and Okinawa. In the mid-1950s, the United States began the deployment to Europe of tactical nuclear weapons: gravity bombs for fighter-bombers, warheads for short-range missiles, nuclear artillery shells, and demolition mines. The military rationale for this deployment, never fully developed, was to force Soviet forces moving forward for attack to remain dispersed rather than to concentrate for breakthrough; to destroy major bridges, airfields, and transportation bottlenecks on the forward route of Soviet reinforcements; and to deter the use of similar Soviet weapons.

In October 1952, the United Kingdom, which had decided that national security required it to have its own nuclear weapons, exploded its first nuclear bomb in the Monte Bello islands of Australia. France would also decide, in 1964, to build its own nuclear weapons. But Federal Germany, as a condition of its entry into NATO, made a commitment to its allies in 1954 not to produce or deploy nuclear weapons. In 1968, along with other countries in Western Europe and elsewhere, it repeated this pledge in a broader commitment in the Non-Proliferation Treaty, in which nations without nuclear weapons pledged not to acquire them. The Non-Proliferation Treaty formalized a situation that had existed since the outset of the U.S. nuclear commitment to the defense of Europe: with the limited exception of Britain and France, the European members of NATO were completely dependent on the United States for defense by nuclear weapons.

It is difficult to exaggerate the ineradicable anxiety, expressed in chronic outbreaks of doubt that the United States would in crisis fulfill its commitment, that this situation of dependence on a dis-

tant foreign country for a contribution considered essential to their
own national defense has caused the nonnuclear members of NATO.
This is so especially for the Federal Germans in their exposed position in NATO's front line. Ideally—it was the French who articulated the point with Cartesian logic, but Germans, Belgians, and
Dutchmen believed it too—the United States should react with a
warning nuclear explosion to the first Soviet tank to cross the dividing line. If the Soviets persisted, the United States should fire
one nuclear warning shot to land on Soviet territory and, if the
attack continued, should move to an all-out U.S. strategic attack
on the Soviet Union. The logic was that Soviet leaders' conviction
that Soviet attack on Western Europe would activate this chain
reaction leading to attack on the home territory of the Soviet Union
with U.S. strategic nuclear weapons would deter them from any
attack on Western Europe. But as Soviet nuclear capability to strike
back directly at the United States grew over the years, the logic of
this concept became increasingly questionable.

Germans and other continental Europeans articulated their recurrent anxieties over the resoluteness of the U.S. commitment to
use nuclear weapons in the defense of Europe in the form of a
doctrine of coupling. At the outset, coupling was less a military
doctrine than a criterion of intra-alliance solidarity for evaluating
U.S. actions as to whether they contributed to or mitigated European anxieties. Gradually coupling became identified with deployment of U.S. nuclear weapons in Europe and with the idea that, in
the event of war in Europe, these deployments would create U.S.
options for use of nuclear weapons short of strategic war, therefore
making a decision to use U.S. weapons more likely. A connected
concept was the idea of escalation dominance, the notion that U.S.
nuclear weapons in Europe should be of a number and type that
could establish superiority over the Soviet Union at every level of
size and range, or at every "rung of the escalation ladder." With
each advance in Soviet weaponry, the continental allies' desire increased to establish a fail-safe system of guaranteeing U.S. strategic
retaliation against a Soviet attack on Western Europe in a seamless
web of deterrence.

The first Soviet response to forward deployment in Europe of
U.S. nuclear weapons in the 1950s was to improve drastically the

air defense system left over from World War II. The Soviet Union also began the long march to nuclear parity, deploying a fleet of about 200 medium-range nuclear-capable bombers at Soviet bases within range of Western Europe. Starting in 1958, the Soviet Union began deploying a force of SS-4s and SS-5s, single-warhead medium-range nuclear-tipped ballistic missiles targeted on Western Europe (and U.S. bases in the Far East), a force that reached about 750 by the mid-1960s. The Soviets threatened to obliterate Western Europe in the event of either NATO ground attack or attack on the Soviet Union by U.S. strategic forces.

In 1957, in a momentous innovation, the Soviet Union launched the Sputnik satellite and, with the same launch, tested the first intercontinental ballistic missile (ICBM). For the first time, the home territory of the United States became vulnerable to Soviet nuclear weapons. The United States had no weapon of this speed and range in its arsenal. European leaders worried over the potential effects on the U.S. commitment to extended deterrence. In response, the United States took one of many fateful actions designed to shore up coupling and European confidence: the deployment in Western Europe of U.S. Thors and Jupiters, intermediate-range nuclear-armed ballistic missiles (IRBMs) capable of reaching Soviet territory. By 1959, sixty Thors were deployed in the United Kingdom and forty-five Jupiters in Italy and Turkey.

The Soviet reaction to this NATO decision to deploy U.S. IRBMs in Europe was agitated and immediate, as it was to be twenty-odd years later when NATO made a parallel decision to deploy a new generation of U.S. intermediate-range missiles in Europe. The Soviets endorsed the Polish Rapacki plan for a zone in Central Europe from which nuclear weapons would be excluded, proposed a summit meeting to discuss a German peace treaty, and launched the second Berlin crisis with Khrushchev's threat in November 1958 to sign a separate peace treaty with the German Democratic Republic, turning over to it all responsibility for access to Berlin. The deployment of U.S. IRBMs in Europe also appears to have led directly to Khrushchev's decision to attempt to equalize the situation by deploying Soviet intermediate-range missiles in Cuba in 1962.

In the course of the Cuban missile crisis, President Kennedy gave some assurances to Khrushchev about the U.S. IRBMs in Europe, which were withdrawn in 1963. The public version of the administration's decision to withdraw the Thors and Jupiters was that U.S. development of its own ICBMs made the IRBMs superfluous. But it would appear that there was some understanding with the Soviet Union not to deploy U.S. IRBMs in Europe, an understanding revoked by NATO's decision of December 1979.[3]

Western Europeans were disturbed by the 1963 IRBM withdrawals and not reassured by the prospect of protection by more distant U.S. ICBMs. In response, France moved to the decision to develop its own nuclear weapons. But for the nonnuclear allies, another solution to restore confidence through visible coupling had to be found. The first restorative action was an offer by the United States to assign to NATO command five U.S. nuclear submarines armed with eighty Polaris missiles. The second was the project for the Multilateral Force (MLF), which envisaged a number of surface ships operated by sailors of European NATO states carrying Polaris missiles whose warheads would be under U.S. control. But like the European Defense Community of a decade earlier, the project foundered, this time because of Western European discomfort at bringing the Federal Germans so close to a nuclear capability of their own. President Johnson killed the project in 1964. After the collapse of the MLF, another action was taken to rescue coupling: the establishment of the Nuclear Planning Group of NATO defense ministers, with the mission of giving nonnuclear NATO members a voice in the development of nuclear strategy, including development of criteria for use of nuclear weapons assigned to NATO. This measure tackled the coupling problem as it should have been handled, on the political level.

Yet Western European worries about coupling were not unfounded. By the early 1960s, steady advances in the quality and amount of Soviet strategic nuclear weaponry had made U.S. leaders apprehensive about any concept of direct resort to use of strategic weapons against Soviet territory in the event of Soviet attack on Western Europe. In the 1960 U.S. election campaign, John F. Kennedy charged that there was a missile gap in favor of the Soviet Union. Later information showed that the Soviets had deployed only four operational ICBMs at the time and that the U.S. lead in warheads was ten to one (two thousand to two hundred). Nonetheless, Soviet development of ICBMs was in fact making U.S. leaders increasingly cautious about their nuclear commitment to Europe.

After four years of discussion, Robert McNamara, the energetic U.S. secretary of defense, finally persuaded the reluctant continental allies to accept a new strategy of flexible response, which represented a compromise between the European and U.S. viewpoints. The continuing European desire was that the United States should threaten automatic, or nearly automatic, U.S. strategic response to Soviet conventional attack on Europe for effective deterrence of any attack, thus avoiding both the expense of matching the Warsaw Pact's conventional forces and the destruction of extended conventional war if conflict came. The United States wanted a European capacity for robust conventional defense of Western Europe in order to decrease the possibility of a requirement to initiate use of U.S. nuclear weapons. The strategy of flexible response was formally agreed in NATO in 1967, as MC 14/3, to the intense distaste of the French, who continued to think that any threat to use nuclear weapons should be automatic. The flexible response strategy, under which NATO is still officially operating, posits that in the event of overwhelming Soviet conventional attack on Western Europe, the United States will among other possible responses consider initiating use of nuclear weapons. The new policy thus continued NATO's earlier doctrine of possible first use of nuclear weapons by the United States to counter a Warsaw Pact attack on Western Europe but in a more attenuated form.

The Crisis of Extended Deterrence

In its various versions, the extended deterrence strategy was quite credible during the years of U.S. nuclear superiority. In carrying out a retaliatory strike, the United States would have little to fear from the Soviets, who were unable to put the U.S. homeland seriously at risk. Moreover, the United States had local superiority in the number and variety of its intermediate-range and tactical nuclear weapons. A great deal has changed since the mid-1960s, however, when the first serious European and U.S. doubts about the validity of extended nuclear deterrence led to the uneasy compromise of the flexible response doctrine. By the late 1960s, the Soviet Union achieved rough equality with the United States in strategic nuclear weapons, an equality codified in the SALT I agreement of 1972. In the 1970s, the Soviet Union greatly increased its intermediate-range and tactical nuclear forces, challenging U.S. superiority in this type of weapon. U.S. nuclear superiority, on which extended deterrence and the first-use strategy have been based, no longer existed.

Moved by the feeling that European interests were not being fully considered in the SALT II talks and also by extremely poor personal relations with President Jimmy Carter, which lowered his confidence in U.S. dependability, in October 1977, Federal German Chancellor Helmut Schmidt went public with his concerns. In a celebrated speech in London, Chancellor Schmidt stated that the SALT talks were codifying the strategic nuclear balance between the Soviet Union and the United States. As a result, the strategic nuclear capabilities of the superpowers had been neutralized. Consequently the significance of Warsaw Pact superiorities in conventional armaments and in nuclear weapons below the strategic range had increased. Chancellor Schmidt said, "Strategic arms limitations confined to the United States will inevitably impair the security of the West European members of the Alliance vis-à-vis Soviet military superiority in Europe if we do not succeed in removing the disparities of military power in Europe parallel to the SALT negotiations." Chancellor Schmidt said there were two ways to deal with the problem: to negotiate the level of Soviet forces down or to raise the level of NATO forces. A major gap in intra-alliance confidence had emerged.[4]

Chancellor Schmidt was speaking for European political leaders. But public realization in the West of the end of U.S. nuclear superiority and its consequences was slow. In fact, the change has not yet been digested intellectually by many in the United States, who are still in one way or another fighting the problem and refusing to acknowledge the factual situation. By the mid-1970s, however, increasingly large segments of the European public had begun to look more closely at what would happen if war broke out in Europe and existing NATO strategy had to be applied. They do not like what they see. This reaction is particularly strong in

Federal Germany, where an exposed location and the searing experience of World War II combine to create understandable sensitivity to dealing with the implications of NATO strategy in terms of fighting a war with Warsaw Pact forces.

More and more Western Europeans, mainly political conservatives, defense officials, and soldiers, have come to suspect that even in the event of overwhelming Soviet attack on Western Europe, the U.S. president would decide not to use U.S. nuclear weapons against the invading Soviet forces because the Soviets might retaliate with their large armory of strategic weapons directly against the United States. These fears have been heightened by the U.S. proposal to build the SDI. Such space-based ballistic missile defenses ultimately might give partial protection to the United States and the Soviet Union against the nuclear missiles of the other country, thus further eroding both the objective value and the credibility of U.S. nuclear deterrence against Soviet attack on Western Europe. The fears of these Europeans are also heightened by discussion of elimination of intermediate-range weapons through arms control.

At the same time, evidence of Soviet nuclear equality has elicited increasing nervousness in broad segments of the Western European public for the opposite reason. They fear that, if the West was losing in a conventional conflict in Europe, the U.S. president would in fact authorize use of U.S. nuclear weapons but against targets in Central or Eastern Europe rather than in the Soviet Union and that the Soviets would respond with nuclear weapons aimed at Western Europe. Each superpower would hold back in resorting to strategic attack on the other's home territory while Europe was devastated by the nuclear exchange.

In sum, the advent of U.S.-Soviet nuclear parity has highlighted the increasingly acute inner contradictions of deterrence theory, making deterrence nearly founder as a conceptual rationale for Western defense. In practice, rough U.S.-Soviet parity, which seems almost certain to continue for the indefinite future, will continue to undermine the validity of extended deterrence and flexible response as far as the European public is concerned. A strategy that requires the United States to commit mutual suicide with the Soviet Union for the sake of a distant European ally cannot reassure the Western European public even if it does retain residual deterrent effect for the Soviet leadership. Yet many Western Europeans who are concerned by the present form of U.S. support for Western European defense do not wish to reject that support outright. After so many years, the strategy of nuclear deterrence is thoroughly identified in Western European thinking with the general issue of U.S. participation in the defense of Western Europe. The result is great ambivalence in European thinking.

In many individual Western Europeans, frustration and anxiety over the role of U.S. nuclear armaments in the defense of Western Europe and the inability to resolve the dilemma it causes have been transmuted into resentment against the United States as the donor of this uncertain and potentially annihilating form of protection. Very often this feeling takes the form of animosity against both superpowers equally for continuing to make the survival of Europe dependent on the uncertain and potentially catastrophic state of their relations. In a British opinion poll taken in fall 1985 that asked respondents to indicate which of the two superpowers constituted the bigger threat to world peace, 33 percent answered the Soviet Union, but 32 percent answered the United States, and 28 percent answered both equally. Thus, 60 percent blamed the United States either directly or equally with the Soviet Union for world tensions.[5] Nuclear dependency, once implicitly accepted by Europeans as the basis of their sheltered position behind the shield of U.S. nuclear power, has become an increasing source of frustrated annoyance, with many potential consequences for relations between the United States and Europe. In a word, U.S. protection has become less effective and less valuable; U.S. nuclear defense, once the binding element of the Western alliance, has been transformed into the potential cause of its dissolution.

The increase in U.S.-Soviet tensions in the late 1970s and early 1980s compounded the strains that nuclear parity imposed on the United States's relations with European NATO members. With the Soviet invasion of Afghanistan and the complete collapse of U.S.-Soviet relations in late 1979 and the election in 1980 of a conservative president, Ronald Reagan, committed to placing restraints on Soviet behavior through increasing U.S. military power, the United States reverted to the containment approach of the early cold war period, sharply downplaying dialogue and negotiation with the Soviets. Despite this renewed U.S. focus on containment, the European countries, even in the face of the Soviet invasion of Afghanistan and the 1981 imposition of martial law in Poland, have tried to continue the two-track approach with the Warsaw Pact that they have adhered to since the mid-1960s.

The clash between the two positions eased materially as the Reagan administration moved to return to U.S.-Soviet arms control negotiation and summit meetings with the Soviet leadership. Yet the events of the early 1980s catalyzed changes in basic European attitudes that appear enduring. As a result of the increase in superpower tensions in the 1980s, Western Europeans came to fear the outbreak of conflict between the two superpowers because of miscalculation or because of competition in some Third World country more than they feared aggressive military attack on Europe initiated by the Soviet Union. A decisive factor in this change has been a marked drop in European respect for U.S. capacity to exercise leadership in international affairs during the Carter and Reagan administrations. This was not because of more favorable opinion toward the Soviet Union; esteem for the United States went sharply down while assessments of the Soviet Union continued uniformly negative. The decline was in part a reaction to the personal style of these two leaders but also in part a reaction to the disillusionment of the failures of the American system in Watergate and in Vietnam.

The significance of individual public opinion polls is open to question, but repeated polls over decades that show confirmed trends must be taken seriously. At the end of 1983, in polls taken recurrently since the mid-1950s, only one in three Britons (32 percent) expressed confidence in the ability of the United States to deal responsibly with world problems; 64 percent did not. Responses to this question over the years have been volatile, reflecting reaction to specific contemporary developments, but this figure expressed the lowest level of public confidence in U.S. leadership for twenty years. The figures for Federal Germany, a country that has traditionally had high confidence in U.S. world leadership, were equally dismaying: at the end of 1983, only 34 percent had confidence in U.S. leadership; 53 percent did not. These negative opinion trends continued after the crisis of missile deployment passed its peak.[6] In the spring of 1986, the same opinion shift was clearly expressed in assessing the U.S. anti-terrorist air attack on Libya: in a *Newsweek* poll, 71 percent of Americans approved of the action; 66 percent of Britons and 75 percent of Federal Germans disapproved.[7] This decline in respect for U.S. leadership was a necessary precondition for the current European tendency to consider the United States and the Soviet Union as equal threats to European security.

Another important factor in European opinion change is declining European fear of the Soviet Union. Even as NATO's nuclear superiority has eroded, the European view of the Warsaw Pact's conventional military might and of the possibility of aggressive attack by the Pact has become less fearful. In the early 1950s, the Soviet Union did have a marked preponderance in conventional forces because of the postwar disbanding of Western European and U.S. forces and the disarmament of defeated Germany. But today such pessimistic conclusions no longer appear valid. Both the quality and the morale of Warsaw Pact troops have come into question, and though Warsaw Pact forces maintain overall numerical superiority in armaments, Western forces have certain specific advantages.

The revised European assessment of the Soviet threat to Western Europe rests not only on an evaluation of military might but also on changed evaluation of Soviet society as a whole. In the 1950s, the key assumptions were that the Soviets had discovered the secret of generating nearly infinite political and military power on a worldwide basis through modern ideological totalitarianism. At that time, a large portion of the Western European population was loyal to communist parties subservient to Moscow. This loyalty posed a serious threat to Western defense in the event of conflict as NATO commanders envisaged large-scale efforts at fifth-column activities. The elites of Third World countries appeared to have a universally strong attraction to Soviet ideology and leadership.

Following much broader direct experience in the 1970s of the Soviet domestic system and its many weaknesses, the present European view of the problem-ridden Soviet system is far different. Following the 1956 Hungarian uprising, the 1968 reform movement in Czechoslovakia, and the Solidarity development of 1980–1981 in Poland, the locus of political crisis in Europe has clearly shifted from West to East. The Soviet Union faces a permanent political challenge in Eastern Europe. It has lost nearly all of its earlier influence over Third World leaders and intellectuals. The world communist movement is so riven by schisms that it has proved impossible for the past several years, despite strenuous efforts by Moscow, to hold a worldwide meeting of communist parties. A parallel development that directly diminished the fears of the 1950s was the waning of the Western European communist parties. Today, only the Eurocommunist Italian party has retained some voter appeal, and it preaches the need for independence from Moscow and even continued NATO membership for Italy.

The evidence of changed European evaluation of the Soviet threat is unmistakable: In the 1950s and early 1960s repeated polls showed that over 65 percent of Federal Germans considered the Soviet Union a military threat to their country. By the early 1980s, that figure had sunk to about 10 percent of the German population, and in the mid-1980s, after the INF crisis had subsided, the approximate average for Western Europe as a whole was also about 10 percent.[8] Thus, to many Europeans, U.S. nuclear protection for Europe now appears not only less valuable but far less needed.

There is an even more fundamental difference between dominant U.S. and Western European views of how to deal with the Soviet Union. Against the background of Europe's long and tragic history of victories and defeats, Western Europeans consider that they are going to have to live with the Soviet Union for the indefinite future in an up-and-down relationship of much competition and friction and some cooperation. Many Americans, on the other hand, are still thinking of some definitive solution of the problems caused by the Soviet Union, perhaps by Western military or technological superiority or through internal collapse of the Warsaw Pact. These Americans tend to see either the United States or the Soviet Union as winning their contest decisively in the foreseeable future. This U.S.-European difference of viewpoint is so central and so important in its future consequences that we will return to it later.

In coming years, the SDI promises to widen the gap between European and U.S. perspectives on defense. This program has great potential to arouse widespread negative reaction in European pub-

lics, largely because it taps directly into the residue of doubt about
the credibility of the U.S. nuclear guarantee left by the long INF
controversy. SDI also hits on the second main neuralgic area of
U.S.-European relations—the greater desire of Europeans to find
some tolerable modus vivendi with the Soviet Union—and has increased European feelings of frustrated, resentful dependence on
the technologically stronger superpowers. Although the rationale
for missile defense that President Reagan has put forward, with its
distaste for nuclear deterrence, will appeal to some segments of
unilateralist opinion in Europe, this appeal is limited by the European suspicion of the administration, by the realization that fully
effective missile defense for Europe is beyond reach, and by vig-
orous Soviet claims that the missile defense program is obstructing
U.S.-Soviet agreement to reduce offensive weapons. President Reagan's decision of May 1986 to repudiate the SALT II agreement
and no longer to abide by its limitations on strategic nuclear forces
elicited the same European fears of being caught in the middle of
mounting superpower tensions and competition in strategic
armaments.

The Heritage of the INF Controversy

These long-term changes in European outlooks were clearly reflected in the controversy of the early 1980s that surrounded the
issue of INF deployment. The NATO decision of December 1979
to deploy U.S. Pershing II missiles and ground-launched cruise missiles in Western Europe was an effort to counter European concerns
about the declining value of U.S. nuclear protection and to maintain the credibility of the U.S. extended deterrent and the NATO
strategy of flexible response. NATO officials argued that deployment of these missiles would reestablish a seamless deterrent link-
ing tactical and intermediate-range nuclear armaments with U.S.
strategic nuclear weapons. They believed that with the capacity of
the U.S. INF weapons to strike Soviet territory from the outset,
these weapons were a safer and more effective link to the U.S.
strategic deterrent than shorter-range tactical nuclear weapons
whose threatened use frightened only the European population, not
the Soviet leadership. But the effort backfired. Many Western Eu-

ropeans feared that INF deployment would instead increase the risk of a U.S.-Soviet nuclear exchange in Europe. Far from reassuring the population of Western Europe, the decision to deploy became a center of controversy, especially in the countries of the Northern Tier of Europe: the United Kingdom, Norway, Denmark, Federal Germany, and the Benelux countries of Belgium, the Netherlands, and Luxembourg.

Assessing the situation in retrospect after the deployment of the INF missiles, which began in late 1983, triggering Soviet withdrawal from the Geneva negotiations, it would appear that both NATO and the Soviet Union lost. Even with a maximum effort of public diplomacy—which included broad threats of an "ice age" in East-West relations and of a "pallisade of missiles" directed against Federal Germany and Western Europe—the Soviet Union failed in a stinging diplomatic defeat to block the deployment or to weaken the resolve of Western European governments. On the other hand, although the INF negotiations resumed in Geneva in March 1985, the political costs of the INF controversy for NATO were great. The entire affair was a disaster in terms of the original Western objective of reassuring European public opinion as to the continued value of the U.S. extended deterrent for the defense of Europe. As for the populations of both Western and Eastern Europe, they ended up just as many of them had feared from the outset: not with more security but with more nuclear weapons deployed by both sides.

For the West, the principal heritage of the INF controversy is that the European defense consensus of the past twenty-five years, supported by all major political parties in each NATO member country, has split down the middle. The mass public demonstrations against INF are no more. But the unilateralist and antinuclear program of the peace movement, as with so many popular movements of the past, has been institutionalized in the programs of political parties, in this case, of the opposition parties of the Left— taken over in most essentials by the Labour and Liberal parties in England, by the German Social Democrats, and by the Belgian and Dutch Socialist parties. These attitudes already heavily influence the views of Norway and Denmark. In particular, loss of the support of the British Labour party and of the German Social Democrats for missile deployment and for NATO's strategy of flexible response, and more generally, for NATO defense budgets of the future, is a serious blow to NATO, equivalent in long-term importance to General Charles de Gaulle's withdrawal of French forces from the NATO integrated command some twenty years earlier.

The underlying trend is serious and seems likely to endure. In their party conference in May 1984, the German Social Democrats rejected extended nuclear deterrence, calling for removal from Federal Germany of U.S. INF missiles and most tactical nuclear weapons, along with U.S. stocks of chemical weapons there. They are also asking for a German right of co-decision for the use of nuclear weapons. The British Labour party continues to advocate that all nuclear weapons should be removed unilaterally from British territory. Already Norway, Denmark, and Spain prohibit peacetime stationing of U.S. nuclear weapons on their territory. One long-term consequence of trends in the Northern Tier of Europe toward restrictions on the role of nuclear weapons could be refusal to permit peacetime stationing of U.S. nuclear weapons in Federal Germany and the Benelux countries, a kind of nuclear Scandinavianization of northern Europe, triggering active and serious pressure in the United States for withdrawal of inadequately defended U.S. forces from Europe.

The problem is not exclusively a left-wing phenomenon. Conservative German leaders Defense Minister Manfred Woerner and Franz Josef Strauss joined the Social Democrats in declaring that deployment of an effective U.S. ballistic missile defense could open Europe to Soviet conventional attack as never before and end the NATO alliance, as indeed it would if developments ever reached this point. The Bavarian leader Strauss has also joined the Social Democrats in the call for a German right of co-decision. Because of pressures from its middle-of-the-road Christian Democrats, the Netherlands had to postpone the decision to deploy cruise missiles on its territory for two years, before finally taking it by a narrow vote in early 1986. Belgium was able to decide only in 1985. The minority Danish government, under pressure from Socialists in the Danish Parliament, refused to contribute to the common fund for INF infrastructure in other countries. Prime Minister Andreas Papandreou says U.S. nuclear weapons have to go from Greece to permit it to participate in a Balkan nuclear-free zone. And he joins others in calling for a freeze on U.S. and Soviet production of nuclear weapons, which also has received the endorsement of the pope.

It is important to follow how the dynamic of this opinion shift, seen first in the peace movement and now in the programs of opposition parties, appears to be operating in the ideas of individual West Europeans. A large number of Europeans have been caught in a classic situation of attitude change: they hold views sharply inconsistent with one another. On the one hand, they have a positive view of the alliance with the United States. Public support for NATO continues high in all Western European member countries (even in Spain, a special case on historical grounds). Moreover, the great majority of Western Europeans distrust and suspect the Soviet Union. Although fear of war has decreased in Western Europe, there has been no increase whatever in sympathy for the Soviets. On the other hand, many Europeans who support the idea of continued military alliance with the United States oppose specific major policies of that alliance or of the United States: INF deployment, the strategy of flexible response, and to some extent the SDI program, as well as U.S. policy on such issues as how to treat communist influence in Nicaragua, economic sanctions against the Soviet Union and Poland, the Mid-East, and a widening range of economic issues where members of the European Community have interests which conflict with those of the United States.

Events have continued to keep this conflict of views salient in the minds of these Europeans. Combined with other opinion trends already described—especially the tendency to discount the military threat from the Soviet Union and decreased respect for U.S. leadership in international affairs—the result has been instability of the whole set of conflicting attitudes. The instability presses toward resolution and consistency by tending to establish the dominance of one set of conflicting beliefs through suppressing the other.[9] In many Europeans, negative attitudes toward specific NATO programs begin to predominate over favorable attitudes toward the NATO alliance itself, toward the concept of military alliance with the United States. The resolution of this conflict for many is the equidistancing "plague on both your houses" phenomenon of

blaming both superpowers, and further along the same path, "independent action" or unilateralism, the conclusion that only through
unilateral action on disarmament in Europe can Europe break out
of the vicious circle of superpower rivalry. This process of change,
which goes on in the minds of politicians and public alike, is severely undermining positive attitudes toward the NATO alliance
with the United States in significant opinion groups, especially ed-
ucated younger people. It is steadily eroding the cohesion of the
NATO alliance.

At issue here is not a temporary fluctuation of public opinion
moved by current developments of limited duration but an ingrained shift in major values, which, if further consolidated, can
exist for decades to come, passing the qualitative divide from an
opinion trend to become a strong political force. The trend is seen
most strongly in Federal Germany, long the most loyal U.S. ally in
continental Europe because of its deep fear of the Soviet Union and
widespread belief that only U.S. power can contain Soviet pressures. In that country, the strongest single foreign policy sentiment
today across the entire political spectrum is increasingly deep-seated
exasperation and resentment over Federal Germany's dependence
on two great powers that are coming to be seen by many as equally
to blame for the continuation of their confrontation.

NATO public opinion is not NATO governments. But the latter follow along, however grudgingly. In the absence of progress
toward arms control or, on the other hand, of some important
negative action by the Soviet Union in the European context, there
is only one direction in which these developments can ultimately
lead, even if slowly and gradually: toward decreased support for
military budgets as most major items become contested on a par-
tisan basis, unilateral force reductions, and unilateral restrictions
on the role of nuclear weapons. Before a stage of determined unilateralism is reached, the trend to blame both superpowers pushes
individuals and governments into a stand-aside, nonparticipatory
role in U.S.-Soviet quarrels. We have seen it already with regard to
Afghanistan and Poland, and we will see it again.

Public opinion polls, especially those testing attitudes of the
under-forty age groups in the Northern Tier populations, who will
be the majority of their electorates in the next ten years, indicate

considerable possibility that unilateralist, antinuclear governments may be elected within the next decade in Federal Germany, the United Kingdom, or the Benelux countries. In Federal Germany, depending largely on the tiny margins of the electorate that will determine whether the Free Democrats and the Greens get the minimum 5 percent of the popular vote required to obtain seats in the Bundestag, a Social Democratic–Green coalition is possible in the 1987 general election or, more probably, in the ensuing general election in 1991. Similarly, a Labour–Social Democratic coalition in the United Kingdom is possible, if not in the elections that will probably take place in the fall of 1987, then in the following general elections. Governments of this kind would be committed to radical cutbacks in nuclear weapons and armed forces in general.

The initial problem if unilateralist governments actually come to power is perhaps not in their efforts to put their programs into effect in isolation. If elected, they are likely to press first for renewed joint efforts at arms control by the NATO alliance and only in the absence of success to move toward fulfilling their commitments to take unilateral action. But the shock effect their election would have on U.S.-European relations would be considerable and immediate.

In fact, the most alarming aspect of these developments, both actual and possible, is the dynamic cycle of reaction and estrangement that they can generate between Western Europe and the United States. Alienation between U.S. and European leadership groups creates openings for expansion of Soviet leverage where relatively little opportunity exists now. And European support for continued political relationships with the Warsaw Pact and tighter restrictions on the use of U.S. nuclear weapons in European defense, as well as the slowness of European NATO countries to improve conventional defense and increasing stand-aside sentiment in Europe on political issues, can strengthen U.S. tendencies to go it alone in world politics.

This may stimulate, among other things, U.S. pressures for unilateral withdrawal of U.S. forces, as shown in the June 1984 proposal by Senator Sam Nunn of Georgia to reduce forces in Europe if European NATO members did not increase their budgetary contribution to improvement of NATO conventional forces. The proposal was defeated but at the cost of continuing a similarly motivated Senate freeze on the level of U.S. forces in Europe. In the early 1960s and 1970s, the Mansfield resolution to withdraw some U.S. forces from Europe was blocked by insistent administration arguments that unilateral reductions would undermine the Western position in the pending talks with the Warsaw Pact on conventional force reductions. (See chapter 5.) But congressional pressures of the 1980s cannot be met by pointing to the mere continuation of NATO–Warsaw Pact force reduction negotiations, now in their thirteenth year without any agreement. As the atmosphere of sourness and mutual recrimination between the United States and Europe diminishes the mutual willingness to cooperate, the United States may slowly be pushed and pulled into relative isolation.

In a sense, NATO's main problem is its continued success in keeping the peace in Europe. The problem posed by the Soviet Union to Western Europe has shifted from preparation to meet possible imminent attack and preventing takeover by indigenous communist parties to the uneasy problem of living next door to a militarily strong great power. In this situation of decreased urgency, some continued drifting apart of the United States and Europe is inevitable. The issue is whether the drift will be orderly and evolutionary, maintaining an underlying disposition to cooperate toward common ends, or whether it will be attended by friction, recriminations, and cross-purposes that hollow out and erode the authority of the alliance and its power, which comes from the capacity to join together the capabilities of its member states in some program of joint action.

A New Defense Consensus?

The Western European debate over NATO strategy will not come to rest, if it does at all, until a new and broader consensus is reached on the two central issues of how best to defend the security of Western Europe and how best to deal with the Soviet Union. On the key question of whether a strategy based on extended deterrence and possible first use of nuclear weapons can receive adequate support over the long run from Western European public and parliamentary opinion, the answer seems an unambiguous no.

The Soviet capacity over the past forty years to overcome a vast U.S. technological lead and to match U.S. performance in most nuclear weapons would appear to indicate that the United States cannot regain decisive and enduring strategic nuclear superiority over the Soviet Union and that rough equality in nuclear weapons will continue. (This conclusion applies also to the more remote possibility of some partial defense against ballistic missiles.) If so, no amount of patching can restore the U.S. nuclear deterrent to its former effectiveness or credibility.

Observers have drawn two main conclusions from the situation described here. One is that the changed U.S.-Soviet nuclear relationship necessitates a change in NATO strategy, a shift away from primary reliance on nuclear deterrence to primary deterrence through conventional forces. This is the conclusion drawn by Supreme Allied Commander Europe (SACEUR) General Bernard Rogers and by most NATO defense ministries. The second conclusion is that the situation calls for broader, more energetic effort in arms control affecting Europe.

This book analyzes both possibilities. If NATO can make real improvement in its conventional forces, it can decrease its reliance on nuclear weapons. In this event, the nuclear weapons issue would become less salient for European publics, and the erosive development of opinion that the nuclear issue is now driving might subside. In the long run, NATO leaders could either drop the concept of first use or allow it to atrophy, wrapped in increasingly restrictive provisos. Ultimately, when Western European opinion is ready, a revised NATO strategy could assign nuclear weapons to the only role that over the longer run public opinion in Western Europe and the United States will support: deterring the use of nuclear weapons by the Soviet Union. To implement this more limited but still vital deterrent function, up-to-date U.S. nuclear weapons of various types would still have to be dedicated to the defense of Western Europe. But the revised strategy would place primary reliance for deterrence of conflict on conventional forces and only secondary emphasis on nuclear deterrence.

In the meantime, a no-first-use commitment on its own, without steps either to improve conventional defense or to reach broader arms control agreements with the Soviet Union, would have purely declaratory effect and for that reason does not seem desirable. If coupled with specific arms control measures, it might make sense and could provide some inducement to the Soviet Union to agree to such measures. At present, however, most NATO governments hold strongly the view that NATO should retain the flexible response strategy as an essential part of the strategy of extended nuclear deterrence, which for them remains the best guarantor of peace in Europe. Consequently NATO is not likely to relinquish flexible response and dependence on nuclear weapons to cope with possible Warsaw Pact attack at least for the next several years.

Nonetheless, events have already made clear that the NATO decision to deploy INF missiles rested on a misconception about the nature of extended deterrence. The real basis for extended deterrence is not the flexible response strategy or the related concept of coupling, which over the years has come to mean efforts to guarantee U.S. nuclear response to Soviet conventional attack on Europe through a hardware solution, by deploying various types of U.S. nuclear weapons in Europe. The real basis for extended deterrence is the continued maintenance of U.S. equality with the Soviet Union in strategic nuclear weapons, the maintenance of a close political relationship between European and U.S. leaders so that each can have confidence in the decisions of the other, and the retention of U.S. ground forces in Europe. The consequent automatic involvement of these U.S. forces in conflict through a Soviet attack on Europe means for the Soviet Union that there would be a worldwide war with the United States, whether nuclear or not, in which the future of the entire Soviet system would be at stake. Conversely the withdrawal or sharp reduction of these forces would signal to European and Soviet leaders alike that the U.S. security guarantee for Europe had been withdrawn. The problem that the INF controversy and the other developments described here have brought is that by unleashing controversy over surrogate remedies, they threaten the continuation of these real U.S. guarantees for European security.

It is probable that the damage to defense morale in Europe and to U.S.–European relations through the INF deployment has already outweighed whatever gain for the defense of Western Europe and for the credibility of extended deterrence may have accrued from the INF deployment. The INF controversy, however, has had two effects on NATO publics that in the long term may be positive. It made many Europeans focus for the first time on defense issues and on the need for defense, leaving an enduring sensitivity to these issues, and has contributed to a long-overdue reevaluation of the nature of the Soviet threat. And it has led to a critical attitude toward the configuration and posture of NATO defense forces and to the development of many imaginative ideas for defense. If well handled, the current dissatisfaction in Western Europe over nuclear deterrence could in the long term have a productive outcome: it could finally convince the Western Europeans, especially the Federal Germans, to take conventional defense more seriously, the topic to which we turn in chapters 2 through 4, and it could convince both the United States and European governments to take arms control more seriously, the subject of part II.

Notes

1. In this book, I do not intend to document each statement of fact or opinion with already published material. In most cases for main points of the argument, I cite a general or specific reference. Regarding opposition to INF deployment, in December 1983, at the height of the controversy over INF deployment, 51 percent of British respondents in a repeated poll opposed INF deployment; 45 percent supported it. In the Federal Republic of Germany, 56 percent opposed deployment and 29 percent supported it. U.S. Information Agency, Office of Research, "Public Image of US Policies Worsens in Britain; German Opinion Remains Largely Negative," research memorandum, (February 6, 1984), pp. 9–12.

2. Details of the evolution of NATO's strategy of extended deterrence can be found in two excellent books: Lawrence Freeman, *The Evolution of Nuclear Strategy* (New York: St. Martin's Press, 1981), and David N. Schwartz, *NATO's Nuclear Dilemmas* (Washington, D.C.: Brookings Institution, 1983).

3. See the four-part series of articles by Walter Pincus in the *Washington Post* in the summer of 1983, particularly "Standing at the Brink of Nuclear War," *Washington Post,* July 25, 1983.

4. Helmut Schmidt, "The 1977 Alastair Buchan Memorial Lecture," delivered October 28, 1977; text in *Survival* 20 (January–February 1978).

5. The British poll, a Gallup poll taken Oct. 10–Nov. 11, 1985, was published in *Gallup Political Index,* Report 304, December 1985. See also U.S. Infor-

mation Agency, Office of Research, "West German Attitudes Toward the US and the Alliance," Research Memorandum, January 5, 1984, pp. 2–3. This report contains the findings of a survey on German opinion commissioned by the opposition Social Democratic Party of the Federal Republic of Germany.

6. Further figures are given in Research Report R-4-82 of the U.S. Information Agency, Office of Research, "Trends in US Standing in West European Public Opinion," February 1982, pp. 11–12. For continuation of attitudes of low confidence in U.S. leadership, see Stephen F. Szabo, "European Opinion after the Missiles," *Survival* 27:6 (November–December 1985), a first-rate survey.

7. *Newsweek,* April 28, 1986, p. 22.

8. See Gregory Flynn and Hans Rattinger, eds., *The Public and Atlantic Defense* (Totowa, N.J.: Rowman and Allanheld, 1985), pp. 116–118, 370.

9. The most convincing theory of attitude change is found in Leon Festinger, *A Theory of Cognitive Dissonance* (Evanston: Row, Peterson, 1957), and subsequent publications. I mention it here because many U.S. and European officials wrongly believe that positive European attitudes toward the general idea of NATO as an alliance with the United States can withstand any amount of negative buffeting and remain unchanged.

2
The East-West Military
Confrontation: War in Europe

How ambitious or modest should be the goals of NATO's conventional defense? In all-out war, on the basis of full mobilization, the United States and other non-NATO countries—among them Japan and possibly the People's Republic of China—would be engaged in air, naval, and ground combat with Soviet forces all around the periphery of the Soviet Union. NATO forces in Europe could not defeat the entire armed forces of the Soviet Union on their own, nor would they be called upon to do so. By reaching for an objective on this scale, even by implication—and sometimes the figures presented to illustrate NATO's mission do imply such an objective—NATO does itself a disservice in terms of defining a defense objective, and defense budgets to carry it out, that can be sustained by European public opinion over decades to come.

On the other hand, NATO forces can and should be expected to deal with a Soviet blitz attack using forces in place in Eastern Europe. NATO forces must also be able to maintain a base for rapid mobilization that could deal with that portion of Soviet forces—those in the western Soviet Union—that could be brought to bear in Europe in the event of worldwide war. Thus the mission of NATO forces in the event of war, difficult as it would be, is more specific and circumscribed than is sometimes thought.

The likelihood of direct attack on Western Europe by the Soviet Union is low. Nevertheless, it is possible that the Soviet Union would attack Europe out of fear of war with the West, perhaps fear of U.S. nuclear attack triggered by conflict in a third area. In such a case, Soviet forces might seek to move into Western Europe in order to hold it as a hostage against U.S. strategic attack on the Soviet Union itself or as an alternative power base of last resort if large parts of the Soviet homeland were destroyed by U.S. nuclear weapons. Because of the common border between NATO and Warsaw Pact troops in Germany, a large-scale uprising in East Germany also presents a possibility of conflict with the Soviets if the Soviet leadership made a panicky decision that the best way to deal with the problem was to move forward in order to prevent effective Western help to East German insurgents. However, Federal Germany's policy in relation to East Germany is keeping the risks of an uprising there to a minimum. (See chapter 11.)

All of these contingencies appear remote—and justly so. In fact, most NATO leaders currently see only a low possibility of Soviet attack on Western Europe. Most, however, also ascribe the absence of Soviet attack directly to the existence of NATO forces and to the U.S. nuclear deterrent. The clear implication is that the Soviet Union might well attack Western Europe if it were not for these obstacles. In fact, it is quite possible, even if there were no NATO at all, that no Soviet attack on Europe would be forthcoming; the costs to the Soviets of such an attack, even a successful one, would be very high.

Nonetheless, powerful, tank-heavy Soviet forces remain deployed in forward position in Central Europe. And although their main purpose appears to be political control and propping up shaky East European communist governments, their armaments and equipment have steadily improved. No responsible Western European leader would want to make the security of his or her country dependent on the assumption that Warsaw Pact forces would not under any circumstances attack Western Europe. Hence, for the indefinite future, there will be a continuing need for counterbalancing NATO forces. The question is whether these forces must be organized as they now are, or be as numerous and as expensive as they now are, to perform their purpose.

NATO's second major purpose is to ensure that Western European governments can make their decisions without fear of ultimate Soviet military intervention. If there were no NATO forces in Europe and Europe were dependent solely on the deterrent effect of U.S. conventional and nuclear forces outside Europe, then Warsaw Pact forces in Eastern Europe might still be deterred from attack, but they might have a considerable capacity to intimidate Western Europe. Even with large NATO forces, the chief concern of NATO's political and military leaders with regard to the Soviet Union remains that Soviet efforts to intimidate Western Europe based on Soviet military power may prove effective.

This issue is discussed more specifically later in the book. It should be emphasized here, however, that the real key to European resistance to Soviet threats is less NATO armed forces at any specific level of manpower or armament than it is the resoluteness of European leaders based on close political understanding with the United States. The combination of NATO forces, including U.S. forces, in place in Europe and close support from a United States insistent on maintaining its own bilateral strategic and naval balance with the Soviet Union can effectively insulate Western Europe against Soviet pressures. Indeed, the Soviet capability to gain decisive influence over Western Europe either by aggression or political pressure is less than it is usually presented.

There remains, however, the residual possibility that real or apparent military or political weakness of Western Europe could present to Soviet decision makers a temptation that does not now exist. Despite divergent assessments as to their quality and potential use, large, well-equipped Warsaw Pact forces are deployed in Eastern Europe. Effective Western European defenses are therefore needed. They have to be real forces, not paper ones, because the assessments of political leaders on both sides are ultimately based on the assessments made by professional soldiers.

NATO's Defense Posture

Later we will discuss more specifically how the intentions and the military forces of the Warsaw Pact, actual and perceived, place certain demands on NATO defense. Yet considerations internal to the NATO alliance raise other, often conflicting, requirements. The West's recurrent internal debate over defense can lead to near despair about the viability of the Western coalition and to the conclusion that the alliance is its own worst enemy, more intractable than even the Soviet Union.

Forward Defense: The Product of NATO's Internal Dilemmas

Among the by-products of the crisis in the West over reliance on nuclear deterrence is increased public rejection of nuclear war fighting as an acceptable means of carrying out defense against actual attack by Warsaw Pact forces. But the search for a more effective conventional deterrent has brought discussion among NATO members right back to the same problem: rejection of war fighting in any form. If there were war in Europe, nuclear destruction would in reality be far greater than the consequences of conventional war, which in today's conditions probably would not involve strategic bombing of cities. Yet serious planning and organization for conventional warfare in Europe evokes the same degree of public and political resistance from Western Europeans as serious planning for nuclear warfare. The reasons are clear: memories of death and destruction in World War II remain active, and protracted conventional defense of Western Europe could result in destruction and loss of life, especially in frontline Federal Germany, at a high level.

NATO's internal dilemma remains ever the same. European opinion naturally wants a deterrent so effective that war will never take place—hence the emphasis over the years on the dire threat of U.S. nuclear retaliation against the Soviet Union. But U.S. defense officials have insisted with equal logic that the United States cannot be expected to resort immediately and automatically to strategic nuclear war with the Soviet Union under all possibilities of Soviet conventional attack on Western Europe—for example, an attack with limited objectives. They have emphasized that effective deterrence also depends on the capacity to fight effectively with conventional forces if conventional attack comes. But European political leaders still contemplate very reluctantly the costs of effective defense, both economic and human, if war actually had to be prepared for and fought.

Senator Sam Nunn authoritatively summarized the prevailing U.S. reaction to these European attitudes in a 1982 report to the

Senate Armed Services Committee. Under the heading "The Heart of NATO's Problem—A Strategy That Cannot Be Implemented," Senator Nunn stated:

> NATO's military strategy has been characterized as one of flexible response and forward defense. Flexible response has implied the use of tactical and/or strategic nuclear weapons in the event of a Soviet–Warsaw Pact conventional attack in Europe could not be contained by non-nuclear means. Forward defense has meant defense as near to the inter-German border as possible, with the aim of conceding minimum West German territory. This strategy was adopted at a time when NATO possessed pronounced strategic and theater nuclear advantages over the Soviet Union and the Warsaw Pact. NATO's quantitative inferiority in conventional forces deployed in or readily available for combat in Europe was deemed tolerable because nuclear superiority permitted the Alliance to escalate a conflict across the nuclear threshold to the disadvantage of the Pact.
>
> During the past decade and a half, however, the Soviet Union has managed to eliminate NATO's nuclear superiority at both the strategic and theater levels, while at the same time expanding its traditional advantages in conventional forces. By attaining strategic nuclear parity with the United States, the Soviet Union has severely undermined the credibility of U.S. strategic nuclear forces as a deterrent to a conventional attack on Europe. By deploying theater nuclear forces that are now superior to NATO's, the Soviet Union has reduced the effectiveness of NATO's tactical nuclear forces both as an instrument for defeating a massive non-nuclear invasion and as a deterrent to Soviet use of nuclear weapons. By enhancing its longstanding quantitative superiority over NATO in conventional forces with greatly improved quality, the Soviet Union has diminished the prospects for a successful forward defense.
>
> Under conditions of strategic parity and theater nuclear inferiority, a NATO nuclear response to non-nuclear Soviet aggression in Europe would be a questionable strategy at best, a self-defeating one at worst. Thus major responsibility for continued deterrence in Europe has shifted to NATO's outnumbered, outgunned and maldeployed conventional forces. Flexible response in theory has become inflexible response in practice.
>
> The United States' loss of strategic nuclear superiority, which

many observers regarded as inevitable, was not in and of itself fatal to NATO's flexible response strategy. Had the demise of strategic superiority been attended by retention of theater nuclear advantages and by creation of conventional defenses unambiguously capable of mounting an effective forward defense of Germany, the basic integrity of NATO's strategy could have been preserved. During the 1970s however, the Alliance chose to rely for the most part on the aging theater nuclear weapons deployed in the late 1950s and the early 1960s. Despite mounting evidence that the Soviet Union was mustering in Eastern Europe the capacity for a conventional blitzkrieg (thereby reducing the degree of warning time so essential for a successful forward defense), NATO's conventional defense posture vis-à-vis the Soviet-Warsaw Pact was allowed to deteriorate further.[1]

This is a classic statement of U.S. dissatisfaction over the uneasy compromise NATO has reached between U.S. insistence since the early 1960s on a robust conventional defense in Western Europe and European abhorrence of war-fighting strategy and consequent emphasis on nuclear deterrence.

NATO forces are a combination of heavily deployed nuclear weapons of all types, mainly U.S., of which only a minority serve a clear military purpose, and conventional forces with everything up front in the literal sense and with limited sustainability in terms of supplies of ammunition and other war stocks. NATO's lack of staying power in ammunition, motor fuel, and replacement equipment for a conventional war lasting more than several weeks has always disturbed U.S. defense planners. It is the basis for SACEUR Commander General Rogers's statement that NATO governments would have to consider use of nuclear weapons after only a few days of combat with Warsaw Pact forces.

But despite these recurrent concerns about NATO strategy and posture, perhaps European NATO governments are closer than U.S. defense planners to defining the right compromise between the low probability of war in Europe and the high costs of fully adequate conventional defense. In fact, NATO's overall flexible response strategy is not only a compromise between conflicting European and U.S. strategic interests, it is a realistic compromise. The same can be said of NATO's plan for fighting a specifically conventional war, the concept of forward defense.

At first examination, the critics are right. Forward defense, at least in its public versions, requires the front line of NATO conventional forces to stand firm and immobile under attack. It would not cede ground. Nor would it move forward deeply into enemy territory, even if successful in defense, lest NATO's defensive posture be misread. Locked into position, NATO forces would absorb the entire impact of a Warsaw Pact attack. They would then have to bring the attack to a halt and defeat enemy units on the spot.

Such a posture is intrinsically unconvincing. Even with heavy numerical superiority, which NATO does not have, success in carrying out such a strategy would be difficult. Despite NATO's lack of defensive depth, with NATO territory at its narrowest only a few hundred kilometers from the dividing line to the ports of the Low Countries, defense in depth still is the orthodox military answer to the desire to have a defense posture that is both effective and visibly defensive in nature. In the West, the doctrine of forward defense therefore contributes to the general belief that successful conventional defense of Western Europe is improbable and thus helps to set the stage for possible early use of nuclear weapons by the West. At the same time, forward defense, which concentrates NATO armored forces along the dividing line between NATO and Pact forces, may to Warsaw Pact leaders look suspiciously like a position for jumping off to a forward-moving attack, just as the tank-heavy Soviet position looks dangerously aggressive to NATO.

Retaliatory Offensive: An Alternative to Forward Defense?

A remedy for these problems of NATO strategy has been proposed by Samuel Huntington, who argues that what is needed is some threat of Western retaliation equal in significance for Soviet leaders to the threat of retaliation against the Soviet homeland, now lost with the loss of U.S. nuclear superiority.[2] Consequently NATO countries should seek some compensating form of conventional retaliation that could place some valued Soviet asset at stake. This compensating move, he suggests, should take the form of a strategy for a NATO retaliatory offensive—a conventional attack deep into East Germany and Czechoslovakia—in the event of Soviet attack on Western Europe, which would threaten the Soviet Union with loss of its control over Eastern Europe.

This strategy has two fundamental defects. First, it needs NATO conventional forces far stronger than present ones to carry it out successfully and at the same time hold Federal Germany against Pact attack. The second defect of the strategy is that although it expresses an objective that would make some sense in wartime if there were resources to carry it out, it is not right for peacetime. Under the proposed strategy, both Federal Germany and its NATO allies with forces on its territory would have to reorganize and redeploy their armed forces. They would have to agree that in case of need, Germany would be used as the point of departure for a mainly German-U.S. retaliatory attack on Eastern Europe. To be effective both as a deterrent to Soviet plans for possible attack and as a vehicle to restore public confidence in NATO defense, these changes would have to be highly public. But the last thing Federal Germany would want for its relations in either Western or Eastern Europe would be to adopt a defense posture that could provide any basis, however farfetched, for concerns that it was placing itself in a position where it could someday attempt to reunify Germany by force.

A publicized NATO strategy of deep counteroffensive would give back to the Soviet Union its one effective political asset in Eastern Europe: the capacity to exploit fears of Germany and NATO as a source of cohesion and public support for Warsaw Pact governments. Such a strategy would serve as a powerful lever for the Soviets to pressure reluctant Warsaw Pact governments for larger defense contributions and could also boost the morale and motivation of non-Soviet Warsaw Pact forces, whose present low state is an important deterrent to possible Soviet aggressive attack against the West.

In sum, forgoing more resolute and militarily effective defense postures like that recommended by Huntington is yet another result of the political restrictions placed on European defense by Germany's peculiar position. NATO forces cannot go backward, but they cannot be seen as poised to go forward either. However, it is already the case that if NATO's forward defense strategy proves successful in the course of Soviet attack, local sector commanders would have to move forward on a tactical basis to secure their positions, with some of the benefits of the proposed strategy. And already among the consequences of successful NATO defense against a Warsaw Pact attack is the implication that failure of that attack could well entail the unraveling of the Soviet system in Eastern Europe.

Living with Forward Defense

It is clear to both critics and adherents that the main reason for adopting the sometimes unconvincing Western military posture of forward defense is political. The main reason for the concept is the position taken by the Federal Republic of Germany—that is, the position of the Federal German government, political party opinion, and the attitudes of the German public. The adult population of the Federal Republic still has vivid memories of the step-by-step retreat of Hitler's Wehrmacht and the advance of the Soviet army, preceded by streams of refugees, through East Russia, Silesia, and Saxony with civilian and military war deaths of over 4.5 million people (about 400,000 U.S. servicemen died in World War II). And in today's Federal Republic of Germany, 30 percent of the population and 25 percent of industrial capacity lie within 100 kilometers—just over 60 miles—of the border with East Germany. It is understandable that there is strong resistance from the Federal Germans to any defense strategy that posits recoiling backward to gain time and space for counterattack, leaving millions defenseless; to any strategy that calls for forward movement in counterattack against the homes of fellow Germans, relatives and friends; and indeed against any form of protracted war, whether nuclear or conventional.

Instead of continually fighting the problem, Federal Germany's allies must accept as a matter of practical politics that NATO strategy for the defense of Europe reflects the values of the member states. Federal Germany, as the most important European NATO state in terms of the strength of its armed forces and its forward geographic location, justifiably has the greatest say.

But even if the principal reason why NATO has adopted the forward defense concept is political, this does not mean that the concept is as wrong as Senator Nunn, Huntington, and other critics would have it. The forward defense concept is not merely a reflection of the German desire to be defended on the spot. It has two clear benefits. First, the forward deployment of allied forces, especially the U.S. component, ensures that these forces would be engaged from the outset of any conflict with Soviet forces. This maximizes the deterrent by raising from the outset the near certainty that Soviet attack on Western Europe would mean worldwide war between the superpowers. Second, it ensures that the first engagement, if it comes, would have to be heavy and serious, no mere skirmish. This too increases the deterrent. Forward defense is therefore a posture that combines defense of the exposed German population with a high degree of deterrence. In fact, this posture, like the strategy of flexible response, is a reasonable compromise between political and military values. There may be conditions of improvements to NATO conventional forces and of arms control in which the strategy of flexible response could be modified. But the forward defense posture represents the best application available of the motives and values underlying Western defense, and it should be maintained in the future.

This short review of NATO strategy has described its rationale and also its weaknesses. Earlier we described how the controversy over the deployment of INF missiles mobilized public awareness of these weaknesses and resulted in a desire to reduce NATO's dependence on nuclear weapons. Before examining possible approaches to improving NATO's conventional defense posture in chapter 3, it will be useful to examine the nature of the East-West confrontation in Europe and the balance of forces between the NATO and Warsaw Pact alliances.

The Military Balance in Europe: What Do the Figures Mean?

Since NATO's foundation in 1949, Western military experts have been nearly unanimous in estimating Warsaw Pact forces as having considerable superiority over NATO forces in numbers of divisions and major armaments. Historically these estimates have been the ultimate justification for NATO reliance on nuclear weapons, as reflected in successive NATO strategies: "massive retaliation" with a tripwire of NATO conventional forces; the similar "sword and shield" concept that succeeded it; and, since 1967, the strategy of flexible response. This numerical superiority has also been the fundamental justification for successive improvement programs for NATO conventional forces.

NATO estimates conclude that the Warsaw Pact states together have a total strength of 6 million active-duty military personnel (ground, air, and navy) as compared to NATO's 4.5 million. These are the standing forces, without reserves. The Warsaw Pact is credited with 115 ground force divisions to NATO's 88; nearly 27,000 tanks to NATO's 13,500; and 2,250 fighter-bombers to NATO's 1,960. Warsaw Pact forces are also estimated to have an impressive numerical edge in fighter aircraft, attack helicopters, artillery pieces, and armored personnel carriers.[3]

But there is controversy over these numbers. Even for the figures on NATO forces, there are difficulties. For political reasons, French and Spanish forces are not assigned to NATO's integrated command. Consequently these forces are not counted in NATO figures, despite France's 10 ground force divisions and considerable air force and Spain's ground forces of roughly 4 divisions and smaller air force.

Not unexpectedly, NATO figures also do not match with those presented by the Soviet Union. It is only in recent years, in order to put its case before Western publics during the INF controversy, that the Soviet Union has departed from its tradition of secrecy in military matters and begun to publish its own force comparison figures. Soviet figures for 1984, the same year as the NATO estimate just cited, show not 115 Pact divisions but 78; not 88 NATO divisions but 94; and rough equality in tanks and fighter-bombers.[4] A comparison of the NATO and Soviet figures is shown in table 2–1.

How Many Warsaw Pact Forces?

What do these conflicting figures mean? How many Warsaw Pact forces would NATO forces have to take on in a Warsaw Pact

Table 2–1
NATO and Warsaw Pact Forces in Europe

	NATO Forces		Warsaw Pact Forces	
	NATO Figures	Soviet Figures	NATO Figures	Soviet Figures
Active-duty divisions	88	94	115	78
Tanks	13,470	25,000[a]	26,900	25,000
Fighter-bombers	1960	NATO has small advantage	2250	NATO has small advantage

Source: See notes 3 and 4 to this chapter.
[a]Includes Spanish forces and tanks in storage.

conventional attack on Western Europe? Consequently, how strong do NATO forces have to be?

The problem begins with the first figure cited: the figure of over 6 million active-duty Warsaw Pact personnel presented by NATO in its compilation of the force balance. For years, force balance figures used by Western experts showed that NATO had somewhat more active-duty military personnel than the Warsaw Pact. For example, the authoritative Military Balance publication for 1982–1983 issued by the International Institute for Strategic Studies in London (IISS) shows 4.9 million NATO forces to 4.8 million Warsaw Pact forces.[5] The editors of the NATO figures and more recent IISS publications have added to the earlier count of Warsaw Pact forces some 1.5 million Soviet general construction troops and other similar forces used by the Soviet government to construct railroads and buildings of all kinds, a useful means of exploiting conscript labor at low wages but not a serious addition to combat power. The more recent Western figures have been changed for presentational purposes to make the Warsaw Pact threat appear more impressive.

A second source of inflation in some Western figures is their inclusion of all Soviet armed forces throughout the Soviet Union, giving the implication that this is what NATO has to deal with in Europe. For example, the 1983 edition of the White Paper of the Federal German Ministry of Defense shows 253 Warsaw Pact divisions—but this number includes 53 Soviet divisions in the Far

East, 12 on the Iranian-Afghan border, and 15 strategic reserve divisions in the central Soviet Union.[6] Only 173 of the divisions are in the European Soviet Union and Eastern Europe. This method of presenting the problem inflates NATO's military mission by geographic distortion, making it appear more difficult or even impossible.

There is a third major distortion in many presentations by Western authorities of the Warsaw Pact threat, a distortion that accounts for many of the wide differences remaining between figures for Warsaw Pact divisions within the European Soviet Union and Eastern Europe: 173 according to the 1983 German White Book but 115 according to NATO's 1984 figures and only 78 according to both the most recent IISS handbook and the Soviets' own figures.[7] The problem here is that for presentational purposes, the German and NATO figures—the NATO figures on Warsaw Pact forces are the same as those used by the United States in its publications on the Soviet threat—overlook the fact that the majority of Warsaw Pact divisions are not combat-ready divisions but reserve divisions and then lump these reserve divisions together with combat-ready divisions in a single total.

A realistic assessment of the Warsaw Pact threat, then, must take readiness level into account. A more complex classification is under development, but NATO experts have long classified Warsaw Pact military forces into three categories according to readiness level, as the Soviet military authorities do themselves. Category 1 divisions are those with over 75 percent of their manpower present and on duty. These category 1 divisions are the only forces that could be used in a classic Warsaw Pact blitz attack with limited time (four to five days) for preparation. Category 2 Warsaw Pact divisions have only 50 to 75 percent of their manpower on active duty. These divisions would take a week or more to be brought to combat readiness. They could be used for reinforcement, but it is doubtful they could be used for a Pact attack with minimal preparation. Warsaw Pact divisions in category 3 are manned by only 10 to 50 percent of the personnel needed for combat. They would take thirty to sixty days to be brought to combat strength and would be involved only in a European or worldwide war of lengthy duration.[8]

How many divisions would the Warsaw Pact have at its disposal in Northern Europe north of the Alps for a sudden attack on NATO with minimum preparation of four to five days? Looking first at Soviet forces, the Soviet Union has available 30 category 1 divisions deployed in Eastern Europe: in East Germany (19), Czechoslovakia (5), Poland (2), and Hungary (4). In addition, there are in the Western Soviet Union (Baltic, Byelorussian, Carpathian, Leningrad, Kiev, and Odessa Military Districts) 2 category 1 Soviet ground force divisions, plus 4 divisions of airborne troops, a surprisingly low number. Adding these divisions together, we get a total of 36 category 1 Soviet divisions. If we add to this figure the 20 Eastern European divisions in Northern Europe classed by IISS as category 1 (6 East German, 8 Polish, 6 Czechoslovak) the total of Warsaw Pact category 1 divisions potentially available for a blitz attack on NATO in Northern Europe is 56.[9] This figure overestimates Warsaw Pact strength, in that some Warsaw Pact forces counted as category 1, including some Soviet divisions in East Germany, are well below 75 percent manning and readiness.

For its part, NATO would have in Northern Europe some 26 active-duty divisions: 12 active-duty Bundeswehr divisions; 6 brigades of combat-organized German territorial forces equivalent to 2 divisions; the equivalent of 6 U.S. divisions (5 divisions plus 3 brigades); 4 British divisions plus one brigade, and one Canadian brigade; one ready Netherlands division, and one ready Belgian division. This figure omits one Danish division which may or may not be ready, and 3 French divisions in Germany and 7 in France (figure 2–1).

These Warsaw Pact figures are imposing, but they are finite figures, not those of a numberless horde. On the average, NATO divisions are much larger than Pact divisions, with 18,000 men in Federal German or U.S. divisions, as compared with 13,000 in recently enlarged Soviet motorized rifle divisions or the 9,500 men of an East German armored division. German divisions actually have 22,000 men at full wartime strength when their assigned replacement personnel are taken into account, about twice the size of the average Pact division.

While diversionary attacks on NATO's northern or southern flanks may take place, any serious Soviet attack on Western Europe would have to win control of NATO's Central Front in Germany;

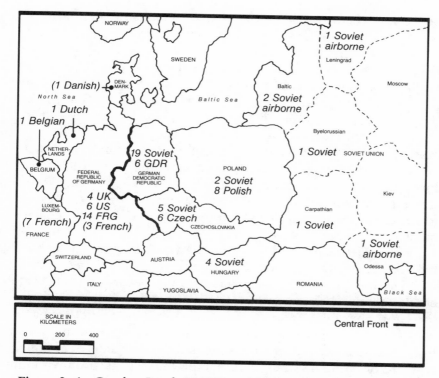

Figure 2–1. *Combat-Ready NATO and Warsaw Pact Ground Force Divisions on the Central Front*

this is the vital area for attack and for defense. Of all the contingencies of Warsaw Pact attack they fear, NATO officials most frequently cite the possibility of a standing-start attack on the Central Front with minimum preparation of four to five days to load ammunition and supplies and ready armaments for combat. But, before we go further in estimating the possible chances of success for such a Warsaw Pact attack on NATO, let us look more closely at the forces themselves.

How Do We Assess Warsaw Pact Forces?

The wide divergences in numerical counts of the East-West confrontation even among Western sources point not only to the unstated use of different criteria for counting and failure to distinguish between Warsaw Pact divisions that are combat-ready and those that are not. They also illustrate the major problem encountered by Western experts in weighing the NATO–Warsaw Pact force balance: the continued difficulty of obtaining reliable information on Warsaw Pact forces. Even inside NATO, there is great difficulty in counting active-duty forces actually present on duty at any given time. British Army of the Rhine forces may actually be in Northern Ireland on antiterrorism duty; Netherlands conscripts may be at home and on leave; part of the Federal German Bundeswehr may be out of the country on training; and the authorized levels of U.S. forces in Europe are often higher than actual levels because of training, rotation, and leave. But official figures for these Western forces are at least published in parliamentary budgets and defense ministry reports.

The Soviet Union and its Warsaw Pact allies consider that the tight security of their closed society gives them military advantage, and over the years they have maintained that security with considerable success. Western estimates of Warsaw Pact forces are therefore for the most part purloined information that remains fragmentary and has to be pieced together in the traditional intelligence mosaic, often through assuming that other units of a similar type are of the same strength or equipment level as a known unit on which specific information is available. For example, when new armaments are introduced, like the Soviet T-72 tank, the Western assumption is often that they will be introduced rapidly through the entire Warsaw Pact force, although it often takes decades before this actually takes place and sometimes it never does. In fact, although the Soviet T-72 tank, as its name indicates, made its first appearance in 1972, the Soviet division withdrawn from East Germany in 1980 was still equipped with T-54/55 tanks of a model introduced twenty-five years earlier. In fact, in 1982, well over half of Warsaw Pact tanks were still of this old model.[10] And as of 1985, only about 40 percent of Soviet units in Germany are equipped with the most modern Soviet tanks: T-64, T-72, and T-80.

U.S. intelligence experts who work on Soviet forces, the main but not only source of NATO figures, include some outstanding analysts with penetrating insights and excellent judgment. The same is true of European analysts. Nonetheless, professionally, intelligence experts are obliged to take a conservative, worst-case view of the capabilities of their adversaries in each individual assessment they make of some aspect of Soviet and Warsaw Pact forces. When these analyses are combined in an overall assessment of Warsaw Pact forces, especially in a situation where a large part of the information is unknown and gaps have to be filled through extrapolation, there is cumulative, built-in bias toward inflation of estimates. The NATO consultative process adds to this bias because the estimates compiled by individual NATO countries must in practice be negotiated between low estimates (often the United States's) and high estimates (often Federal Germany's).

How Good Are Warsaw Pact Forces?

A further difficulty of Western analysis of Warsaw Pact forces is that it focuses almost exclusively on quantifiable data. Yet information that can be put in figures deliberately excludes as unquantifiable a number of key factors of military evaluation, almost all of which bear on force quality. In its latest assessment of the East-West conventional balance in Europe, the IISS states, in a standard formulation of this point, "There are a number of elements which it is impossible to evaluate: the quality of units or equipment, geographic advantages, doctrine, military technology, deployment, training, logistic support, morale, leadership, tactical initiative, terrain, weather, political will, and alliance cohesion."[11]

Despite the difficulties of obtaining reliable information on Soviet and Warsaw Pact forces, over the years a good deal has in fact become known of these qualitative factors in Warsaw Pact forces. The inflationary bias of Western intelligence is especially evident in the evaluation of the quality of new Soviet equipment. Since only fragments of information on new models become available through tight Soviet security, Western experts are forced to extrapolate and to theorize about probable performance. For example, on its first appearance, the Soviet T-72 tank was described as remarkably effective in performance and armor. Ten years later, in Israeli-Syrian fighting in the Bekaa Valley of Lebanon, where Syrian forces were equipped with these tanks, their many defects were revealed: inaccurate cannon, ineffective motor, and engine block of highly inflammable aluminum. Many similar faults are reported for the new Soviet armored personnel carrier, described on its first appearance as a breakthrough in design that would decisively increase the effectiveness of Soviet conventional forces in Europe. Soviet aircraft, too, when in combat or examined after capture, have performed far less well than advertised in Western intelligence reports.[12]

A good deal is also known, primarily from émigrés and defectors, about difficulties in the leadership and organization of Soviet forces: rigid traditional leadership inhibits the development of flexibility and initiative by junior commanders; a hierarchical commissioned officer–enlisted man relationship brings poor morale; there is a shortage of noncommissioned personnel with long service experience to train conscripts; many non-Russian conscripts have poor knowledge of Russian and are nearly illiterate. When they are brought into East Germany in large batches for their service with the active-duty units of Soviet forces there, most of the conscript personnel of these crack category 1 divisions spend much of their time gaining basic skills like driving and literacy. These troops are far inferior in both skills and morale to Federal German conscripts. In fact, there are grounds for the assessment that the Soviet forces in East Germany are qualitatively inferior to the Bundeswehr, as well as to U.S. and British forces in Federal Germany.

The tank-heavy organization of Warsaw Pact forces, especially of Soviet forces in forward positions in East Germany, has long been a source of concern to NATO. Yet some experts with experience of German blitzkrieg tank warfare in World War II consider that, despite changes, Soviet forces still have too many tanks and too few of the support troops—armored infantry, combat engineers, repair and logistic forces—that made it possible for the Wehrmacht tank forces to move rapidly. Former Bundeswehr General Christian Krause points out that Soviet armored divisions have had three tank regiments and only one rifle regiment, a ratio of three to one, while German Bundeswehr tank divisions have a tank-unit-to-infantry-unit ratio of one to one, with strong service support units. This ratio has changed in the last five years with reorganization of Soviet active-duty divisions, but Krause still considers that the Soviet armored division organization lacks sustainability and can cause units to bog down easily.[13]

Quantitative analysis of the NATO–Warsaw Pact balance in air forces also omits NATO advantages in better-trained forces and superior equipment. For example, NATO pilots are better trained than Warsaw Pact pilots, putting in many more hours of flight training. Individually their aircraft are superior and carry far larger payloads of missiles and bombs. With the exception of some Greek and Turkish forces from NATO's southern flank, NATO ground forces are also better trained than Pact forces, and they train considerably more in the field than their Warsaw Pact equivalents. NATO leaders argue that as a coalition of independent states with their own military traditions, NATO has to exercise more than the more homogeneous, Soviet-dominated armies of the Warsaw Pact. Yet it is notable that, for whatever reason, the Warsaw Pact over the past thirty-five years has conducted far fewer joint exercises between the forces of the Soviet Union and those of its Warsaw Pact allies than has NATO among the Western allies. NATO's annual exercises of 250,000 men and more are over twice the size of the largest Warsaw Pact exercises. They give troops and commanders good training, although their sheer size may make them appear threatening in the East.

On the crucial NATO Central Front in Germany, the key area for the success of any Warsaw Pact attack on NATO, terrain generally favors the defender. Two-thirds of the 800 kilometer dividing line between Federal Germany and East Germany and Czechoslovakia is wooded, broken terrain, which includes the Bavarian Forest and Harz Mountains. Along the remaining third of the dividing line, the flat North German plain, often assumed to be ideal country for tank attack by Warsaw Pact forces, in fact has many towns and cities that would be tank traps, as well as the Elbe River and the Lueneburg Heath, with many small watercourses and bogs.[14] NATO forces are frequently said to be poorly deployed, with the bulk of U.S. forces concentrated in the more easily defended South, which constituted their zone of occupation at the end of World War II. Yet Soviet forces in East Germany, currently in garrisons they have occupied since World War II, would have to move farther to combat positions than would German, U.S., and British defending forces.

Above all, traditional quantitative analysis fails to take into account the morale and political attitude of the Eastern European armed forces. The 1968 Soviet invasion of Czechoslovakia left the spirit of the Czechoslovak forces so crushed that extensive personnel changes in the officer corps were required, but real recovery was never effected. The Solidarity development and political turmoil in Poland create serious doubt about the pro-Soviet loyalty of the Polish armed forces. The East German forces have been kept small because of Soviet distrust of Germans, even their own allies. The loyalty and cohesion of the East German forces is open to question in any military action that allowed time for contact and polarization between East German conscripts and the Federal German population or in which the personnel of Federal German units made local advances into East Germany.

Weaknesses of NATO Forces

This discussion of the NATO–Warsaw Pact force balance is intended as a deliberate corrective to often-exaggerated presentations of the Warsaw Pact threat to Europe. Nevertheless a powerful Warsaw Pact force does face NATO in Europe. And it is a Warsaw Pact force that, though its manpower has remained at roughly the same level for the past decade, has made impressive progress in improvement of its armaments.

Although NATO was the first to introduce ground attack helicopters, the Warsaw Pact now has more of them than NATO. NATO's qualitative edge in air forces is being eroded. Warsaw Pact air forces for decades deployed large numbers of interceptor aircraft unsuitable for supporting a forward-moving ground attack. Now, for the first time, the Warsaw Pact has an increasingly numerous force of fighter-bombers that can give ground support to advancing troops and attack targets on the NATO side. Its already heavily developed antiaircraft defenses with interceptor aircraft and surface-to-air guns and missiles, which reflected Soviet fears of an attack by U.S. nuclear bombers from Western Europe from the early 1950s on, have become still denser, making it increasingly difficult for NATO's superior fighter-bombers to penetrate. This development accounts for NATO's continuing preoccupation with interdicting Soviet forces moving West to reinforce an initial attack by Soviet forces in position in Eastern Europe. Previously the NATO air forces could be relied on to get through in attacks on bridges, airports, rail lines, and other transport choke points that would slow the forward advance of reinforcements from the Soviet Union. In fact, together with keeping Warsaw Pact forces dispersed and deterring use of nuclear weapons by the Warsaw Pact, this would have been the logical role for NATO's tactical nuclear weapons in an extreme case.

The Warsaw Pact's new tanks and armored personnel carriers, though not as good as sometimes described, do represent an advance over earlier models. Self-propelled artillery that can support and keep up with a rapid advance has been introduced in increasing numbers. With deployment of the improved SS-20 intermediate-range nuclear missile, modernization of the Frog (SS-21) and Scud (SS-23) short-range nuclear missiles, forward deployment of a modernized Scaleboard (SS-12/22) nuclear missile of about 900 kilometer range, and introduction of nuclear rounds for Soviet artillery, Soviet nuclear capability directed at Europe has greatly increased. Soviet and Warsaw Pact forces have also improved their logistics and are tackling problems of leadership and organization.

While these improvements in Warsaw Pact forces have been taking place, NATO has deployed U.S. INF missiles, but it has been making only slow progress toward dealing with its own ingrained conventional force weaknesses. In particular, these are shortages of ammunition, motor fuel, and other combat supplies. Several NATO national forces have only a three- to four-day supply of ammunition and fuel despite NATO requirements to build a supply of at least thirty days. This is the main reason for SACEUR Commander General Rogers's complaints that NATO countries were meeting only 70 percent of their stated force goals and for his repeated statements that he would have to consider recommending the use of nuclear weapons after less than a week of conventional conflict in Europe. These war stocks are expensive. And war stocks are sacrificed by all armed forces, including those of the United States, in order to buy more heavy armaments. Beyond this is the antipathy of European parliaments and military commands to obligating funds for lengthy conventional conflict.

Moreover, as we have already seen in discussing the flexible response and forward defense strategies, there is also some under-lying logic in European reluctance to invest in war stocks. A former senior European commander of NATO forces makes the point that faced by a choice between buying a maximum number of tanks to deploy on the German border with only a few days' ammunition supply, and buying fewer tanks with more ammunition to sustain them, he would deploy the maximum number of tanks every time because for him the first few days of combat would be decisive. Faced by the need to choose in a situation of limited resources, he chooses the force capable of making an immediate contribution at the outset of conflict.

Among other NATO shortcomings, there is still no remotely guided light Western antitank weapon that does not require the user to remain in the open to guide the missile to its target; there is nothing to counter the heads-down reaction of troops to intense artillery fire of the kind that would accompany Soviet attack. There is a need to improve NATO antiaircraft capabilities to meet the increasing capacity of Warsaw Pact air forces. Starting in 1987, NATO's strongest national component, the Federal German armed forces, will be faced by a shortage of conscript personnel. By the mid-1990s, this shortage will amount to 100,000 men in each year's cohort of men of conscription age unless resort is made not only to an increased period of service for conscripts but also a series of expensive inducements to increase the number of volunteers. A ma-jor weakness of NATO forces, and a serious one, is the shortage of operational reserves, active-duty units that can be deployed di-rectly behind NATO frontline units and can move rapidly to counter breakthrough by Soviet forces.

Beyond this, NATO still suffers the typical weakness of a co-alition army: lack of standardization and interoperability of equip-ment, both for ground and air forces. NATO's coalition structure has a further weakness of potentially serious dimension: decision making. Experts continue to fear that the NATO Council will not be able to decide rapidly on NATO actions to react to evidence of Warsaw Pact preparation for warfare. However, in the present analysis, it is assumed, probably quite realistically, that in case of need, the United States, Federal Germany, and the United Kingdom will be able to reach timely decisions among themselves to defend against a Pact attack and would not wait for a possibly tardy response from Portugal or Denmark.

A further problem of increasing importance is the mounting costs of defense. As figures presented in Department of Defense annual reports have repeatedly shown, NATO has been outspending the Warsaw Pact for defense for decades—almost certainly from the establishment of both alliances—and getting far fewer combat forces for its money. The Warsaw Pact may enjoy some advantages as a command economy in the production of military equipment, although low worker production rates plus poor-quality production machinery cut into these often-cited advantages. But in the West the problem is clear: the RAF's Spitfire cost 5,000 pounds sterling per aircraft in 1939; the new Tornado fighter-bomber, produced by a Western European consortium, costs 17 million pounds, 172 times more, even after allowing for inflation.[15] The lack of standardization and the absence of economies of scale in the NATO alliance, a coalition of autonomously organized national forces, is an important reason for these higher costs.

War in Europe

The U.S. intelligence community has repeatedly found that a standing-start Soviet blitz attack limited to the Central Front, without prior preparation of all Soviet forces (including nuclear forces) for involvement in war on a worldwide basis, is improbable. Nevertheless, the main fear of NATO commanders continues to be a conventional Warsaw Pact standing-start attack on the Central Front with brief preparation of four to five days to load ammunition and supplies and to ready armaments for combat use. The aim of such an attack would be rapid deep penetration of NATO defenses, holding off Western use of nuclear weapons through the rapidity and short duration of the conflict. Rapid penetration by Warsaw Pact ground forces, including diversionary airborne attack behind the lines and quickly gained air supremacy, would be used to destroy NATO nuclear weapons, airfields, and command and control systems. The attack would be designed to prevent escalation and to cut off rapid reinforcement from the United States and Britain—all of this in order to face the United States with a fait accompli before its nuclear and conventional potential could be thrown into the balance and also before major problems began to emerge in Eastern Europe. The up-to-date versions of this scenario posit preemptive attack on NATO ports, airfields, nuclear storage sites, and command posts by conventionally armed Soviet cruise and ballistic missiles. (The possibility is less dramatic than appears at first sight. The missiles are expensive, costing about a million dollars apiece, a cost justifiable in terms of the destructive power of nuclear weapons but not for a 2000 pound warhead of high explosives. The major virtue of the weapon is its terminal guidance. But this can be spoofed with decoys, leaving a very expensive bomb delivery system.)

Now that we have looked at some of the weaknesses of both alliances, let us return to assessing the chances for success of a Warsaw Pact attack of this standing-start type on NATO's Central Front in Germany. For this type of conflict, with four or five days' preparation at most, the Soviet Union would have to use its own category 1 forces, which total 36 divisions, as described above. But of these category 1 Soviet forces, those in the Soviet Union would be of little practical utility: the 2 airborne divisions in the northern Leningrad Military District and the more southerly Odessa Military District have missions directed at the NATO flank states in the North and South; withdrawing them for a blitz attack on Central Europe could expose the Soviet Union's own flanks. The 2 category 1 ground force divisions in the Byelorussian and Carpathian Military Districts, though committed to the Central Front, would be too far away for a blitz attack, as would the 4 divisions in Hungary. Their movement toward the Central Front would take over a week and would give unambiguous warning of pending attack. The 2 Soviet divisions in Poland would be needed to guard land communications to the Soviet Union and might well have to be reinforced if conflict continued. So the Soviet Union might use for such an attack the bulk of its 19 divisions in East Germany, some of its five divisions in Czechoslovakia, perhaps with one airborne division from the Baltic District for behind-the-lines attacks—in all, a force of perhaps 21 divisions, which would be without immediate reserves.

What about non-Soviet Warsaw Pact forces? Whether or not

East Germany's category 1 divisions could be used in such an attack is questionable, in view of their doubtful loyalty when in contact with fellow Germans in the West. But let us assume that 4 East German divisions are used. Perhaps 4 of the 8 Polish category 1 divisions might make a weak push at Federal German and Danish forces in Schleswig-Holstein and Denmark to try to open the Baltic for the Soviet Navy, moving along the Southern coast of the Baltic Sea and also making an amphibious attack on Denmark. Four of the 6 Czechoslovak category 1 divisions might try to push into Bavaria to tie down German and U.S. forces there. It is unclear whether the Soviets would want to use these questionable Eastern European units for a standing-start attack on the West or whether they could be organized to participate within a four- to five-day period. But we will count them for a worst-case hypothesis. If we do so, adding them to the 21 Soviet divisions already described would give us Warsaw Pact force of about 33 divisions for a blitz attack on the Central Front (figure 2–2).

At the outset of a Pact attack with minimum preparation on the Central Front with 33 divisions, NATO would have about 24 active-duty divisions to meet them. This worst-case count includes only Federal German, U.S., British, and Canadian forces in Germany. It excludes all reserve units, three French divisions already in Germany, one Danish division, and one Belgian and one Netherlands division normally stationed in their home countries with forward elements in Federal Germany. (The Belgian and Netherlands divisions are supposed to move to forward readiness positions in Federal Germany within 24 to 36 hours.) The ratio of NATO to Warsaw Pact combat personnel here is about 1:1 on the first day of mobilization. (Crediting the 14 German division equivalents with 18,000 men each, which is low, and 6 U.S. divisions with 18,000 each, and 4 British divisions with 10,000 each, for a total of 400,000 divisional personnel; and 33 Warsaw Pact divisions at an average of 12,000 each or 396,000, the forces are nearly equal in divisional manpower, with the qualitative superiority on the NATO side.)

Under the circumstances, NATO forces should be able to hold the attack, especially given the many qualitative weaknesses of Soviet and Pact forces. Even so, it would be wasteful to use active-

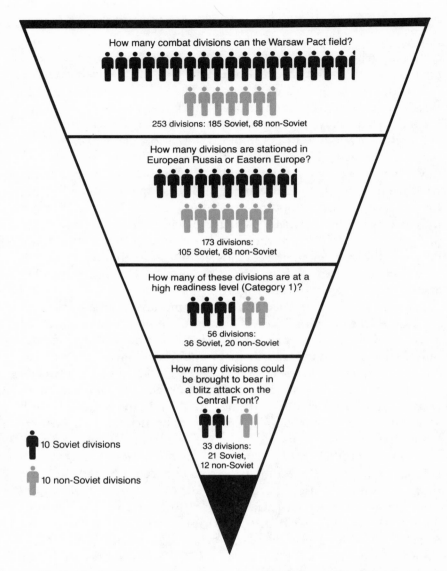

Figure 2–2. *Warsaw Pact Forces Available for a Blitz Attack on NATO's Central Front*

As forces that could not be used in a minimum-preparation attack on NATO's Central Front are excluded step by step, the Warsaw Pact threat appears progressively more limited.

duty NATO divisions, mainly Federal German and U.S. divisions, to cope with the manpower-consuming but militarily unconvincing Czechoslovak and Polish diversionary attacks. The right way to deal with them is properly organized and equipped German Territorial Forces, which, except for six combat brigades, are not included in our count of NATO divisions.

As noted, both Warsaw Pact and NATO forces have severe weaknesses in their ability to sustain conventional combat once a conflict has started. To get a more complete picture of the prospects for Warsaw Pact success, it is necessary to use a more dynamic form of analysis than the static comparisons we have been making thus far. Dynamic analysis takes into account factors like firepower, losses, consumption of ammunition, and mobilization rates.

The attacking Warsaw Pact forces would of course be reinforced. Applying dynamic analysis, several studies indicate that the Warsaw Pact could mobilize and bring to bear additional personnel faster than NATO, and that the highest point of danger to NATO could come in seven to fourteen days, with a force ratio that could approach 2:1 in favor of the Warsaw Pact.[16]

Warsaw Pact victory even under these conditions is far from assured. One weakness of many mobilization estimates is that they assume full mobilization of non-Soviet Warsaw Pact forces and their commitment in action. This is unrealistic. It is improbable that East German, Polish, and Czechoslovak forces will see action in a short war except on the limited scale described. Moreover, if Federal German forces in limited counterattacks move into East Germany, they could be supported from the outset by some elements of the East German population. This support would increase the longer the hostilities continued. These Federal German forces could create far more disruption behind Warsaw Pact lines than East German, Polish, or Czechoslovak units could in a hostile environment in Federal Germany.

Meanwhile, the more serious Eastern reinforcements—two Soviet category 1 divisions in the Western Military Districts—would begin their move forward soon after conflict began. In addition, five category 2 Soviet divisions in the same military districts could begin to move forward in about ten days, for a total of seven Soviet reinforcement divisions arriving in combat position within two weeks or so. The twenty-nine category 3 Soviet divisions in these military districts would not be ready to move for at least four weeks. The Soviet reinforcing forces would have to move forward 800 to 1000 kilometers, mainly by rail, with a change in railroad gauge from broad-gauge Soviet trains to the narrower European gauge at the Polish border. The East-West rail and road lines cross two major rivers, the Vistula and the Oder, with vulnerable bridges, among a small total of some twenty transportation choke points that are likely targets for NATO interdiction attack.

On the NATO side, Federal Germany alone would mobilize about 700,000 ground force personnel within a week, over seven times the total of the personnel of the reinforcing Soviet divisions. A portion of these reservists would already have filled in active-duty units of the Bundeswehr field force, some of which are manned at only 60 percent of the wartime level. A portion would have filled in the six territorial defense brigades. But there is a large remainder, many of them organized into lightly armed home defense units. If properly organized and equipped into combat units, which is not now the case, the remaining German reserve personnel alone should eventually be able to cope with Soviet reinforcements. In any event, a considerable portion of the three active-duty Belgian, Danish, and Netherlands divisions mentioned above and of the further two Netherlands divisions, one Belgian division, one British division, and six U.S. divisions promised for two weeks after the NATO mobilization order is given would be on hand to reinforce NATO standing forces, even if none of France's ten active-duty divisions and eight reserve divisions was committed. The chances for Warsaw Pact success remain quite uncertain.

This brief account of possible conflict on the Central Front has focused on ground force elements. In a short engagement, NATO naval forces would retain local superiority. Air power would be more in the balance, but it continues probable that NATO air forces would retain air superiority over the NATO area and over the forward edge of the battle area. It seems probable, given shortages of ammunition and war supplies and replacements for major armaments on both sides, that a purely conventional war on the Central Front would peter out in about four weeks, creating an opportunity for negotiation to end hostilities or for their continuation on a less massive scale.

Other types of Warsaw Pact attack are possible. In a full mobilization war preceded by sixty to ninety days of preparation sufficient to mobilize most reserve forces on both sides, the Warsaw Pact in Northern Europe is credited with ninety divisions and NATO with about 49 divisions.[17] NATO would be outnumbered. But the outcome would remain uncertain. Moreover, full mobilization and a gradual buildup of forces over a two- or three-month period without earlier hostilities is a most improbable situation in a nuclear age. The idea that the United States and the NATO countries would for two months limit themselves to mobilization of their reserves while the Soviet Union was manifestly committed to war and was taking every step needed to deploy its maximum military potential is implausible—and the same goes for the Soviet Union.

If Soviet leaders contemplate an attack on Western Europe, they must calculate not only the possibilities of winning that war as such but also the worldwide war that would probably ensue. Such a conflict could include worldwide naval warfare, in which Western navies would be superior, attacks on Soviet territory from the Black Sea area and in the Far East, and the participation in the conflict of Japan or even China, developments that could threaten the survival of the Soviet system. In addition, Soviet attack on Western Europe incurs the possibility of escalation to nuclear war. Taken together, these risks are enormous. As the IISS concludes in its latest assessment of the military balance, "Our conclusion remains that the conventional overall balance is still such as to make general military aggression a highly risky undertaking for either side—there would still appear to be insufficient strength on either side to guarantee victory. The consequences for an attacker would still be quite unpredictable and the risks, particularly of nuclear escalation, incalculable."[18]

Our own conclusion here must be that the evaluation by NATO commanders and NATO governments that the possibility of Warsaw Pact attack on Western Europe is very low is correct and well founded because NATO forces would be considerably more evenly matched with Soviet forces than most analyses allow for and because of the potential worldwide consequences of such actions.

However, purely rational considerations may not govern decisions on both sides at all times. It cannot be excluded that Soviet attacks on Western Europe could be triggered in consequence of an internal power struggle in the Soviet Union; as a panicky reaction to fear of nuclear war with the United States or to widespread political unrest in Eastern Europe, especially East Germany; or as a consequence of U.S.-Soviet conflict in some third area. Moreover, a confrontation involving about 10 million active-duty military personnel and thousands of aircraft, tanks, and missiles entails a built-in risk of human error, misperception, and miscalculation that could result in conflict.

Beyond the current risks of war for reasons of this kind, force improvements on both sides are continuing, and theoretically the Warsaw Pact could in the future gain such a large edge militarily that aggression might appear more profitable than it does today. Against this background, in the next chapter we will examine some of the main proposals for improvement of NATO military forces as regards their feasibility, their potential impact on the force balance, and, not least, their effects on the stability of the East-West confrontation in Europe.

Notes

1. U.S. Senate, Armed Services Committee, 97th Cong., 2d sess., Committee Print, May 13, 1982. Two good short discussions of NATO military problems are William P. Mako, *US Ground Forces and the Defense of Central Europe* (Washington, D.C.: Brookings Institution, 1983), and Roger L.L. Facer, *Conventional Forces and the NATO Strategy of Flexible Response* (Santa Monica, Calif.: Rand Corporation, 1985).
2. Samuel Huntington, "Conventional Deterrence in Europe," *International Security* 8:3 (Winter 1983–1984): 32–56.
3. *NATO and Warsaw Pact Force Comparisons* (Brussels: NATO Information Service, 1984), pp. 8, 11.
4. *Whence the Threat to Peace* (Moscow: Military Publishing House, 1984).
5. International Institute for Strategic Studies, *The Military Balance, 1982–1983* (London: IISS, 1982), p. 132.
6. Federal Republic of Germany, Ministry of Defense, *White Paper 1983* (Bonn, 1983), p. 66.
7. International Institute for Strategic Studies, *The Military Balance, 1985–1986* (London: IISS, 1985), p. 186.
8. See the interesting discussion in William W. Kaufmann, "Non-Nuclear De-

terrence," in John D. Steinbrunner and Leon Sigal, eds., *Alliance Security: NATO and the No-First-Use Question* (Washington, D.C.: Brookings Institution, 1983). The figures cited in the text as to time needed to bring the various categories to readiness are my own, based on repeated discussion with Western experts on Soviet forces.

9. Figures on Warsaw Pact forces in the three categories of readiness are drawn from *The Military Balance, 1985–1986* and from my own discussions with Western experts. See also Kaufmann, op. cit., and Mako, op. cit.
10. See *Defense Electronics* 14:1 (January 1982).
11. IISS, *Military Balance, 1985–1986,* p. 182.
12. See Andrew Cockburn, *The Threat* (New York: Vintage Books, 1984), for a discussion of these and other biases in evaluation of Soviet forces. Also see Andreas von Buelow, *Die Eingebildete Unterlegenheit* (The imaginary inferiority) (Munich: C.H. Beck, 1985), an account by a German Social Democratic leader. These books focus on weaknesses in Western estimates of Soviet and Warsaw Pact forces and are therefore one-sided in their own way. But they are a useful corrective to cumulative overevaluation.
13. Christian Krause, *The Balance between Conventional Forces in Europe* (Bonn: Friedrich Ebert Stiftung, 1982).
14. Steven Canby, "Territorial Defense in Central Europe," *Armed Forces and Society* 7:1, Fall 1980; John J. Mearsheimer, "The Conventional Balance on the Central European Front," *International Security,* Summer 1982.
15. Cited by Gwynne Dyer, *War* (New York: Crown Publishers, 1985), p. 191.
16. See Carnegie Endowment for International Peace, *Challenges for U.S. National Security, Part II, Assessing the Balance-Defense Spending and Conventional Forces,* Washington, D.C. 1981, Chapter 2; Mearsheimer, loc. cit.; Kaufmann loc. cit.; and Fen Osler Hampson, "Groping for Conventional Panaceas," *International Security,* 8:3, Winter 1983-84.
17. See Kaufmann, op. cit.
18. See *Military Balance, 1985–1986,* p. 185.

3
Shifting the Emphasis to Conventional Deterrence: A Critical Evaluation

M any ways of improving NATO's defenses have been suggested, ranging from modest improvements in existing forces to radical revisions of the forward defense posture. But any revision to NATO's conventional defenses—in addition to diminishing Europe's dependence on nuclear deterrence—should meet two further criteria. It must make the conventional defense of Europe more feasible in a visible way, with impact on both Warsaw Pact leaders and the West European public, and it must do so in a way that is not destabilizing, a way that will hold to a minimum the inducement to Warsaw Pact leaders to introduce compensatory improvements in their own forces and that will not result in a force posture on both sides more liable to miscalculation and human error.

Deep Interdiction Using Emerging Technologies

One group of proposals for improving NATO's strategy involves using high-technology weaponry—the so-called emerging technologies—to allow conventional strikes deep into Warsaw Pact territory, with the goal of interdicting second- and third-echelon Soviet reinforcements. We have already seen the importance of these reinforcements for possible Soviet attack on Western Europe and have also noted that continuing improvement of Pact air defenses makes penetration by NATO fighter-bombers to these targets increasingly

difficult. Moreover, the bulk of the targets for NATO bombers—
bridges, airfield runways, and transportation choke points such as
major crossroads and railroad yards—would logically be the targets for tactical nuclear weapons. If NATO wishes to move toward
less reliance on nuclear weapons, some substitute for these air sorties with nuclear weapons will have to be found.

In theory, the new emerging-technology weapons, most of them
still in development, could be used in the event of conflict to destroy these fixed targets and ultimately even concentrations of tanks,
personnel carriers, or trucks in motion. By exploiting the West's
technological superiority to increase the effectiveness of conventional firepower, these weapons theoretically could place Warsaw
Pact forces at something like the degree of risk that could once be
achieved only with nuclear weapons.

Emerging Technologies Defined

Several types of technical advance have come together in the emerging technologies, with many applications on the battlefield in addition to deep interdiction. Conventional munitions themselves have
developed rapidly in recent years. They have increased in explosive
power and have been made more effective by being tailored to
particular uses (such as shaped charges to penetrate tank armor
and charges configured to break up airfield runways). New submunitions have been developed that are delivered in clusters dispersed near the target. These clusters may be delivered at relatively
short ranges by artillery or, for heavier salvos, by a multiple-launch
rocket system.

Accurate delivery of the new munitions can be ensured by precision guidance systems. For example, target-seeking devices such
as infrared sensors may be applied to submunitions; these smart
submunitions, after dispersal, can home in on individual targets.
At longer range—and this includes any deep interdiction application—smart submunitions could be delivered by aircraft. Or warheads equipped with terminal guidance targeting devices may be
delivered at long range by cruise missiles using terrain-following
guidance and ultimately by ballistic missiles now under development. The great advantage of the missiles is that they could more

effectively penetrate increasingly effective Warsaw Pact air defenses. In theoy, this would be at a cost per missile that is far less than the cost of more vulnerable manned aircraft and their pilots, if total loss of aircraft in combat is assumed.

Advances in munitions have been aided by major advances in finding targets through computer-aided surveillance and target acquisition (sophisticated airborne radar feeding its findings to land-based computers). Proponents claim that by using modern methods of surveillance, target acquisition, and precision guidance to ensure accurate delivery, these weapons could obviate the need to use nuclear warheads to compensate for inaccuracy.

More specifically, the new weapons consist of improved anti-tank guided weapons for hand use, using infrared sensors that can home in on their targets; laser-guided antitank projectiles mounted on helicopters and vehicles; the multiple-launch rocket system now being deployed by NATO forces (this self-propelled system can fire twelve rockets per minute at a 30 to 40 kilometer range, and each rocket warhead carries thousands of explosive projectiles that can kill personnel and stop lightly armored vehicles); unmanned drone aircraft equipped with sensors for target identification and targeting; aircraft-mounted combined radar systems believed capable of detecting moving ground targets like tank or truck columns; a modified longer-range Lance ballistic missile armed with a conventional warhead; and a cruise missile with a conventional warhead. The full weapons combination now proposed for deep interdiction would include airborne radar systems, automated ground systems to correlate information, and—the key item—ballistic and cruise missiles of up to 600 kilometer range, armed with conventional warheads with various types of terminal guidance.

Deep-Strike Strategies

Two variants of a deep-strike strategy using these emerging technologies have already been developed. The Air-Land Battle doctrine, espoused by the U.S. Army and Air Force, could involve use of nuclear as well as conventional weapons in strikes deep into Warsaw Pact territory in response to Pact attack. This concept, which U.S. officials point out was formulated in the abstract rather than for specific application to Europe (but where else could it be used?), has elicited controversy in Europe, where it appears overly militant. It has also become a focus for Warsaw Pact accusations that NATO has aggressive intentions. These reactions have ensured that the Air-Land Battle doctrine as such will not be adopted by NATO.

Consequently, that doctrine has given rise to the less far-reaching doctrine of Follow-On Force Attack (FOFA) advanced by General Rogers and already adopted by NATO as a long-range goal. This doctrine calls for deep strikes at the outset of conflict in Europe. These strikes would use only conventional warheads, delivered by dual-capable aircraft, artillery, and missiles. For the most part, their intended range would be considerably less than in the Air-Land Battle concept—100 kilometers or less.

Interdiction of fixed targets behind the Warsaw Pact lines has always been a feature of NATO wartime planning, but, because interdiction would take place in enemy territory, it has never been publicly emphasized in describing NATO strategy. Several factors already mentioned here have come together to bring a shift to greater publicity: NATO publics want less reliance on nuclear weapons and more emphasis on conventional weapons. Interdiction of reinforcements is an area of potential substitution of conventional for nuclear weapons, but it will cost a great deal, and so a publicity campaign is needed to focus generalized public support for conventional force improvement on this program. This is what has taken place. But in focusing public attention on an aspect of NATO defense previously not salient, the campaign has backfired to some extent by conjuring up in European publics the image of a long conventional war fought with reinforcements.

High-Tech Solution or Costly Error?

In evaluating the military value of deep-strike strategies, the natural first question is whether the new weapons will work. Critics have claimed that the weapons are not robust enough for the battlefield, where smoke, dust, and bad weather would severely degrade the performance of the sensors used for precision guidance, and also that the weapons may be rendered ineffective through cheap defensive measures like decoys and roof-mounted umbrella-like shields on tanks. The terrain-following guidance systems used in cruise missiles to deliver weapons at relatively long range are now useful only for known, fixed targets, such as bridges, airfields, or rail junctions. Target identification and location for moving targets at long range are still problematic and are likely to remain so for some time. The favorable cost figures for missiles can be deceptive. Even in difficult combat conditions, it will be possible to reuse many aircraft for multiple sorties, while warheads carried by the missiles become less impressive when they consist of conventional explosives; conventional explosives, no matter how improved, do not have destructive capacity remotely comparable with that of nuclear warheads.

But other questions are more fundamental and also less amenable to solution. Which Warsaw Pact follow-on forces are involved in the deep interdiction concept? Are they operational reserves from forces already on hand in East Germany or reinforcements moving forward from the Soviet Union itself? There is a difference not only in the range of the armaments required (perhaps 30 to 40 kilometers on the one hand, 1000 on the other), and therefore in the armaments that would be involved, but also in the strategy of war fighting. Moreover, to some extent, the Soviet doctrine of attacking in wavelike echelons seems to have been replaced or at least supplemented by a more active use of dispersed operational maneuver groups, designed to cut through defensive lines wherever they find an opportunity and operate disruptively behind NATO lines. If evolving Soviet strategy calls for bringing combat power forward and relying less heavily on second and third echelons deployed behind the initial line of battle, then a deep interdiction strategy becomes less useful to NATO, which should focus more on the first wave.

Finally, introduction of these new weapons systems, like all other technological innovations, will not be confined to NATO. There seems no reason to doubt that the Warsaw Pact will eventually develop these weapons. Certainly Soviet technology can in time duplicate the electronic processors and computer guidance components that are the distinctive features of these new weapons. If both alliances deploy these new systems extensively, large numbers of conventional deep interdiction weapons could be deployed on both sides, aimed at the adversary's transport choke points, command and control facilities, airfields, and nuclear weapons sites. There would be great military advantage in using the new weapons preemptively against these targets at the outset of a conflict in Europe. There would also be great advantage for each side in early strikes to destroy these same weapons before they were used against its own forces. Here is a real case of "use 'em or lose 'em," the problem of forward-deployed tactical nuclear weapons—but without the inhibitions attached to the use of nuclear weapons. These destabilizing effects are illustrated by the Syrian deployment in the spring of 1986 of Soviet-made SS-21s and possibly SS-23s targeted on Israel; a debate is already in progress in Israel over whether Israel should try to destroy them by preemptive air strikes.

This comment makes clear the most important defect of the deep-strike strategies, which applies even to the less far-reaching FOFA concept. Although they may be conceived by their supporters as a purely defensive response to possible Warsaw Pact attack, if deployed in large numbers these weapons can be used for attack. Already the Soviet force posture, with heavy armored forces concentrated in a forward position in Central Europe, creates great ambiguity as to Soviet intentions. Although this deployment pattern reflects announced Soviet strategy for defense against Western forces in the event of war in Europe—a massive armored counterattack on the aggressor force—it could also be used to launch an aggressive attack on Western Europe. It should be the object of Western policy through arms control and political negotiations to bring the Soviet Union gradually to change this deployment pattern. Yet the tank-heavy equipment of NATO forces concentrated in forward position currently forms a mirror image of Warsaw Pact forces, creating a strong inducement to competition in force improvements on each side. With both NATO and Pact forces structured and equipped to carry them out, the adoption of deep penetration strategies on both sides would increase the possibility that tensions in Europe, or a conflict outside Europe, would lead to a panicky Pact decision to launch a preemptive attack against the West. Moreover, if conflict breaks out, expanding the battle area on both sides from an early point in the conflict through use of deep interdiction weapons could make it more difficult to bring hostilities to a close.

Deep-strike weapons could also be destabilizing in another way: instead of raising the nuclear threshold in the event of conflict, they might actually make resort to nuclear weapons more likely. Because many delivery vehicles for longer-range interdiction weapons may be dual capable (with both conventional and nuclear warheads), simply moving them out of garrison for possible use could lead an adversary to conclude that the deploying side was about to use nuclear weapons. For first-strike preemptive use, the missiles would be fired from garrison position. But if the conventionally armed missiles were used in combat, their flight pattern would be identical or closely similar to that of nuclear-armed missiles, and the adversary might well respond immediately with nuclear weapons.

Prospects for Deep Interdiction

For the most part, European political reaction to the possibility of deep interdiction strategies for NATO has not been positive. Most of the problems posed by these strategies—their destabilizing effects, the threat they pose to arms control, their capacity to increase East-West tension—have been grasped and probably even exaggerated by segments of the European public sensitized by the debate over deployment of the U.S. Euromissiles. Against the background of that controversy, the new weapons are likely to present a political problem of some dimension. Deep interdiction weapons are already perceived by some to have an inherently aggressive character because of their range. This aspect has already brought heavy criticism in Federal Germany, and the Social Democrats have rejected the deep interdiction concept.

No agreement has yet been reached as to who will produce weapons using emerging technologies, and European suspicions continue active that the intensive NATO discussion of new weapons sponsored by the United States is part of a campaign to exploit U.S. microchip technology by selling large quantities of U.S.-manufactured weapons to European governments. General Rogers has suggested that production might be by joint European-U.S. consortia, but these too are only in the discussion stage for most of the weapons under consideration. Indeed it will take from five to ten years before most of these systems are ready for deployment, and in terms of large-scale deployment of the deep interdiction systems, we are talking of the weapons of the next century.

There is no doubt that these weapons will be expensive. The European Security Study group estimated the cost of equipping NATO with long-range interdiction capability at $10 billion to $20 billion, including the cost of some 5000 ballistic missiles with conventional warheads. We can assume the actual cost would be far higher if the program were carried out in full.[1]

From the viewpoint of political support for military budgets, the issue is not only the high cost of these systems against a background of continuing high unemployment in Europe and a pervasive low in public willingness to spend more money for defense. It is a question of priorities for existing defense budgets, and there are many claimants for additional money within the framework of existing NATO strategy. Among the leading ones are items like those already agreed upon by the NATO Council: larger ammunition stocks, revetments to receive reinforcement aircraft from the United States, and improved antiaircraft coverage for NATO, an expensive program now in progress. Then there are the competing operating costs of existing forces for training and so on. And almost all of these claims have higher priority with national defense ministries in Europe than do emerging technologies for deep interdiction. Interdiction of Warsaw Pact second- and third-echelon reinforcements will be of little use, critics argue, if the battle has already been lost at the front against the first wave of attack because too little money was spent there.

These economic factors—along with the political defects of the deep interdiction strategies and weapons—mean that these new weapons are likely to be introduced very slowly even if they are satisfactorily developed. Nonetheless, slow introduction of at least some of the new interdiction technology, including perhaps new missiles of 100 to 200 kilometer range equipped with conventional warheads, is likely over time. It will be difficult to argue against aircraft that can provide fuller information for early warning, against computers that can organize the information from these radars in readily understandable form, or even against munitions that can break up the runways of Pact airports and reduce the sortie rate of Pact aircraft, and indeed the NATO governments have accepted these items in principle and have already developed munitions to destroy runways. There is a definite benefit in long-range weapons of assured penetration capacity, given that improvements in the Warsaw Pact's already highly developed air defenses make NATO air penetration increasingly difficult. In a sense, too, there is no stopping the introduction of as pervasive an item as a silicon chip.

Thus although deep interdiction systems are not likely to be introduced rapidly on a large scale as components of a decisively effective new defense strategy, NATO forces are still likely to deploy them piecemeal over coming years. The main problem with gradual introduction of computerized conventional weapons may come less from the weapons themselves than from the claims and counterclaims generated by the publicity campaign that has already been launched to finance them. This could elicit public opposition in Federal Germany and other Western European countries, with the Soviets jumping into the public dispute, as they did with telling contributory effect in the INF controversy.

There is a further, more serious complication: improvement in Warsaw Pact fighter-bombers and the possibility of increased deployment by the Pact of its own conventionally armed deep interdiction missiles has already caused European NATO leaders, especially the Germans, to discuss the need for improved defenses against shorter-range ballistic and cruise missiles, a new system of point defenses protecting airfields, nuclear weapon sites, and command posts in Western Europe. The Warsaw Pact is already deploying some additional defenses against the new U.S. ground-launched cruise missiles deployed in Europe. Presumably the Warsaw Pact will in time also imitate the innovative aspects of a NATO antimissile system.

It is difficult to forecast what the net outcome will be of deployment of conventionally armed missiles and antimissile defenses by both alliances. Clearly the civilian population on both sides will remain vulnerable to both the new weapons and nuclear weapons. For the armies of both alliances, the prospect of some interdiction damage in the early stages of conventional war may provide an additional reason for forward deployment of combat forces. It also provides an additional reason for believing that the battling forces will run out of supplies relatively rapidly if war comes. But amid the uncertainties, one point is already clear: instead of financing one major wave of new technology, NATO taxpayers (and the citizens of Warsaw Pact countries) are confronted with funding two major waves.

As the forces of the two opposing alliances enter the next century, there will probably be increasing deployment of missiles with conventional warheads and increasing deployment of missile defenses. Costs will be high, but there will be no clear gain in security for either side. Military experts will argue the fine points of who has the advantage from deployment of these systems. There are better answers than these to the problems of European defense. Force modernization on both sides is often a euphemism for engaging in the arms race. If arms control agreements or less formal arrangements covering these armaments could be achieved, they would be a far cheaper and preferable way of improving the stability of the huge East-West military confrontation.

Other Approaches to Improving NATO's Forces

After looking at deep interdiction, then, we are left with the NATO forward defense strategy as the strategy that, despite its major defects, most closely meets the overall political-military requirements of the situation in Central Europe. It is a strategy that reassures public and political opinion in Federal Germany and provides a framework for participation by other allies in the defense of Europe, especially on the Central Front. And because it is defensive, it provides a basis for a political approach to East-West relations, in the long run the only key to solving NATO's defense problems. What is left to do is to make NATO's forward defense strategy more effective.

The most orthodox and the most necessary improvement of NATO conventional forces would be to carry out existing NATO programs for building up ammunition supplies to a thirty-day level. Evident NATO capability to carry out a four-week war would meet the requirement defined at the outset of this discussion for NATO to deal with a blitz attack by Soviet forces in the forward position and their immediate Soviet reinforcements, and thus to deter such an attack. This objective is already partly secured, and progress is being made toward its completion.

The United States urges that NATO countries should build a ninety-day stock of ammunition and war supplies. There is no doubt that achievement of this goal would add to the Western deterrent by making it clear that NATO countries were willing and able to continue fighting indefinitely in the event of Pact attack. But given European antipathy to extended war, it is more realistic to focus on the achievable short-term target. Capacity to fight a four-week war is reasonable both in the sense that it would adequately meet the challenge that NATO most fears—Soviet blitz attack on the Central Front—and that it corresponds to the concept of European defense leaders of a short, decisive conflict.

NATO conventional defense for the Central Front could also be strengthened if a greater number of Federal Germany's ground force reserves were organized into combat units. Four and one-half million men have gone through military training in the Federal German forces since their inception in 1955. Two and one-half million men who have performed military service as conscripts are still required to report their whereabouts to Federal German military authorities. Of these, about 800,000 are already on call for return to duty at short notice; with them, Federal German forces could reach their wartime strength of 1.34 million within a week of mobilization. Of the 800,000 reservists, some 500,000, a large number, are being held for replacement of wartime casualties. Only 300,000 would be called to fill out existing active-duty divisions, which are manned at 60 percent of their wartime strength, or to form part of the German Territorial Forces, whose main task is to maintain operational freedom of the area behind the front line of combat against penetration by Soviet maneuver groups or airborne troops and to deal with smaller-scale diversionary incursions of commando type. Of the Territorial Forces, six brigades (the equivalent of two divisions) are organized into combat formations and would probably be assigned to NATO command in the event of conflict.

The question is whether a larger number of the German reservists could be organized into combat formations by drawing down on the pool of reservists for combat replacements. Doing so would cost money for equipment, training, and possibly payment to the reservists themselves. If conscript training is handled in the optimal way, with conscripts first trained in active-duty units and then immediately thereafter moved together with their training cadres into reserve formations held together for the next eighteen months or two years, they will not need to be called up for training during that period while their skills are still fresh and therefore would not have to be paid.

The Netherlands has pioneered in a type of conscript training in which the same cadre of professional personnel stays with a unit in its active-duty phase and in its reserve phase, at considerable savings and with high effectiveness. As former conscripts grow older, the reserve phase can be divided into two stages: younger reservists can be organized into reserve combat units, and older conscripts can serve in units with home guard functions in rear areas.[2] If additional combat units are formed from German reservist personnel over a longer period of ten years or more, Federal Germany could implement this program with a limited increase of its annual defense budget.

In theory, further reserve combat units could also be formed by drawing down active-duty personnel from some active-duty units and converting them to reserve units, using the surplus active-duty personnel to establish still more reserve units. The result in this case would be a somewhat smaller force of active-duty units but a considerably larger force of combat units on short-term mobilization. This procedure, however, would have to be used selectively with certain units of active-duty German divisions, or the level of active-duty forces available to counter possible Warsaw Pact attack with limited preparation would sink too low.

A third improvement to NATO's conventional defense could be brought about by France, which in theory could do a great deal to strengthen NATO defenses at low cost to itself. For example, an official statement by the government of France that in the event of Soviet attack, French forces would come to the support of NATO forces would do a great deal to invigorate NATO conventional defense. Such a statement would not require France to rejoin the NATO integrated command, nor would it cost anything in economic terms. But it would enable NATO political and military leaders, and Western European public opinion, to count on the French to help in the event of war rather than merely to hope that they will do so. France would not only be placing its ten active-duty ground force divisions and eight reserve divisions at the disposal of NATO in the event of conflict, it would also be guaranteeing use of its logistic infrastructure and airfields. This assurance would make the prospects for successful conventional defense appear more solid to Western European public and political opinion, and it would enable NATO force planners to make firm plans for basing reinforcement aircraft from Britain, Canada, and the United States and bringing forward war supplies from French ports.

Specialization by country could open the way to further improvements in NATO defense. Although NATO has an integrated military command, NATO's forces are not integrated forces. Rather they are a combination of national forces, each the product of a separate history and tradition with its own institutional roots and each with its own army, navy, and air force. It has long been clear that a certain degree of specialization among these forces could result in a much increased NATO force. For example, one expert has calculated that continental countries with forces in the NATO Central Front—the Netherlands, Belgium, Denmark, and Federal Germany—could find the men and money for twelve additional active-duty ground force divisions for the Central Front by cutting back somewhat on their air and naval forces. To make up the shortfalls, the U.S. Air Force could move 400 to 500 of the aircraft from its large fleet of 3500 held in the United States to Europe, and the U.S. Navy could use some of its expanded forces to make up the decrease in naval forces of European countries.[3]

Some supporters of this approach point out that it would make NATO's own force of combat-ready divisions on the Central Front much stronger and decrease the need for rapid reinforcement from the United States. These U.S. rapid reinforcements appear increasingly unlikely because of the poor state of U.S. reserves and the continuing vulnerability of European ports and airfields to attack by Soviet nuclear and conventionally armed missiles.

A further area of potential improvement of NATO defenses is the construction of light field fortifications and tank barriers at the most vulnerable points of the dividing line between the two German states. Stocks of remote-controlled scatter mines with specialized deployment equipment—rocket launchers and helicopters—could be built up near the border. Plastic pipes can be laid at vulnerable points to be filled with slurry explosive from tank trucks in mobilization and detonated if conflict seems certain, creating highly effective tank obstacles.[4] In some more complex versions of improved static defenses, territorial militia with specialized antitank equipment is deployed in front of existing mobile active-duty forces, which then can take over the role of operational reserves.

This general approach has several virtues. It would create an impact zone to take the first shock of possible attack, enabling more rational use of NATO's present active-duty forces as operational reserves. It would decrease the mirror-image competitive effect of NATO's present tank-heavy forward defense and result in a far more clearly defensive posture. Finally, it would also lend itself to an arms control application.

In one sense, the split in the NATO consensus on defense issues that has been the product of the INF controversy has had a positive aspect: it has generated a skeptical review of the existing NATO force posture and strategy and a large number of proposals for alternative defense. Most would involve thorough reorganization of NATO defenses. One such approach is the area defense model, in which a network of static light infantry units of twenty to thirty men would defend specified areas throughout Germany using a system of camouflaged, preplaced artillery rockets randomly distributed to avoid detection. A second concept is of a forward fire barrier composed of antitank guided weapons on elevated fighting platforms and mortars and rockets with terminally guided munitions.[5] One advantage of all of these concepts is that they fall into the category of nonprovocative defense. They are postures that are unambiguously defensive and move away from a NATO force that is a mirror image of Warsaw Pact forces, with the resulting tendency toward competition in force improvements. A serious defect of most of these approaches, however, is that most are essentially a home defense concept using German personnel and with no feasible role for participation by NATO allies in the defense of Germany. Indeed many are explicitly intended as methods of defending a neutral Federal Germany that has withdrawn from NATO. Whatever the real state of the Soviet threat, however, radical change through departure of Federal Germany from the NATO alliance is wholly improbable during the next decades.

Improbability of Significant Improvements in NATO Defenses

Clearly there is no shortage of possibilities for improving NATO's conventional defense, including some very effective ones. In fact, the theoretical answers to NATO's shortcomings have long been known. The problem is that, other than some practical improvement of NATO's ammunition stocks, none of them will be put into effect in any large-scale, decisive way in the foreseeable future.

A major addition to German reserves would cost more money than German taxpayers will spend. As it is, keeping up the level of active-duty personnel at anything near their present level in a period of demographic decline will cost billions of marks to increase inducement for long-service personnel to remain on duty. Within the next two decades, the aging demographic pattern of the Federal German population and the resulting pension burden will bring a major increase in Federal Germany's already high level of social payments and bring much heavier pressures on the German defense budget. The entirely logical suggestion that the number of active-duty NATO ground force divisions in Central Europe could be increased through a limited degree of specialization and contraction of the Belgian, Danish, Dutch, and Federal German air forces and navies will not be implemented because of institutional opposition within these countries. The Belgian Air Force effectively resisted the idea of including a modest reduction of air force manpower in Western proposals for the Vienna force reduction negotiations by claiming that even a small reduction would result in its elimination as a viable autonomous force. None of the smaller Western European countries with World War II experience of German occupation would be enthusiastic about larger Federal German armed forces, and the Germans themselves are sensitive to these feelings.

The NATO Council has for decades pressed for standardization of NATO military equipment, interoperability, and rationalization of military production through joint production or coordinated specialization. Modest progress has been made. The U.S. Army has bought Italian pistols and French communication equipment. But progress is likely to remain modest. Many more projects for joint production of armaments among European NATO countries—aircraft, tanks, artillery, antiaircraft weapons—collapse than are carried through. Because of economies of scale in U.S. armaments production and because of congressional pressures, the two-way street of U.S. purchases from Europe and European purchases from the United States is a one-way highway in favor of the United States. Over the years, U.S. sales to Europe have been ten times larger than U.S. purchases from Europe, although there has been some recent improvement. There is little chance that these programs can do more than hold their own in the area of new technology. At best they will advance modestly.

There has been much discussion in France, motivated by concern over the antinuclear development in Federal Germany, of increased Franco-German defense cooperation. But now that antinuclear sentiment has receded in Germany, so has this discussion in France. France is prepared on economic grounds to collaborate with Germany in the production of military equipment; coproduction of a new helicopter has been agreed. But there was no response in France, official or otherwise, to former Chancellor Schmidt's proposal of June 1984 of Franco-German cooperation to create a combined force of thirty ground force divisions to reduce NATO's dependence on nuclear weapons. France has created a rapid intervention force, the Force d'Action Rapide (FAR), of attack helicopters, light armor, and infantry, which it has implied could be used in the defense of Germany. But in reality, this force is planned for use outside Europe, and the publicity surrounding its establishment—through reorganizing existing units, not creating new ones—was designed to meet well-substantiated public criticism in France of a decline in France's own conventional forces to pay for the expansion of French nuclear forces. French contingency plans for conflict in Europe apparently envisage deployment of the bulk of French ground forces on French territory in northeastern and eastern France to block the traditional invasion route from Belgium and Germany against advancing Soviet forces while a decision is made to use French nuclear weapons; it is a plan for autonomous defense rather than alliance defense. Although basic French autonomy-centered values appear to be slowly changing, there is little prospect within the next decade of real help from France to improve NATO's conventional defense.[6]

A screen of static defenses on the Federal German border with East Germany and Czechoslovakia would absorb part of the impact of sudden Warsaw Pact attack and makes eminent military sense. But for years Federal German authorities have turned away such suggestions with the argument that they would deepen the division of Germany, send the German public into panic because of the presumed approach of conflict, raise objections from ecologists, and do great harm to economically poor border areas that live mainly from tourism, hiking, and outdoor sports.

For political and economic reasons, then, unless the Soviet Union engages in some major action with directly negative consequences for Western Europe, few of the approaches to force improvement described in this chapter—emerging technologies, more combat units in German reserves, an increased role for French forces, increased specialization among NATO forces to create stronger NATO ground forces, or standardization and joint production of equipment—are likely to take place on a major scale. Some aspects of all will be carried out but none in decisive measure. For the indefinite future, NATO is likely to continue with barely adequate defenses.

This situation is militarily unsatisfactory. Two reasons for it have been mentioned in earlier chapters: the European disinclination to have conventional forces so capable as to make lengthy conventional war feasible or possible and the unspoken European fear that if they develop genuinely capable conventional forces, the result will be withdrawal of U.S. conventional forces from Europe. But the main reason for it is quite apparent and less illogical than it may appear: the conclusion, vocal or tacit, by European leaders and electorates that the risk of Soviet attack is low and consequently that the problems of NATO defense are not so urgent as to justify the political and economic dislocation required to make major reforms. European NATO countries are now paying all the insurance they are willing to pay to guard against unlikely contingencies. Indeed every weekend and every holiday, at least 50 percent of the personnel of the armed forces of the most exposed NATO country, the Federal Republic of Germany, go on leave. Under pressure from their own public, German authorities in recent years have with increasing emphasis requested U.S. forces in Germany to stop their practice of exercise firing at night and on weekends for U.S. army tanks and artillery at approved target ranges because too much noise is generated for the public in the surrounding areas. It is hard to imagine a clearer indicator of the low degree of urgency felt by Europeans.

Notes

1. *Strengthening Conventional Deterrence in Europe,* Report of the European Security Study (New York: St. Martin's Press, 1983), pp. 240–243.
2. Steven L. Canby, "Military Reform and the Art of War," *International Security Review* 7:3 (Fall 1982), discusses the reserve concept.
3. Steven L. Canby and Ingemar Dorger, "More Troops, Fewer Missiles," *Foreign Policy* (Winter 1983–1984).
4. H.H. Von Sandrart, "Forward Defense and the Use of Barriers," *NATO's Sixteen Nations* 1/85 Vol. 30. Canby, "Military Reform."
5. Hans Gunther Brauch and Lutz Unterseher, "Getting Rid of Nuclear Weapons: A Review of a Few Proposals for a Conventional Defense of Europe," *Journal of Peace Research* 21:2 (1984). Frank Barnaby and Egbert Boeker, *Defense without Offence; Non Nuclear Defense of Europe,* Peace Studies Papers 8 (London: Housmans, 1982). Michael Clarke, *The Alternative Defense Debate,* ADI Occasional Paper 3 (Brighton, Sussex: Armament and Disarmament Information Unit, University of Sussex, August 1985), contains an exceptionally useful and balanced account of most proposals.
6. For valuable background on French views of conventional defense in Europe, see David S. Yost, *France and Conventional Defense in Central Europe,* EAI Papers 7 (Marina del Rey, Calif.: European American Institute for Security Research, Spring 1984).

4
Beyond the Watershed in Europe

T he Federal German Army's holiday practices and, more seriously, continuing European resistance to force improvements that are intrinsically feasible cause concern to many Western military experts, especially U.S. experts. It is proper for these experts to point to the many continuing defects of NATO defenses. That is their function. But the prevailing European assessment of the overall balance between defense efforts and defense risks appears to be roughly correct.

The Chance of Soviet Attack on Europe

Many segments of the European public—probably a majority of the adult populations of the Northern Tier countries—seem to have reached a conclusion about the Soviet Union that is still highly controversial in the United States. In the prevailing U.S. view, the Soviet Union is an expansionist power in a general sense, expansionist in all settings that permit it, but realistic enough to suspend its ambitions temporarily where circumstances require it, as in Europe, only to resume them as soon as it is feasible. In practical terms, this means that Western Europe continues to be directly threatened by Soviet attack at the moment and more surely if it lets its military guard down and, of course, is also threatened by continuing Soviet efforts to gain increased influence over Western European policy through pressures generated by its military power. The divergent European view is that although the Soviet Union probably remains prepared to use military force in Third World countries, militarily at least, the Soviet Union is a status quo power in Europe. That is, the Soviet Union would defend itself if attacked, could react irrationally in some circumstances, but will not on a deliberate and considered basis launch an aggressive attack on Western Europe for the purpose of conquering and holding Western Europe.

European public opinion has developed more rapidly than that of most European governments, which officially still share the U.S. view. Yet the prevailing European public view of the Soviet Union is probably correct. Over the years, the Soviet leadership has absorbed the significance of nuclear weapons for warfare, making attack on Europe not worth the ultimate risk. It has achieved nuclear parity with the United States, which makes a U.S. attack on the Soviet Union improbable and almost excludes a repetition of attack by a German-led European coalition army. The Soviet leadership has observed the effects of its aggressively activist policies during the Stalin and the Khrushchev periods in increasing NATO's cohesion and military strength. The Berlin blockade was the final Soviet action that crystallized U.S. and Western European determination to establish the NATO alliance, and in retrospect this is obvious to Soviet leaders. Soviet leaders have also observed the decidedly nonaggressive phenomenon of antinuclear sentiment in Western Europe. The Soviet regime has drawn its conclusions from all this. The recurrent heavy-handed political moves against Western Europe that made the task of maintaining NATO cohesion easier in the past are no longer probable.

NATO forces probably are an adequate match for most possible forms of Soviet attack, and it is essential that this should remain the case. But above and beyond NATO's capacity to resist, it is improbable that a Soviet attack on Europe would be carried out to gain enduring control of European productive resources since this objective might well be frustrated through immense destruction whether the war was won or lost. There is no longer any possibility, if there ever was one, of the Soviet Union's using local communist parties as their agents, backed by Soviet armed forces, to gain lasting political control over Western Europe. Moreover, even if a Soviet attack on Western Europe were successful, the requirement for Soviet occupation forces would be enormous at a time when worldwide conflict still raged. The task of quelling resistance would be immensely difficult, as the Soviets know from experience in Afghanistan and elsewhere. Soviet leaders also know that a Soviet occupation would in due course create grave problems of morale and political control not only for the personnel involved but ultimately for the Soviet system itself.

Rationally there are no offsetting national Soviet gains from attack on Western Europe and no form of attack on Europe that would not entail some risk of both nuclear war and worldwide conflict. Attack and occupation of Western Europe would bring fewer economic and political benefits for the Soviet Union than trade and credits from Western Europe. The Soviet Union has much more to gain and far less to risk from continuing its present policy of accommodation with Western Europe. This conclusion does not mean that the Soviet Union might not launch an aggressive attack on Western Europe if the whole range of costs were much lower. There is nothing in the Soviet record to suggest principled restraint against the use of armed force or squeamishness about spilling blood to further national aims. But militarily, on the basis of rational considerations, the Soviet Union has become a status quo power in Europe.

Skeptics will correctly say that this conclusion assigns great weight to the effect of rationality in Soviet thinking. As long as the Soviet Union possesses enormously powerful military forces, the possibility of war through irrational Soviet actions or through miscalculation remains and, for this reason also, the need for NATO defenses in Europe. Moreover, it is evident that the Soviet Union will continue to attempt to increase its influence over Western European governments, just as the Western coalition will continue its efforts to increase its influence over Eastern Europe and the Soviet Union. Whether these Soviet efforts are motivated by the continual desires of a conservative great power to improve its security by gaining influence over countries on its periphery or whether they are motivated by expansionist ideology is a secondary issue; the efforts will continue. But as long as Western European countries can maintain a rough military parity with those portions of Soviet forces committed to the Soviet Union's western approaches and maintain a reasonably close political relationship with the United States, they can deal with these attempts. The Soviet Union will not go to war in Europe if it cannot achieve its political objectives by political means.

Soviet Political Intimidation

The concept of intimidation by the Soviet Union as a means of increasing its influence over Western Europe is central to Western thinking. In the period directly after the end of World War II, the main fear of Western policymakers was that the Soviet Union would act directly with aggressive military force. As developments showed this possibility to be increasingly remote, their greatest fear has been that the Soviet Union could somehow use its military power to intimidate Western European political leaders. This apprehension is so central to the thinking of NATO leaders that any treatment of the East-West military confrontation must analyze whether it is well founded.

The concerns of U.S. leaders about the steadfastness of others in the face of Soviet pressures often reflect a supercilious assessment of the superior toughness of Americans and the lesser fiber of foreigners, as well as some exaggeration of Soviet capabilities. But these concerns are too widely shared by respected European leaders to be dismissed out of hand. In November 1983, at the special convention of the German Social Democratic party in Cologne on the INF issue, former Chancellor Helmut Schmidt, who despite his disclaimers comes as close as any Western leader to being the initiator of the entire project for deployment of new intermediate-range U.S. missiles in Europe, made a last vain appeal to his Social Democratic colleagues not to withdraw their support for deployment of the missiles. The clinching argument Chancellor Schmidt sought to advance was the heightened risk of Soviet intimidation of Western Europe if the planned deployment did not take place.

Moreover, it is a matter of record that the Soviet Union does indulge in threats based on its military strength and has done so repeatedly in Western Europe. In 1948 and 1958, the Soviets tried to use overwhelming local superiority in military forces to pressure the Western allies out of Berlin. In 1981, the Soviet Union carried out massive military exercises around the borders of Poland with the manifest intention of intimidating supporters of the Solidarity movement. As the dispute over INF deployment peaked in 1983, the Soviet Union used every potential pressure it could squeeze from its military forces, threatening to increase its nuclear forces in Europe, to withdraw from the Geneva arms control talks with the United States, and to cut off the developing relationship between the two Germanies, which has deep emotional and symbolic importance for Federal Germans. It carried out its first two threats, but all the pressures did not sway a vote of a single deputy of the Kohl coalition government, even those of Free Democrats skeptical of the merits of missile deployment.

This Bundestag vote took place under adverse conditions in a situation where the original decision to deploy INF missiles in Europe was flawed, a technical response to a crisis of political confidence, and where U.S. conduct of the INF talks was not fully convincing to Europeans. When the issue is clearer, as in the case of Soviet military pressures on Berlin in 1948 and 1958, Western European public opinion has given full support to the NATO and U.S. position.

No country in the world has been the recipient of more direct Soviet threats to burn it to a crisp with nuclear weapons than the Federal Republic of Germany. A few recent threats have been mentioned, but they are only recent ones. For example, the Soviet note of February 5, 1963, to the Federal German government states, "One can imagine without difficulty that, in the event of a thermonuclear war, powerful and concentrated blows of missiles and nuclear weapons would inevitably fall on Federal Germany, which would not survive a third world war." In October 1963, Khrushchev said in East Berlin with customary bluntness that the Federal Republic, "if a war broke out, would burn up like a candle at the very outset." Yet these repeated threats, as brutal and heavy-handed as any threat of use of military force could be, have not altered a single significant decision of the Federal Republic: membership in NATO, establishment of the Bundeswehr, or equipping the Bundeswehr with nuclear-capable aircraft and Pershing I missiles (with warheads remaining in U.S. custody). In the mid-1960s, massive Soviet threats did not cause the Germans to relinquish the project for a multilateral nuclear force. In its note to the Federal German government of July 11, 1964 on the MLF project, the Soviet Union accused the Germans of being the ringleaders of the project and threatened that, in so doing, the German government was converting its entire territory into a target zone for massive nuclear retribution. Despite this Soviet pressure, the decision to end the MLF project was not a German decision, but a political decision by President Johnson that the project would cause more friction with non-German members of NATO than it was worth. And in 1978, it was the United States that dropped the plan to deploy neutron warheads in Europe, not the Germans, although they had been pressured by the Soviet Union in a broad campaign of threats.

Soviet efforts to influence Federal German elections have been so frequent as to be customary. As the elections of September 1957 approached and there was discussion of deploying new dual-capable U.S. nuclear weapons to units of the German Bundeswehr, Soviet Prime Minister Bulganin publicly warned that a nuclear war would turn Germany into a cemetery. The Federal German electorate reacted by giving Chancellor Konrad Adenauer victory by the largest margin he ever received. A similar campaign of threats and intimidation by the Soviet Union in the spring of 1983 in connection with deployment of the U.S. intermediate-range missiles is credited by most experts with helping Chancellor Helmut Kohl and his Christian Democrats to a strong election victory over the Social Democrats, who were openly favored by the Soviet Union.

There is a clear pattern in this record. It is one of repeated Soviet attempts to influence Western European, especially Federal German, policy, using Soviet military power as a basis for these efforts—and of repeated failure of these attempts. This is the reality of the Soviet intimidation issue, and it seems likely to continue. It would not be right to be too categorical about this subject. Living in the neighborhood of a large, powerful Soviet Union has instilled prudence and caution in the Western European countries. Many individual suggestions for NATO force improvements have been rejected by European NATO states as provocative toward the Soviet Union. In the late 1950s, for example, Chancellor Adenauer is reported to have rejected the idea of deploying U.S. Thor intermediate-range missiles in Federal Germany because of potential problems with German domestic opinion and friction with the Soviet Union. But on most major issues, the Western Europeans have resisted Soviet pressures.

Some U.S. experts worry about the possibility that the Soviet Union might attain a greater capacity for intimidating Western European governments now that it has achieved nuclear parity with the United States and U.S. nuclear protection is less convincing for the European NATO states. Some worry in particular that Federal Germany could be vulnerable to Soviet or East German pressures on West Berlin. But such action would cause East Germany to forego the important economic benefits of Federal German payments for access and services to Berlin and Federal German trade with East Germany, with consequent severe damage to the viability of the East German system, while it would mobilize Federal Germany and Western Europe toward greater cohesion with the United States, as well as intensified military efforts. No one can deny that Soviet achievement of nuclear parity with the United States has downgraded the value of U.S. nuclear protection for Europeans, but the last two unsuccessful Soviet efforts, in connection with the neutron warhead and INF, took place in the age of parity.

The Soviet Union as a Status Quo Military Power in Europe

The conclusion that the Soviet Union has become a status quo power in Europe in the military sense has major significance for the future. It means that the NATO–Warsaw Pact military confrontation has passed its peak and is now on the downward slope— that the watershed has been passed. In a sense, the NATO countries approached acceptance of this point in 1967 when they adopted the Harmel report committing NATO to a two-track policy of defense and negotiation with the Warsaw Pact. (See chapter 5.) But the Soviet invasions of Czechoslovakia and Afghanistan and the repression of the Solidarity movement in Poland intervened to suspend that conclusion. All three developments once again demonstrated what was already known: that the Soviet Union would use or threaten to use military force to maintain its dominant position in areas it considered belonging to its sphere of influence. They did not, however, demonstrate increased Soviet militancy in the sense of readiness to attack Western Europe. The increase in Soviet armaments, especially nuclear weapons, that can be targeted on Western Europe may have been motivated by defense considerations. It may also have been motivated by a desire to seek advantage in the East-West balance of forces. But it is not evidence of desire to attack Europe. Gorbachev's proposal of January 1986 to reduce Soviet SS-20s in Europe to zero has propagandistic aspects, but the move clearly recognizes that the original SS-20 deployment was counterproductive for the overriding Soviet aim of protecting its western flanks and of increasing Soviet political influence over Western Europe. In fact, the East-West military confrontation in Europe appears well on the road to becoming "routinized" in the sense of the term developed by Max Weber, with a loss of ideological impetus on both sides.

If the Soviet Union is indeed a status quo power in Europe in the military sense and the East-West military confrontation there is in fact on the downgrade, then NATO will have an increasingly political rather than military function. Even so, no abrupt change will occur in the East-West military confrontation. It will continue for decades, as will the two alliances, even if the trend toward decline becomes more evident, for governments in East and West will not know how to manage the ensuing situation. The insoluble problem of reconciling a declining threat with continuing vigilance and readiness to defend will of itself tend to maintain the confrontation. Moreover, a confrontation in decline has its own dangers and risks, which should be studied and evaluated.

Above and beyond these provisos to the conclusion that the Soviet Union is a status quo power militarily in Europe, the evidence for that conclusion is admittedly ambiguous and heavily disputed. No Westerner can afford to be dogmatic, certainly not in so vital a matter, on interpreting the intentions of a Soviet leadership whose decision-making process is largely impervious to Western analysis.

There is one clear test of the nature of Soviet policy toward Western Europe, whether militarily expansionist or status quo. This is the arms control test, the test of Soviet willingness to enter into significant, verifiable arms control agreements. Up to now, the evidence here has also been ambiguous.

This ambiguity and the underlying divergence of U.S. and European political opinion as to the nature of Soviet policy, specifically Soviet policy toward Europe, is already evident in differing European and U.S. assessments of the imposition of martial law in Poland, the Soviet intervention in Afghanistan, and East-West economic sanctions. The divergence is likely to increase in coming years. The United States, faced with the task of coping with Soviet political expansionism in the Third World, has not yet learned that these Soviet efforts, like U.S. interventions in the Third World in favor of Western democracy, will continue indefinitely. Instead, the United States is still looking for some definitive solution to a problem that has no definitive solution. Consequently it has not focused on the main task: that of reducing the military component of the competition.

Conscious of the friction and distrust that divergent assessments of the Soviet Union and of Western tactics toward it have caused in European-U.S. relations, the governments of European NATO countries are likely for years to come to resist publicly stating that the Soviet Union has become a status quo power in the military sense. Yet each passing year without war in Europe, beyond the forty peaceful years that have already passed, will add weight to the status quo interpretation—and will progressively increase the difficulty of maintaining NATO defenses.

This difficulty will take various forms, among them increased voter resistance to defense budgets and to specific NATO policies like nuclear deployments. In the long run, it is likely to lead European NATO countries, among other things, to shift more and more of their active-duty forces into reserves—a wholly logical way to dismantle a military confrontation—if these actions are reciprocated in Eastern Europe and the Soviet Union. But they may not be reciprocated, at least not for a long time to come.

U.S. forces in Europe, which are expeditionary forces assigned abroad, cannot be converted to reserve status and still be kept in place in Europe. No one can now say what specific continuing effect efforts to reduce the U.S. budgetary deficit will have on U.S. forces in Europe. But it has become a traditional reaction of the U.S. Congress when the military budget is under pressure to seek increased European effort and to threaten U.S. troop withdrawals if this does not occur. Emotional reactions in the United States to policy divergences with NATO Europe are as likely, perhaps more likely than economic considerations, to generate pressures for withdrawal of American forces. If Western European governments, as distinguished from European public opinion, move closer to acceptance of the idea that the Soviet military threat to Europe has peaked and that Europe can afford to ease back on defense, the potential for friction on this issue will be even greater than in the past. No substantial body of American opinion now urges reduction of U.S. forces in Europe, but pressures for cuts may grow, and some reductions may take place. That development might finally galvanize European governments to overcome political resistance and to take some eminently rational steps toward NATO force improvement. But otherwise, U.S. withdrawals from Europe would have unfortunate consequences, including detracting from whatever long-term possibility may exist for slow decline of the NATO-Pact military confrontation.

Once again, the residue of the INF controversy is a key factor. The importance of the INF controversy is not only that it brought the consequences of U.S.-Soviet nuclear parity to the forefront of European consciousness. It also caused Europeans to reassess traditional concepts of the Soviet threat and to conclude that the threat had receded. In the eyes of many Europeans, U.S. nuclear protection became not only less valuable but less necessary.

But this is just the juncture where conventional U.S. troop presence in Europe becomes more, not less, necessary: necessary to maintain the forward defense strategy and necessary to maintain the deterrent threat of worldwide conventional war between the two superpowers in the event of conflict in Europe, and with it the residual deterrent threat that if NATO forces are losing a conventional war in Europe, U.S. nuclear weapons might be used.

A New and More Demanding Mission for NATO

Let us sum up the discussion thus far. NATO's two main functions are military and political: insulating Western Europe from increasing Soviet influence or from Soviet attack and ensuring cohesion on major policy issues among members of the alliance, especially policy toward the Soviet Union and Eastern Europe. On the military side, NATO's concept of forward defense and flexible response has many serious shortcomings. But the forward defense strategy at least has an inner logic, and NATO is not likely to get a better one. In practice, regarding strategy and force posture, the alliance will have to continue to live with the limitations imposed by European political opinion; fortunately, the risk from doing so does not appear extreme. Given its steady if modest force improvements, NATO should be able to deal adequately with its military problems in coming years.

For the future, the most important area of difficulty for NATO, far more important than the problems of NATO force posture, will be in alliance cohesion. A considerable gulf has developed between the United States and its Western European allies over defense strategy for the West and relations with the East. Against this background, arms control agreements with the Warsaw Pact are not only a response to the threats posed by the military confrontation itself but also a political necessity for the West, to demonstrate the capacity of Western governments to deal with the problem of relations with the Soviets and to restore alliance cohesion on defense issues.

The current situation poses an extremely difficult task for both U.S. and European political leadership, a task to which they have not fully adjusted. For reasons already described, European public opinion has been more rapid than European governments to recognize that the nature of the military problem the NATO alliance is called upon to deal with has changed, probably fundamentally. Unlike the 1950s, when there was genuine concern in Western Europe, whether justified or not, over the possibility of direct Soviet attack on Western Europe, effective NATO defense forces are now needed for the much narrower and less dramatic mission of preventing success for Soviet efforts to exploit in political ways the weakness of a poorly defended Western Europe. These forces will have to be maintained for years to come in a situation where the possibility of outright Soviet attack will appear increasingly remote—and will actually be remote—where costs of new equipment are mounting, possibly against a background of continued high structural unemployment; and where, because of deep-seated attitude change, support by the European and also the U.S. publics for high defense expenditures is flagging. This is a different and far more demanding mission for the NATO alliance, to which one response at least must be a genuine, not merely symbolic, dual approach of defense and negotiation with the Soviet Union and the other Warsaw Pact countries.

What are the prospects for real progress in this field of negotiation, results that could help with the problems of NATO cohesion and divergent interpretations of Soviet policy by providing clear evidence of Soviet willingness or unwillingness to engage in serious efforts to make the East-West confrontation in Europe less risky and less costly? This is the subject to which we will now turn.

Part II
Managing the European Confrontation through Arms Control

5
Arms Control in Europe: A Disordered Puzzle

T he various segments into which arms control in Europe is being negotiated form only a haphazard disarray. This disorderly pattern reveals the underlying truth that there is no integrating concept to hold together these diverse activities, no overall Western scheme of arms control negotiation with the East, and no comprehensive coverage in arms control negotiation of all important aspects of the East-West military confrontation.

Today European arms control in the broad sense is being pursued in three separate forums. First, alliance-to-alliance negotiations between NATO and the Warsaw Pact are taking place in Vienna on the Mutual Reduction of Forces and Armaments and Associated Measures in Central Europe; the "associated measures" in this official East-West title relate to verification and confidence building. In NATO terminology, these talks are called the negotiations on Mutual and Balanced Force Reductions (MBFR). Second, in Stockholm, thirty-five nations are participating individually in the Conference on Confidence- and Security-Building Measures and Disarmament in Europe; in the West, this is called the Conference on Disarmament in Europe (CDE). Third, bilateral U.S.-Soviet negotiations in Geneva on reducing intermediate-range nuclear forces—known in the West as the INF negotiations—are one segment of the broader U.S.-Soviet negotiations also covering space weapons and strategic nuclear weapons. The United States and the Soviet Union participate in all three of these negotiations, but otherwise participants vary. Two of the negotiations, CDE and

MBFR, overlap in geographic area and in subject matter. Yet many important aspects of the NATO–Warsaw Pact confrontation—notably naval forces, air forces and air defenses, nuclear weapons of range under 1000 kilometers, and the entire range of conventional armaments—are not actively covered in any of the forums. In addition, although the United Nations Committee on Disarmament, also meeting in Geneva, is discussing a possible worldwide ban on the production of chemical weapons, there is no negotiation on chemical weapons in Europe, the only place where known stocks of chemical weapons are held outside the home territories of the United States and the Soviet Union.

Why do we have the particular array of European arms control negotiations that we do? What was the impetus for each negotiation? Why does each have the participants and the format—bilateral, multinational, or alliance-to-alliance—that it does? Of all the aspects of the European confrontation, why does each forum cover what it does (both subject matter and geography)? And what is the effect of the present configuration in terms of incomplete or overlapping coverage of issues and lack of evident interrelationship?

This chapter discusses the early history of the three European negotiation forums. But the short answer to these questions is that arms control in Europe in its present form is the product of a divided Europe. It arose haphazardly in response to specific political pressures and not as part of an overall plan. As regards nuclear weapons, the thread is from multilateral negotiations to bilateral U.S.-Soviet negotiations. In the immediate postwar period, the issue of nuclear arms control was negotiated multilaterally in the United Nations framework under the heading of general and complete disarmament. This pattern ended, and a period of effort, mainly bilateral, to achieve partial results came after the Cuban missile crisis of 1962 seriously frightened the leadership of both the United States and the Soviet Union and brought the Limited Test Ban Treaty of 1963.

With some overlap, arms control dealing with conventional armed forces in Europe has been discussed in two distinct functional and chronological contexts. During the fifteen years from the end of World War II to the 1960s, arms control was discussed in terms of a solution of the problem of the division of Germany and of withdrawal of U.S. and Soviet forces from Europe. From the early 1960s on—we can date the change more specifically with the August 1961 construction of the Berlin Wall and the Cuban missile crisis in 1962—East-West discussion of arms control in Europe has been on the basis of accepting the status quo of a divided Germany and of the continued existence of the Warsaw Pact and NATO alliances and has sought to deal directly with the existing East-West military confrontation, although in a fragmentary, haphazard way.

Early Arms Control Efforts

Less than a year after the end of World War II, in the beginning of 1946, deep divisions of opinion over the treatment of occupied Germany and over Soviet actions in installing communist governments in Eastern Europe arose between the Soviet Union and its Western wartime allies. In 1947, the Western allies decided to establish separate economic administration of their zones of occupation in Germany and to reject Soviet demands for reparations and a share in control of the Ruhr area, the major concentration of German industry. In 1948, the Western allies established a separate German government for their zones of occupation. During the conference where this was being decided, communists took over the government of Czechoslovakia. In June 1948, the Soviet Union blockaded land routes to Berlin with the apparent objective either of forcing revision of these Western decisions or of pushing the allies out of Berlin. The NATO alliance was established in the next year, and Federal Germany became a member in 1955.

During the decade that followed the events of 1948–1949, both the Soviet Union and the Western allies made repeated proposals to overcome the division of Germany; all of them had troop withdrawal features, some quite complex. In March 1952, for example, as the West was deciding in principle to establish new German armed forces, the Soviet Union presented Western governments with a draft peace treaty for Germany proposing a reunified Germany with its own military forces on the basis of enforced neutrality, a status like that later agreed for Austria. At the October–November 1955 meeting of the foreign ministers of France, the United Kingdom, the United States, and the Soviet Union in Geneva, the Western allies presented a plan for German unity calling for a zone on both sides of the line of demarcation between a united Germany and East European countries in which limits would be set on armed forces. In a second, narrower, zone closer to the line of demarcation, there could be special restrictions on deployment of military forces and installations. Participants were to provide data on their armed forces in this zone in progressively greater detail. There would be on-site inspection, also of progressive intrusiveness, to verify these data and provide assurance against surprise attack. In order to give further protection against surprise attack, the Soviet Union and its Warsaw Pact allies were to operate a radar system in the Western part of the zone, and NATO would operate a radar system in the Eastern part.[1]

At the July 1955 summit meeting, in which the heads of the governments of the four wartime allies participated, each of the participants introduced proposals for mutual inspection as a means of confidence building. Premier Nikolay Bulganin, the Soviet representative, proposed an agreement among the participants not to be the first to use nuclear weapons, a proposal that still has currency today. He also proposed a system of ground control posts at ports, railroad junctions, and airfields to report whether there were dangerous concentrations of military forces. This point has been taken up in Western proposals in MBFR for fixed exit-entry points to Central Europe manned by personnel of the opposing alliances. President Eisenhower advanced his Open Skies proposal for aerial inspection of the United States and the Soviet Union to give confidence against surprise attack. The West has also proposed low-flying aerial inspection in the MBFR talks.

In 1957 came the first of several plans by Polish Foreign Minister Adam Rapacki for a zone in Central Europe, composed of the territory of Federal Germany, East Germany, Poland, and Czechoslovakia, from which nuclear weapons were to be removed—a subject now under active discussion between the Federal German Social Democratic party and the Socialist Unity party, the communist ruling party of East Germany. Later versions of the Rapacki plan also provided for reduction of conventional forces in this area.[2]

At the initiative of President Eisenhower, a conference to study measures to prevent surprise attack met in Geneva in November–December 1958. The Western participants presented a theoretical scheme for detecting preparations for surprise attack by missile, ground, or air forces. The proposal on ballistic missiles introduced for the first time the concept of controlling nuclear weapons through limiting their delivery systems, which formed the basis for the later SALT I and SALT II agreements. The Soviet proposal at the conference was based on the later versions of the Rapacki plan and provided for a three-stage procedure: freeze nuclear weapons in Federal and East Germany, Poland, and Czechoslovakia; reduce conventional forces; and then eliminate completely nuclear weapons from the zone. The Soviets proposed a system of aerial and ground inspection of a zone in Central Europe, as well as a zone composed of Siberia and the western half of the United States. They also proposed a system of fixed ground inspection points at major transport points, including six in the Soviet Union and six in the United States. Ground posts would be manned and aerial inspections carried out by mixed teams of the two alliances. In the 1958 Soviet proposal, there was also to be a joint center for development and interpretation of aerial photographs, the partial precursor of some contemporary proposals for crisis reduction centers.[3]

Thus although none of the numerous conferences that took place in the late 1940s and the 1950s came even close to achieving specific results, they did generate a wide range of arms control proposals for Europe that formed the intellectual basis of proposals actively negotiated on in the 1970s.

The main focus of negotiation in the 1940s and 1950s was the intractable problem of the division of Germany. In essence, it was only when the division of Germany was accepted as an enduring condition and only when the two leading countries of the rival alliances became sufficiently concerned about the dangers of nuclear weapons to break through their cold war distrust and conclude their first arms control agreement that it became possible to negotiate on arms control in Europe separately from the German question. The turning point in negotiating arms control in Europe came in the early 1960s. The erection of the Berlin Wall by the East Germans in August 1961 under diplomatic and military cover from the Soviet Union and without military resistance from the

United States was a central turning point in Federal German thinking about the reunification issue. Following as it did the earlier
repression by Soviet forces of the Hungarian uprising without
Western military intervention, the construction of the Berlin Wall
admitted of only one reasonable conclusion: to accept the division
of Germany as a fact of indefinite duration and to try to work
around it—as Willy Brandt later put it, to accept the status quo
and to try to improve it. After many years of connection between
the German question and arms control, this conclusion gradually
eroded previous Federal German reluctance to accept measures of
arms control not connected with progress toward solution of the
German unity question.

The second decisive development of the early 1960s was the
Cuban missile crisis of October 1962 resulting from Khrushchev's
foolhardy effort to equalize with a single move U.S. superiority
over the Soviet Union in nuclear weapons, specifically, the introduction of U.S. intermediate-range Thor and Jupiter missiles into
Europe. The crisis frightened both countries into rapid conclusion
of the Limited Test Ban agreement of 1963 limiting nuclear tests
at sea and in the air, the first arms control agreement since the
beginning of the cold war.

In a third decisive development, in 1964 a new coalition of
Soviet leaders headed by Leonid Brezhnev deposed the impetuous
Khrushchev because of his "harebrained schemes," not least among
them the scheme to deploy Soviet missiles in Cuba, as well as
Khrushchev's much-resisted reform of the Communist party structure in the Soviet Union. The new Soviet leaders made an evident
effort to appear conciliatory to the West, seeking increased political
and, above all, economic contacts with the West to gain access to
Western technology and credit. Later, Soviet clashes with the
Chinese, like the fighting on the Usuri River in the spring of 1969,
intensified Soviet motivation to stabilize their western approaches
through negotiation.

The statements of the new Soviet leaders made a positive
impression in the West. In 1966, in an action that marks the beginning of German efforts to deal with security issues separately
from the German question, the Federal German government headed
by Chancellor Erhard proposed to the Soviet Union and the other

states of the Warsaw Pact conclusion of bilateral treaties on nonuse of force, a concept similar to that which the Soviets had advanced a decade earlier at a Four-Power Conference. The Germans proposed that other nonnuclear states enter an international commitment not to produce nuclear weapons, to freeze and reduce nuclear weapons in all of Europe, to conclude a mutual declaration of nonuse of force, and to exchange observers at military exercises. The last two items are actively under consideration today at the Conference on Disarmament in Europe in Stockholm.[4]

Maneuvering toward Negotiations on Force Reductions and a European Security Conference

These indications of East-West relaxation were not without effect on the U.S. public and Congress. Moreover, as U.S. involvement in Vietnam deepened, the U.S. defense budget mounted, and the U.S. balance of payments became more unfavorable. Although the MBFR negotiations did not begin until 1973, mounting pressure in the United States to reduce U.S. forces in Europe was apparent by the mid-1960s. In an exchange with Senator Robert Kennedy during a Senate hearing in July 1966, Secretary of Defense Robert McNamara had said the Johnson administration would be prepared to reduce its forces in Europe if the Soviets made reductions in East Germany. In August of that year and in subsequent years through 1972, Senator Mike Mansfield introduced resolutions calling for unilateral withdrawal of substantial U.S. personnel in Europe in the light of increasing U.S. commitments in Vietnam. Although support for the Mansfield resolutions reached a high point of only forty-two votes, they did push the Johnson administration further toward negotiating force reductions with the Soviet Union.

In October 1966, President Johnson in an important policy speech supported the idea of a gradual and balanced revision of force levels on both sides. The communiqué of the semiannual NATO Ministerial Council in December 1966 picked up this signal and repeated it in almost the same words. In their June 1967 meeting, the NATO foreign ministers made it more explicit, stating, "If conditions permit, a balanced reduction of forces by the East and

West would be a significant step toward security in Europe."[5] The key word *balanced* that appeared in all these statements is the same one used in the NATO title for the Vienna force reduction talks, Mutual and Balanced Force Reductions. This concept represented an early NATO determination to try to achieve parity with the Pact in arms control negotiations and not to sign any agreement with the Warsaw Pact that would contractualize in treaty form any Warsaw Pact numerical advantage. Put another way, it represented NATO's determination, understandable given NATO's conviction that the Warsaw Pact had numerical superiority in men and weapons, to make the Warsaw Pact give more than they received in any agreed troop reductions. Aware of this connotation of an otherwise unobjectionable word, Soviet and Warsaw Pact negotiators would later refuse to accept it as part of the official title of the force reduction negotiations.

The pressures on the United States to reduce its forces in Europe were real. In 1967, the United States and the United Kingdom reached an agreement whereby Federal Germany would pay a larger share of the costs for maintaining troops in Germany. As part of this Trilateral Agreement, the United States withdrew two brigades from Germany, and the United Kingdom also reduced the Army of the Rhine. Canada cut in half its small force in Europe. Federal Germany announced plans to reduce its forces from 461,000 to 400,000 over a period of years. (Germany had not yet reached the 500,000-man limit on its personnel contained in the 1955 London and Paris treaties that had agreed on establishment of new German armed forces, although it was to do so in the détente period under Chancellor Schmidt.) The Netherlands and Belgium also wanted to cut their forces. The United States was able to persuade Federal Germany and the other continental European states not to reduce their forces in the absence of agreement with the Warsaw Pact, but these U.S. efforts increased the United States's own commitment to negotiate force reductions with the East.

Yet even as the NATO countries were becoming more convinced of the desirability of negotiating force reductions with the Warsaw Pact, the Warsaw Pact itself appeared to be moving away from this concept. In January 1965, the Political Consultative Committee of the Warsaw Pact, the Warsaw Pact's equivalent of the NATO Council of Ministers, called for an all-European security conference, with China and the United States as observers, along the lines of the conference they had proposed as early as the four-power foreign ministers' meeting of 1954. The declaration issued by the committee's Bucharest meeting in July 1966 called for good neighborly relations on the basis of peaceful coexistence, dissolution of existing alliances, liquidation of foreign military bases, withdrawal of foreign troops, nuclear-free zones, recognition of existing frontiers, and conclusion of a German peace settlement and for convening an all-European security conference to apply these principles of cooperation. The European communist parties meeting in Karlovy Vary, Czechoslovakia, in April 1967 repeated the call for a conference of all European states on the question of security and cooperation in Europe. The underlying purpose of this conference—the United States was conspicuously omitted from those invited—was to ratify the postwar boundaries in Eastern Europe, especially of Poland and of the Soviet Union, both of which incorporated large segments of pre-Hitler Germany; it was not to reduce forces.

Meanwhile the movement within NATO toward force reductions continued. The Harmel report, *Future Tasks of the Alliance,* approved by the NATO Ministerial Council in December 1967, mentioned that the allies were studying balanced force reductions. The report officially added a second main function to NATO's long-standing mission of maintaining adequate military strength and political solidarity to deter aggression by the Warsaw Pact: "to pursue the search for progress toward a more stable relationship in which the underlying issues [for example, the division of Germany] could be solved."[6] It was essential and necessary for the NATO alliance to take this step toward broadening its functions under the pressure of growing interest in Europe and the United States in improving relations with the Warsaw Pact states, but the report amounted to an explicit acknowledgment that NATO's future task would be to reconcile these often irreconcilable objectives or, rather, to seek some uneasy and temporary compromise between them.

The NATO Ministerial Council at Reykjavik, Iceland, in June 1968 took yet another step toward negotiating force reductions.

Deciding to make all necessary preparations to discuss mutual force reduction with the Warsaw Pact, the ministers issued a series of principles that should govern reductions: (1) reductions should be balanced in scope (with the connotation already discussed) and in timing (which meant in practical terms that the Soviets and the United States would be expected to reduce first); (2) reductions should be substantial but not so large as to risk destabilizing the situation in Europe (a formula later worked out to mean a reduction of no more than 10 percent of NATO forces); and (3) reductions should be consistent with the security interests of all parties. This last point is ambiguous. In practice, as seen by NATO, "all parties" turned out to mean all members of both alliances that were willing to participate in the MBFR talks, a concept that greatly complicated the negotiating task.

Nearly all of the early NATO moves on MBFR were at Federal German initiative, namely Social Democratic initiative. In June 1966, the Social Democratic party adopted a resolution calling for negotiated force reductions based on a speech by Helmut Schmidt, who was to become defense minister in the Kiesinger-Brandt Broad Coalition that took office in November 1966 and who has often referred to himself as the father of the MBFR talks. Both the Harmel report and the "signal of Reykjavik" in the June 1968 ministerial communiqué were the direct result of the work of Foreign Minister Willy Brandt and the head of the policy planning section of the Foreign Ministry, Brandt's close associate Egon Bahr.[7]

The August 1968 Soviet invasion of Czechoslovakia to reinstitute communist orthodoxy once again revealed the Soviet Union as willing to use armed force to prevent any decrease in its control over Eastern European countries. Other than a barely seemly delay, this utterly repugnant action had scarcely any practical effect in decreasing Western desires to negotiate arms control with the Soviet Union. But the underlying situation was still one of crossed purposes: NATO wanted force reduction negotiations, while the Soviet Union wanted a political negotiation confirming the postwar borders of Poland and the Soviet Union to serve as a substitute for the peace treaty with Germany which the Soviet Union had so often proposed in the years before 1960. In their May 1969 communiqué, the NATO ministers made progress toward convening the

European security conference desired by the Soviets dependent on achieving a Berlin agreement, on which diplomatic soundings were just beginning, as well as on a move toward MBFR talks.

With the September 1969 election of Willy Brandt as chancellor of Federal Germany, these different elements began to fall into line in a complex system of linkages. In March 1970, four-power negotiations on Berlin began. In June, the Warsaw Pact indicated that the United States and Canada could participate in the all-European security conference. In August, the Brandt government concluded a treaty with the Soviet Union and in November with Poland accepting the postwar borders of these two countries and thus their incorporation of prewar German territories. Once the Soviet Union received this formal indication of acceptance of the postwar status, the necessary precondition for Soviet agreement to negotiate arms control in Europe was fulfilled, and in March 1971, Brezhnev indicated willingness to negotiate on force reductions in Central Europe.

In May 1971, Senator Mansfield submitted a new version of his resolution calling for unilateral withdrawal of U.S. forces from Europe. As the vote approached, he believed he had put together majority support. But only five days before the scheduled Senate vote on the Mansfield resolution, in full knowledge of the importance of his step, Brezhnev destroyed its chances in a speech in Tiflis commemorating the fiftieth anniversary of the founding of the Georgian republic. Brezhnev said political leaders in the West had expressed worry about what type of reductions might be involved in East-West force reduction negotiations. But, he said, they resembled "a person who tries to judge the flavor of wine by its appearance alone without imbibing it. . . . Translated into diplomatic language, this means—to start negotiations."[8] The message was unambiguous—the Soviet Union was ready to start talks on force reduction—and it brought the defeat of the Mansfield resolution in Congress by sixty-one to thirty-six votes. Senator Mansfield tried once again in the summer of 1972, but by then it was evident that arms reduction negotiations with the Warsaw Pact would take place, and most senators were not willing to undercut the U.S. position at the outset of these negotiations.

Brezhnev's statement derailing the Mansfield resolution was an action designed to retain U.S. forces in Europe, perhaps in order to head off the increase in Federal German forces that unilateral U.S. withdrawal could have ultimately entailed. Together with the June 1970 agreement to invite the United States and Canada to the proposed European security conference, it suggested that the Soviet Union at this time considered an important U.S. role in Western Europe as an element of stability, perhaps in a dual role with the Soviet Union. Whatever motive they reflected, these Soviet moves were not the actions of a government seriously interested in creating conditions for Soviet military action against Western Europe. The logical thing in that case would have been to seek to help the Mansfield resolution, not hinder it.

Brezhnev's actions with regard to the all-European security conference make clear that it was a favorite project for him. The German treaties with the Soviet Union and Poland, along with the written endorsement of these treaties by the three Western allies, already entailed acceptance of the postwar borders of Poland and the Soviet Union. The endorsement of smaller European states, such as Malta, that would participate in an all-European conference could add little additional authority to this confirmation. Yet Brezhnev persevered with the European security conference project, and he was willing to pay for it—first, by accepting the Western idea of a troop reduction negotiation that prior Soviet actions showed they did not particularly want, and, second, by accepting in the Helsinki Accords that the European security conference produced commitments on human rights that cause continuing difficulty for the Soviet Union.

The way was now clear to holding both conferences: the all-European security conference, which became the Helsinki Conference on Security and Cooperation in Europe (CSCE), and a NATO–Warsaw Pact negotiation to reduce armed forces, the MBFR talks. The remaining developments leading to the two conferences took place smoothly. In September 1971, the Four-Power Agreement on Berlin was concluded, fulfilling NATO's main precondition for accepting a European security conference. What remained was to pull the threads together into a finished deal.

This was the more necessary since the Soviet Union had refused to receive the NATO Secretary General, charged by NATO with conducting exploratory talks on force reduction negotiations, on the grounds that the Soviet Union, which continues to support dissolution of the two alliances as part of its long-term program, did not want an alliance-to-alliance forum of negotiation on force reductions but a wider circle of participants. The European NATO countries wanted an alliance-to-alliance format to enable direct Western European participation in East-West arms control negotiation and to ensure a unified alliance position at the negotiations. All the NATO countries considered at this stage that if the negotiation was to be multilateral, only an alliance-to-alliance format would bring real results—negotiated reductions instead of Soviet rhetoric. The Soviet intention to avoid an alliance-to-alliance format persevered through the preparatory talks for MBFR, where the Soviet Union explicitly reserved the option of inviting other participants to the main negotiations. It may well be that at this stage, the Soviet Union intended to do the main military business of CSCE in the Vienna force reduction talks.

In May 1972, when President Nixon went to Moscow to sign the SALT I agreement, the Soviets tentatively agreed to start preliminary talks on MBFR in return for starting CSCE preliminary talks in the summer of 1972 in Helsinki. In September, Secretary of State Henry Kissinger visited Moscow, and at the conclusion of his visit, it was publicly announced that the Soviet Union had accepted the Western position to hold a separate East-West conference on force reductions at about the same time as the CSCE began.

MBFR Gets Underway

Within seven months of the signing of SALT I, preparatory talks for the MBFR negotiations began. During this period, the ranks of NATO MBFR participants swelled considerably, but strenuous efforts to gain an especially important recruit, France, for the negotiations failed. France's NATO allies—Federal Germany, then Britain, and then the United States—did their best to persuade France to participate in the MBFR talks. The Soviet Union did the same during President Georges Pompidou's visit to the Soviet Union in January 1973 and subsequently, but the French government was not to be swayed. It was convinced that the MBFR talks were

founded on an erroneous concept. If successful, they would result
in a special zone in the center of Europe, an area where the Germans would be subject to restraints and controls and to a Soviet
right of oversight to which other Western European states would
not be subject. Sooner or later Germany would resent this treatment, and its resentment would give rise to instability. The Netherlands, Belgium, and Luxembourg took sufficiently seriously the
negative aspects of leaving Germany isolated in a zone of control
to agree to add their territories to German territory to form the
Western part of the reduction area.

France also believed that ultimately, if reductions continued,
this special zone might in practice become a zone of neutrality,
taking the heart out of NATO defense. (France, following its 1966
withdrawal from NATO's integrated command, remains a member
of the NATO alliance and of the NATO Council, where it has
occasionally commented in the negative on the MBFR talks.) Subsequent French reactions to the anti-INF demonstrations of the
early 1980s in Germany showed that France was indeed sensitive
about possible moves toward German neutrality. But equally strong
motives in eschewing MBFR were France's desire not to have its
troop presence in Germany subject to international agreement with
the Soviets. French officials considered that French occupation rights
in the Federal Republic gave France the right unilaterally to increase its forces stationed there as a last guarantor against negative
political developments in Germany, and they had no intention of
surrendering or limiting these rights through an agreement with the
Soviet Union.

Finally, France recognized from the outset that the other allies
wanted to have a rule of unanimity in the force reduction talks—
principally to limit any possibility of U.S. deals with the Soviet
Union at the cost of Western Europe—and it had no intention of
sacrificing its hard-won autonomy within NATO to go into lockstep again in the negotiation field. Later France successfully insisted
that the policy of NATO members only be loosely coordinated in
the Stockholm Conference on Disarmament in Europe rather than
coordinated to the last detail as in MBFR.

But if France did not wish to participate in the MBFR talks,
many other NATO members did. In the original NATO concept,

the NATO participants in Vienna were to be those countries with forces in the Central European area that NATO had decided should be the focus of negotiations. These countries were Belgium, Canada, the Federal Republic of Germany, the Netherlands, Luxembourg, the United Kingdom, and the United States. As originally conceived, these countries would report results in the talks to their allies at NATO in Brussels.

But this was not to be. Turkey, a country that had aspired to a direct connection with Europe since the days of Kemal Ataturk, was insistent on playing a direct role in the MBFR talks; it wanted to participate in any East-West agreement on European security issues. Senior Turkish ministers threatened to resign demonstratively if the United States and other NATO participants did not agree to Turkey's presence in the MBFR negotiations as a participant. In the end, the United States and the larger NATO states did agree, and that meant inviting the other states of NATO's southern flank, Greece and Italy, as well as Norway and Denmark, the two flank states in the north. Of the remaining NATO countries, France had refused to participate; Spain was not yet a member; Portugal, then in the throes of revolution, had no forces in Central Europe; and Iceland has no armed forces at all.

On the Warsaw Pact side, the list of participants also grew. At the last moment, the NATO states had decided to attempt to gain Hungarian participation in reductions because of the Soviet divisions stationed there—in other words, to increase the total Soviet reduction—although NATO experts believe Soviet forces in Hungary have the mission of moving south against Yugoslavia in the event of war rather than west over neutral Austria to attack NATO's Central Front. NATO had already decided to invite the Soviet Union, Poland, Czechoslovakia, and East Germany as those Pact countries directly involved in the critical Central European area. So the last-minute NATO decision to invite Hungary meant that the West also had to invite the remaining Warsaw Pact states, Romania and Bulgaria. NATO would have had to justify an invitation limited to Hungary alone with an explanation of its intentions with regard to Hungary, and this would have brought Pact rejection. In any event, when the Soviet Union made inclusion of Italy the price for Hungarian inclusion in the reduction area—

something the Hungarians visibly wanted—Italy and other NATO states drew back from their demands regarding Hungary and merely reserved the right to bring up the subject of direct Hungarian participation at a later date. (If this were ever done, it probably would be in the form of a noncircumvention clause barring the Soviets from increasing their forces in Hungary while decreasing their troops in Central Europe.)

Once the entire membership of the Pact and most NATO states were assembled in Vienna, it seemed logical to give decision-making powers at the conference only to those states that would be reducing their forces, and so participants were divided into the categories of direct participants and special, or flank, participants, on these grounds (figure 5–1). Two countries, Romania and Italy, were unhappy at this decision; they thought all participants ought to have equal status. As far as NATO deliberations are concerned, the distinction rapidly became a meaningless formality, and NATO developed a consensus rule for all statements to the Warsaw Pact negotiators made in both plenary and informal sessions, as well as statements made to the press.

The preparatory talks for the MBFR negotiations began in January 1973 in Vienna and ended in June 1973 with adoption of agreement on the subject matter and geographical area of the main negotiations. The participants agreed on a reduction area to consist of the territory of the Benelux states and the Federal Republic of Germany in the West and of the German Democratic Republic, Poland, and Czechoslovakia in the East (figure 5–1). They agreed to exclude naval forces from the scope of the forthcoming conference as an undesirable complication, and they agreed that the subject matter of the negotiations should be the mutual reduction of forces and armaments and associated measures in Central Europe.

The Warsaw Pact negotiators insisted on specific inclusion in the agreed description of the subject matter of the concept of armament reductions. NATO participants were reluctant to include the term, and this difference of view over armament reductions foreshadowed one of the major difficulties in the negotiations proper. For their part, the Soviets were somewhat mystified by the term *associated measures* until it was explained that it would cover matters like postreduction information exchange, advance notification of military movements, verification, and measures against

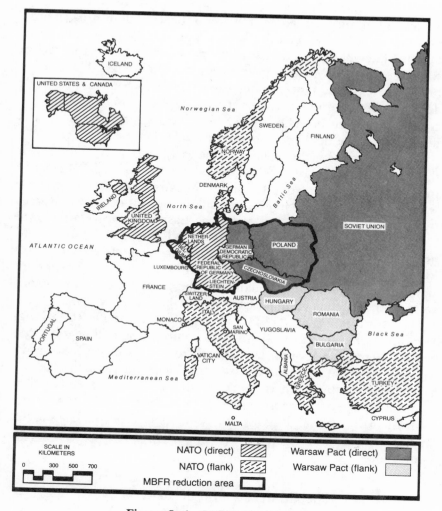

Figure 5–1. *MBFR Participants*

surprise attack. The Soviets then insisted that the associated measures as well as reductions take place in Central Europe. Their
successful insistence on this point, against the efforts of NATO
negotiators already speculating on the possibility of extending some
of these measures to the Soviet Union, meant that later NATO
moves in the main negotiations to extend to the entire western

Soviet Union the requirement for prenotification of out-of-garrison movements would exceed the agreed mandate of the negotiations. But this later NATO action was taken mainly in order to develop some aspect of an MBFR agreement that could be signed by NATO flank participants. Once again, the decisive factor was Turkey's desire to be a formal participant in agreements on European security; corporate NATO interest in achieving an agreement was weaker than the desire to accommodate Turkey.

These arrangements reached in the early 1970s for dealing with the major problems of war or peace between East and West and the huge military confrontation in Europe are more noteworthy for what was not included than for the small segment of military forces they did cover. In practical terms, as East-West negotiations are still organized over a decade later, naval forces, air forces, and armaments of all kinds except for nuclear weapons of over 1000 kilometers in range are omitted from coverage in reductions, as are the northern and southern flanks of the great European confrontation. And already in this early period, there was evidence of differing attitudes among NATO participants: in the North, a long-standing Scandinavian inclination to compromise and negotiation; robust skepticism about arms control from France and Britain; divided opinion in Germany; status considerations among the representatives of the southern flanks; with the United States skeptical and cautious even when supportive of efforts to negotiate arms control in Europe and always far more interested in U.S.-Soviet nuclear negotiations dealing with questions of survival of both countries.

The Conference on Security and Cooperation in Europe

Intra-alliance maneuvering leading up to MBFR also brought a good deal of agreement on the scope of a Conference on Security and Cooperation in Europe (CSCE). NATO's December 1969 communiqué suggested that the subject matter of a European conference might be freer movement of people, ideas, and information and nonintervention in the affairs of any state, whatever its political and social system (an indirect reference to the 1968 Soviet intervention in Czechoslovakia). NATO also suggested measures like advance notification of military movements, the presence of observers at maneuvers, and possibly the establishment of observation posts. In May 1970, the NATO Council suggested that the agenda of a security conference should include principles governing relations among states, including nonuse of force and cooperation in the cultural, economic, technical and scientific, and human environmental fields.

The June 1970 Warsaw Pact foreign ministers meeting at Bucharest not only agreed to U.S. and Canadian participation in a European security conference but suggested the agenda should include the topics of safeguarding European security and renunciation of the threat or use of force; expanded trade; and economic, scientific, technical, and cultural exchanges. The Pact did not accept or even address the NATO concept of freer movement of peoples. In its meeting of May 1972, the NATO Council agreed to the opening of multilateral preparatory talks at Helsinki for the CSCE in Helsinki in November of that year.

Thirty-five nations participated in the preparatory talks at Helsinki and have remained active in subsequent years in continuing consultations that have become known as the Helsinki process. The participants are all the European states, including small states like San Marino and the Vatican, and Canada and the United States. Albania, pursuing its lonely course, refused to participate. The list of participants comprises the full membership of NATO (sixteen states), the full membership of the Warsaw Pact (seven states), and twelve neutral and nonaligned states (see figure 5–2).

The CSCE preparatory talks concluded in June 1973 (the same month that the MBFR preparatory talks were concluded in Vienna). As a result, the Conference on Security and Cooperation in Europe opened with a four-day conference of foreign ministers in July 1973 in Helsinki. Active negotiation took place from September 1973 to July 1975. The results were ratified by a three-day summit meeting of heads of state and government that ended on August 1, 1975.

During the CSCE conference, it was decided that its outcome should take the form of a declaration of political will rather than of a binding treaty. A major reason was the reluctance of the United States, influenced by émigré groups, to accept formal ratification of the postwar borders of Europe because this would have formally

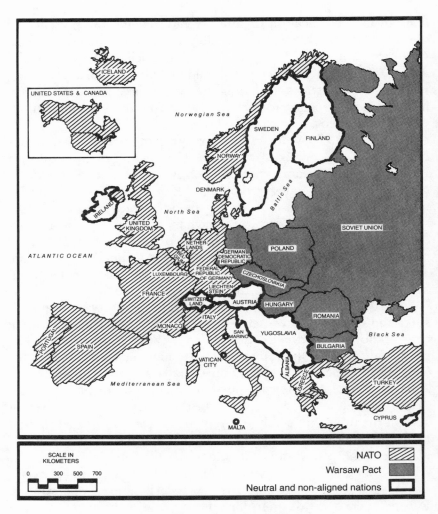

Figure 5–2. *CDE Participants*

ratified Soviet incorporation of the Baltic states Latvia, Estonia, and Lithuania into Soviet territory. Federal Germany too was not enthusiastic over the domestic repercussions of further treaty commitments on borders, and the Soviet Union was reluctant to put human rights commitments into treaty form.

The main outcomes of the CSCE conference, known as the

Helsinki Final Act or the Helsinki Accords, were embodied in several documents.[9] The first, a "Declaration on Principles Guiding Relations among Participating States," contains ten principles, including nonuse of force in border disputes. These principles contain the broad endorsement of the postwar borders the Soviet leadership had been seeking.

A document entitled "Confidence-building Measures and Certain Aspects of Security and Disarmament" contains a political obligation, not a treaty commitment, to give twenty-one days' advance notice of major maneuvers exceeding 25,000 troops and also to provide details on the designation, purpose, states involved, type and numerical strength of forces involved, area, and duration. The NATO countries and the neutral and nonaligned states sought to extend coverage of this measure to "all of Europe from the Atlantic to the Urals," but only a 250 kilometer strip of the western Soviet Union and of Turkey was covered. The Soviets objected to including all of the European Soviet Union because the territory and forces of the United States were not covered in the agreement. It was also agreed that participants could invite military observers to these maneuvers but on a fully voluntary basis. The document also contains three other recommended but not obligatory measures: advance notification of major military movements, a more comprehensive coverage than a definition limited to maneuvers (both the United States and the Soviet Union opposed making this a requirement); prior notification of smaller maneuvers; and exchanges of military personnel.

This document represented the first East-West agreement on a new type of measure, a confidence-building measure. Confidence-building measures as they have become understood in the CSCE context differ from classic arms control, which consists of reduction and limitations of armed forces. Confidence-building measures are intended in the first instance to contribute to the flow of information about the armed forces of participating countries, increasing visibility and diminishing the secrecy of routine military activities, thus providing participants with assurance that preparations for attack are not underway. A second category of confidence-building measures applies restrictions of various kinds on force deployments (e.g., on their size or area).

The Helsinki Final Act also contained measures on cooperation in economics, science and technology, and environment, as well as the document "Cooperation in Humanitarian and Other Fields," encouraging freer movement of people, ideas, and information and facilitating family reunification. This is the human rights component of the Helsinki Accords. The Final Act also provided for indefinite continuation of the consultations on its entire subject matter in the Helsinki process, a series of review meetings of which two, Belgrade 1977–1978 and Madrid 1980–1983, have been held, and a third is scheduled for November 1986 in Vienna.

The 1975 Helsinki Final Act gave the Soviet Union most of what it had wanted from the European security conference it had been pressing for since 1954. Most important was endorsement of the postwar borders of the Soviet Union and Poland. It also gave the Soviet Union a continuing forum in which European governments could be called on to react seriously to Soviet arms control concepts like no first use of nuclear weapons and nuclear-free zones for which the Soviet Union had been pressing for decades. It is somewhat more difficult for NATO governments to avoid detailed discussion of these themes in a forum of this kind than if they are restricted to presentation to the United Nations or to exchange of diplomatic notes. NATO governments have tended to pass off these Soviet concepts as mere propaganda. And most of these themes do lend themselves to propagandistic treatment as topics of public diplomacy designed to gain public acceptance of the Soviet Union in the West as sincerely interested in arms control and to elicit demonstration of public support for the Soviet position. But their regular recurrence in Soviet positions on arms control over the past three decades suggests that some serious underlying interest is being reflected.

The Soviets have had to pay for the Helsinki process in terms of accepting human rights obligations that cause them recurrent difficulty, reflected in continuing Soviet efforts to restrict the Helsinki process to a dialogue on security issues. The economic aspects of the Helsinki Accords never came up to apparent Soviet expectations; the more serious economic business with the Soviet Union continues bilateral.

The Western Europeans (and the Eastern Europeans too) are pleased with the Helsinki process. Western Europeans insisted on including the human rights provisions, to the great skepticism of the United States, which in the ensuing Belgrade and Madrid review conferences tended to act in its dealings with the Soviet Union as if these provisions had become a monopoly of the U.S. government. But for the Europeans, the ongoing conference is their forum for dealing with the division of Europe.

Aside from the human rights aspects, the United States has been the odd man out in the Helsinki process. The United States saw no virtue in endorsing the postwar borders or in the grandiloquent principles of relations. It resists being one among many in the East-West dialogue. It has tended to suspect conclusion of confidence-building measures as a means of misleading Western European opinion and diverting it from what the Soviet Union is actually doing with its armed forces.

Nevertheless, all thirty-five participating countries joined in the consensus to accept the Helsinki Final Act. Among the subsequent outgrowths of the Helsinki process has been the Conference on Disarmament in Europe. (See chapter 8.)

In the 1970s, NATO states carried out no organized analysis of the connection between the CSCE and MBFR negotiations. Even after the Helsinki Accords were concluded in 1975, their content on security issues was so modest that there seemed no real need to do so. It was only after 1978, when France began a campaign to gain agreement on a follow-on conference to CSCE whose subject matter might overlap with or with conflict with MBFR's, that this issue appeared more important.

The SALT Talks and the Road to INF Negotiations

The SALT I talks, which had begun in 1969, ended at the Moscow summit of 1972 with modest but immensely important accomplishments: the Treaty on the Limitation of Anti-ballistic Missile Systems (the ABM Treaty), then as now a requirement for agreement on limiting or reducing offensive strategic weapons; and the SALT I Interim Agreement putting a ceiling on the strategic delivery systems of both sides, a necessary basis for further agreements. In relation to the size of the forces of both superpowers, it was indeed a modest outcome. But at the same time it was a remarkable achievement—the first agreement between the two adversary superpowers directly limiting the weapons that could destroy both.

Early in the SALT talks, the Soviets indicated a desire to limit ABM systems. They also brought out from the outset their desire to cover in the limitations all strategic weapons, which they defined as all weapons capable of nuclear attack on the Soviet Union or the United States, including U.S. forward-based aircraft in Europe, U.S. carrier-based aircraft, and French and British nuclear forces— a problem that continues in the current U.S.-Soviet talks in Geneva. The main action of the SALT I negotiation, which derived its primary dynamic from successive changes in the U.S. position, was on the issue of how many ABM systems each side should be permitted. Two systems were finally decided on, reduced to one in 1974 by mutual agreement. The second major variable was what types of delivery systems should be covered by limitations. The United States resisted inclusion of carrier-based systems but sought to gain agreement on inclusion of ballistic missiles of strategic range, both ground launched and submarine launched, and this was the outcome. This aspect of the SALT I agreement contained a major defect in that the ceilings were so high that they entailed no real restraint on the arsenal of either side. Moreover, administration leaders decided early that they would receive more domestic political support for limits on ABM systems than for limits on multiple independently targetable reentry vehicles (MIRVs), and the effort to use the agreement to limit warheads was dropped.[10]

The great significance of the SALT I agreement was not only that it was the first agreement limiting nuclear weapons. It was also in its acknowledgment that the Soviet Union had finally achieved rough parity in nuclear weapons with the United States and that the United States had lost its nuclear superiority, probably definitively. This was an unpleasant fact to Americans but nonetheless probably the most significant development in U.S.-Soviet relations since the cold war and a fact of great significance for U.S. relations with the NATO allies.

Wide awareness in the European public of the changed U.S.-Soviet nuclear balance and its possible consequences was postponed until the widespread debate in the United States in 1979 over ratification of SALT II and the beginning of the INF debate in Europe. In 1972, European political opinion was well satisfied with the ABM and SALT I agreements as a first step. For European leaders, the main point was that the United States and the Soviet Union had been able to reach any agreement on nuclear weapons, and the success of these U.S.-Soviet efforts encouraged them in their efforts to have East-West negotiation on arms control with Europeans participating directly.

Two aspects of the SALT I negotiations did leave European governments unsatisfied. One was NATO consultation, which had been close and informative. Between January 1969 and June 1972 there were forty-five oral or written communications on SALT to the NATO Council.[11] But the European NATO states wanted a form of consultation that would give them an opportunity not merely to keep abreast of U.S. negotiations but to affect formulation of the U.S. negotiating position, a desire that continues to this day. European NATO states reasoned that they were so dependent on U.S. extended deterrence for their security that they should have a direct voice in changes in that deterrent made by treaty with the common Soviet adversary. For them, as they so often asserted, NATO security was indivisible, composed of shared security and shared vulnerability. The U.S. administration, then and now, did not want to accord Western Europeans any direct voice in the superpower relationship on which the national security of the United States directly depended. As we will be seeing when we look more closely at the INF negotiations in chapter 6, the consultation issue continues unresolved to the satisfaction of Western Europeans.

The other issue on which European NATO governments were not fully satisfied was the U.S. position on excluding forward-based systems from the coverage of the SALT I agreement (and subsequently from SALT II). European governments supported the logic of U.S. insistence on not equating less destructive U.S. short-range systems with Soviet strategic systems. But the European interest was in Soviet intermediate-range missiles, the SS-4s and SS-5s aimed at Western Europe. They believed that if the threat to the United States by Soviet strategic missiles was to be limited and later reduced by U.S.-Soviet agreement, then the United States should also seek to reduce the Soviet threat to its Western European allies.

The most insistent of the NATO states on this subject was nonnuclear Federal Germany. In July 1968, when it still appeared that the planned summit meeting between President Lyndon Johnson and General Secretary Leonid Brezhnev to start the SALT negotiations would take place, the Federal German Foreign Office informed the American embassy in Bonn in detail that the Federal Republic wanted the issue of shorter-range Soviet missiles dealt with in the coming negotiations. Alliance security should be indivisible. At the time, these desires were limited to Federal German officials dealing with security affairs, and the topic was not one of broad public interest. But the determination of Federal German officials to do something about the problem hardened over the years, and the broad public did become vividly aware of it.

The Soviet view, however, was at variance with this Federal German concern over Soviet intermediate-range missiles. Although U.S.-Soviet parity in strategic launchers was codified in the 1972 agreement, in Europe the situation was different. The SS-4s and SS-5s were aging; the Soviet Union had replaced some 180 of them with variable-range SS-11s by the time SALT I was signed. But in that agreement, the SS-11 was classed as an ICBM. Consequently, its numbers could not be further increased, even to replace SS-4s and SS-5s. At the May 1972 Moscow summit, President Nixon and General Secretary Brezhnev had made it clear to each other that each country would proceed with weapons systems not limited by SALT I, and in 1976 the Soviets began to deploy a new intermediate-range missile in Europe, the SS-20.

Over the coming years of intensive public diplomacy, NATO leaders would increasingly justify the deployment of the new U.S. Euromissiles by the threat to NATO posed by mounting SS-20 deployments until this began to look like the only reason NATO had to deploy U.S. INF missiles. But in fact SS-20 deployment was not the decisive factor in the NATO decision. That decision had two bases: an objective one—that Soviet achievement of strategic parity with the United States had undermined extended deterrence—and a subjective one—the dishearteningly sharp decline in European confidence in U.S. leadership in world affairs, aggravated by President Carter's poor relationship with allied leaders, especially Helmut Schmidt.

By December 1976, the NATO defense ministers had decided that a new push to improve NATO forces, including NATO nuclear forces, was necessary. They had earlier decided to establish the High Level Group of senior officials to examine specific requirements for NATO theater nuclear force modernization. (Later, during the Reagan administration, under the impact of the antinuclear movement, European NATO leaders were to reject the term *theater* as too suggestive of nuclear warfare in Europe. The term *intermediate-range nuclear force,* or INF, was settled on instead and used to designate negotiations on this subject. Despite the anachronism, for the sake of clarity, we use the INF designation here.)

The year 1978 was a fateful one for NATO. In meetings of the High Level Group, senior European defense officials urged with increasing intensity deployment of U.S. INF missiles capable of reaching Soviet territory. U.S. officials were divided. The Defense Department supported modernization, as did opponents of the SALT negotiations in the Congress and in the nongovernmental Committee on the Present Danger. The Carter administration had decided in 1977 to develop a follow-on ballistic missile to the 700 kilometer range Pershing I missile in Germany. The Pershing II would have a range of about 1800 kilometers and much improved accuracy. It was also decided to start development of a slower-moving ground-launched cruise missile of 2400 kilometers range.

But Secretary of State Cyrus Vance told a congressional committee in October 1977 that existing U.S. submarines and forward-based systems were adequate to defend Europe and that no new systems were required. At the December meeting of NATO foreign ministers, Vance proposed an East-West negotiation on INF to be included in SALT III. NATO European governments were thus assured that Soviet INF systems would be covered in forthcoming negotiations.

The development that precipitated a change in the U.S. position was the crisis over deployment to Europe of the neutron warhead, a newly developed reduced-blast, enhanced-radiation nuclear charge intended for antitank use by artillery and short-range missiles. In mid-1977, details of the new weapon leaked to the U.S. press. The news caused a furor in Europe, where Soviet propaganda intensified European charges that deployment of the neutron warhead would make nuclear war in Europe more likely. After erratic, in-effective handling of the issue, President Carter decided in April 1978 to defer production of the neutron weapons just as Chancellor Schmidt had won a difficult struggle inside his Social Democratic party to approve deployment if Germany was not the only country where the weapons were deployed.

This intra-alliance fiasco illustrated the crucial importance of good personal relations between the U.S. president and other alliance leaders. It also reflected politicization of the nuclear weapons issue in three respects. First, the European public's opposition to U.S. nuclear deployments in Europe, quiescent since the mid-1950s, was again mobilized. Second, President Carter insisted for the first time in the history of U.S. nuclear deployments in Europe that explicit approval of the European governments where deployment was to take place was a precondition; all previous changes in U.S. nuclear armaments in Europe had been discussed and debated in the NATO Council, but no approval at the political level had been required. This requirement, repeated with regard to deployment of INF weapons, made approval of changes in U.S. nuclear weapons a matter of internal politics in the deployment countries because individual NATO governments had to go to the political parties in their parliaments to gain their agreement. Third, the neutron warhead episode led to determination within the U.S. administration to avoid any repetition in terms of both domestic U.S. criticism and indecisiveness of the allies. This determination catalyzed opinion among senior administration officials in favor of deploying modernized U.S. INF weapons in Europe and in favor of an energetic campaign of implementation with no slipups.

At the January 1979 summit meeting of President Carter, Chancellor Schmidt, President Valéry Giscard d'Estaing of France, and British Prime Minister James Callaghan on the island of Guadaloupe, the decision was taken to deploy new U.S. INF missiles in Europe. Chancellor Schmidt insisted that Federal Germany not be the sole deployment country. Giscard agreed with him that there should be a parallel effort to negotiate arms limitations with the Soviet Union. Further alliance meetings during 1979 finally led to the NATO two-track decision of December 1979 to deploy 572 new INF missiles and to negotiate for INF limitations with the Soviet Union.

Significantly, NATO also decided in 1979, adopting a schedule suggested by the High Level Group, that this deployment should begin by 1983, whatever the fate of the arms control negotiations with the Soviet Union. As part of the overall decision, NATO decided under Netherlands pressure to withdraw 1000 U.S. nuclear warheads from Europe (these 1000 warheads had been offered in MBFR in December 1975 and that offer was now withdrawn) and, in addition, one warhead for each new single-warhead INF missile deployed. Belgium and the Netherlands made their final decisions on cruise missile deployment dependent on the progress of arms control talks with the Soviets.

NATO decided on a figure of not over 600 U.S. missiles to come close to the total of 700-plus Soviet INF missiles without equaling it (because in the arcane logic of coupling, equality in INF forces would tend to decouple the INF deterrent from the U.S. strategic force) or exceeding it (because this would be considered provocative by NATO publics). The 572 figure represented 108 Pershing IIs (to replace the 108 Pershing Is already in U.S. Army hands in Germany) plus 464 cruise missiles (29 flights of 16 missiles apiece, with 4 missiles mounted on each of 4 launch vehicles). It was agreed that the Pershing II missiles would be deployed in Federal Germany and that the ground-launched cruise missiles (GLCMs) would be deployed in the United Kingdom (160), Italy (112), Belgium (48), the Netherlands (48), and Federal Germany (96).

The two-track decision represented real success for long-held continental, especially German, aims. Optimally German officials wanted some continuing European deployment of U.S. INF missiles combined with some reduction of Soviet INF weapons. The United States was ready once again to deploy missiles in Western Europe that could reach Soviet territory, while the Soviet Union itself had repeatedly stated that it would respond with strategic weapons aimed at the U.S. homeland to any U.S. nuclear attack on Soviet territory. INF deployment was therefore the ultimate coupling, the closest thing yet to the seamless web of deterrence that the Germans had been seeking for years. NATO officials had decided that the new missiles should be deployed on land rather than at sea in order to be a more determined deterrent to the Soviets and a more visible reassurance to European publics. In a remarkably inaccurate misreading of European public opinion, these officials thought the public was motivated mainly by their own concern—that the United States might not use nuclear weapons in the event of conflict in Europe—rather than by the public's actual concern—that the United States would use these weapons.

The Soviet Union reacted as galvanically to the emerging NATO decision to deploy new U.S. INF missiles in Western Europe as it had in the late 1950s to the prospective deployment of Jupiter and Thor missiles. Following the pattern of its successful public campaign on the neutron warhead, the Soviet Union launched what became the largest of many postwar campaigns of propaganda and public diplomacy directed at Western Europe. The Soviet campaign did not create the attitudes underlying public demonstrations of hundreds of thousands of opponents of missile deployment, but did help to mobilize the demonstrations.

In a major speech in East Berlin in October 1979 in an effort to influence the pending NATO decision, Brezhnev announced the unilateral withdrawal of 20,000 Soviet troops and 1000 tanks from East Germany. Despite Soviet efforts at the outset to publicize this withdrawal, the effect of this gesture was undermined by the secrecy that surrounds Soviet troop movements. Western observers were not permitted to see that these troops had indeed left East Germany and entered the Soviet Union; only later was it confirmed that a net reduction of manpower had indeed taken place in 1979–1980. Brezhnev also offered to reduce Soviet INF weapons in the western Soviet Union if NATO would freeze its INF forces and relinquish the plan to deploy the new U.S. missiles. It was the first of many Soviet freeze proposals in the INF context. But Brezhnev did not then explicitly offer to freeze the deployment of the new Soviet SS-20s, as he did after the December 1979 decision. If the latter offer had been made before the NATO decision on INF, it might well have influenced NATO governments to decide against deployment.

The bilateral INF negotiations that were the second track of NATO's two-track decision form the subject of the following chapter. In chapters 7 and 8, we will pick up the thread of the European negotiations on force reductions and European security issues.

Notes

1. Details of the modified Eden plan are found in U.S. Senate, Committee on Foreign Relations, *Documents on Germany, 1944–1970*, May 17, 1971, pp. 279–282, which also contains details of other Soviet and Western proposals described here.
2. Ibid. John G. Keliher, *The Negotiations on Mutual and Balanced Force Reductions* (New York: Pergamon Press, 1980), chap. 1, contains a good short account of highlights of early East-West moves on Germany.
3. Bernard C. Bechhoeffer, *Post-war Negotiations for Arms Control* (Washington, D.C.: Brookings Institution, 1961), pp. 466–486.
4. The text is in Boris Meissner, *Moskau-Bonn* (Cologne: Verlag Wissenschaft und Politik, 1975), pp. 1041–1045.
5. *NATO Final Communiqués, 1949–1974* (Brussels: NATO Information Service).
6. Ibid.
7. See Reinhard Mutz, *Konventielle Abrustung in Europa* (Conventional disarmament in Europe) (Baden-Baden: Nomos Verlagsgesellschaft, 1984), pp. 157–172.
8. U.S. Arms Control and Disarmament Agency, "Address by CPSU General Brezhnev at Tbilisi (extract) May 14, 1971," in *Documents on Disarmament, 1971* (Washington, D.C.: Government Printing Office, 1972), p. 293.
9. The text is in Department of State publication 8826, General Foreign Policy Series 298 (August 1975). See also John Borawski, Lynn M. Hansen, and Suzanne Parry, *From the Atlantic to the Urals* (McLean, Va.: Pergamon-Brassey's, forthcoming 1987), chap. 1.
10. See Raymond Garthoff, *Detente and Confrontation* (Washington, D.C.: Brookings Institution, 1985), chap. 5. Garthoff's account of SALT I is definitive.
11. Ibid., p. 197.

6
INF: The Crisis of
Extended Deterrence

When in December 1979, the NATO ministers endorsed bilateral U.S.-Soviet negotiations on INF, they assumed that this negotiation would take place in the framework of SALT III. But only days after NATO's dual-track decision, the Soviet Union invaded Afghanistan, and President Carter requested the U.S. Senate to suspend consideration of the SALT II agreement. With SALT II unratified and hopes for SALT III extinguished, the INF negotiations were left in limbo. Yet the dauntless Chancellor Schmidt, on a visit to the Soviet Union in June 1980, succeeded in obtaining the agreement of General Secretary Brezhnev to conduct separate U.S.-Soviet talks on the subject. Preliminary exchanges began in October 1980 in the last months of the Carter administration, at the height of the Carter-Reagan presidential election campaign. They lasted only a few weeks after President Carter's defeat in those elections, but the issues raised then continue to play a role in the INF talks in one form or another. The United States presented basic criteria for an agreement drawn from principles approved by NATO in connection with its 1979 decision on INF. The criteria called for coverage of INF weapons on a global basis, including Asia, and placed priority on nuclear missiles, leaving aircraft for subsequent negotiations. The draft treaty tabled by the Soviets focused on Europe alone but did include aircraft, including U.S. carrier-based aircraft capable of only a one-way mission to the Soviet Union, as well as British and French nuclear forces.[1]

Various definitions of *intermediate range* have been used in the

INF negotiations, but the prevailing U.S. definition of "long-range INF," the focus of the Geneva negotiations, has been the range of Pershing II—1800 kilometers or more—while the Soviet definition has been a range of 1000 kilometers or more. As the Soviets counted European INF weapons—those capable of reaching Soviet territory and those capable of reaching European NATO territory—rough parity existed in the late 1970s. It seems doubtful that in deploying the SS-20, the Soviet Union, with great power imperviousness to reactions of its neighbors to its actions, had objectives beyond replacement of the seriously aging SS-4s and SS-5s and creating a substitute weapon for the SS-11. But the Soviets did consider that the NATO INF deployment would increase NATO forces in a significant way. In emotional public presentations, Soviet experts stressed that the range, short flight time (they claimed a flight time of six to eight minutes for the Pershing II), and accuracy of the new U.S. INF missiles made them capable of a decapitating first strike against Soviet command and control installations. They also claimed that the Pershing II had a range (or improved versions could be given a range) of 2400 kilometers, as compared to the 1800 kilometers claimed for it by Western experts, so that it could reach Moscow and its environs, and that the slower GLCM already had a range of 2400 kilometers and could be made much faster in future versions.

For their part, Western governments argued that the SS-20 had brought a qualitative change in the Soviet nuclear threat to Western Europe because of its longer range, mobility, and accuracy; because it was MIRVed (three warheads); and because its solid fuel made it far quicker to launch than the liquid-fueled SS-4s and SS-5s (which took from eight to twenty-four hours to fuel and could not be kept at the ready for more than five hours before they had to be topped up again). Some NATO experts considered these changes made the SS-20 a counterforce weapon that could be used for preemptive strikes on NATO command posts, ports, and nuclear weapons storage sites. Consequently, they regarded it as a Soviet effort to acquire regional nuclear superiority.

Today, after nearly six years of episodic negotiations, the INF talks have slowly moved into sight of a first agreement. The main issues dealt with in the negotiations can be described as follows:

1. Which Soviet and U.S. systems should be included. From the outset, the U.S. position, approved by the NATO allies, was to limit the scope of the negotiations to land-based INF ballistic missile systems of both sides. The United States has wanted to postpone consideration of aircraft (considered a complicating factor because of the numerous different types deployed by the two countries) and sea-based missiles—that is, the existing U.S. forward-based systems in Europe. The Soviets have wanted to include aircraft. They insisted on coverage of all U.S. fighter-bombers, including not only intermediate-range F-111s, but also the short-range F-4s and carrier-based A-6s and A-7s. In the figures presented to the public, both sides openly stacked the deck. The Soviet count of their own aircraft included only their INF bombers (Badger, Blinder, and Backfire), while omitting fighter-bombers of short ranges, comparable to the U.S. types it wished to include. In U.S. data presenting total INF forces of both countries, the United States included nearly all short-range Soviet fighter-bombers as nuclear-capable despite the fact that only certain Soviet air force units train for use of nuclear weapons, but only its own nuclear-capable F-111s and F-4s. In its missile counts, the United States included not only Soviet SS-4s, SS-5s, and SS-20s, but also the shorter-range SS-12/22s, while omitting from its figures and from its proposed freeze on shorter-range INF its own similar Pershing I missiles. (See tables 6–1 and 6–2 for current figures for both sides.)

2. Geographic coverage. The United States has wanted to include INF missiles in the whole of the Soviet Union, both Europe and Asia, including Soviet nuclear weapons directed at China, about which Soviet leaders continue to be nervous. The Soviet Union wished to include only armaments deployed in that part west of the Urals.

3. Third-country forces. The Soviet Union has insisted on taking account of British and French nuclear forces. Reviving a classic Soviet position for which they had failed to gain acceptance in the SALT I or SALT II agreements, Soviet

Table 6–1
U.S. Count of INF Systems

United States		Soviet Union	
Missiles		*Missiles*	
81	Pershing IIs[a]	270	SS-20s in Europe
128	GLCMs (32 launchers with 4 missiles each)	171	SS-20s in Far East
209	INF missiles (with one warhead each = 209 warheads)	441	SS-20s (with three warheads each = 1323 warheads)
		100	SS-4s (with one warhead each = 100 warheads)
		541	INF missiles (with 1423 warheads)
Aircraft		*Aircraft*	
222	U.S. medium-range bombers (with about 850 weapons)	884	Bombers (with 3536 weapons); includes Backfire, Badger, and Blinder bombers with Naval Aviation and deployed in Far East
1417	U.S. tactical fighter-bombers (with about 3140 weapons)	2500	Tactical fighter-bombers (with 4800 weapons)
1639	Aircraft (with about 3990 weapons)	3384	Aircraft (with 8336 weapons)
Total		*Total*	
1848	Total medium-range delivery systems (with 4199 weapons)	3925	Total medium-range delivery systems (with 9759 weapons)

Source: *New York Times*, October 4, 1985.
Note: Count as of October 1985. Count reflects U.S. approach to INF and is on a global basis, covering systems of both countries wherever deployed, in Europe, the Far East and the United States. The present U.S. negotiating position does not provide for reduction of aircraft; figures on aircraft are included only for purposes of comparison. British and French nuclear forces are not shown since they are excluded from U.S. proposals.
[a]Had increased to 108 by end of 1985.

negotiators insisted on equal security for the Soviets—specifically, equality between total Soviet INF and the total number of INF weapons of all countries that could be used against the Soviet Union in Europe. The consequence would be to permit the United States fewer weapons than the Soviet Union. U.S. negotiators refused to codify such inequality and also argued that Britain and France were sovereign countries for which the United States could not speak.

4. The United States has stressed the need for full verification

Table 6–2
Soviet Count of INF Systems

United States		Soviet Union	
Missiles		*Missiles*	
81	Pershing IIs	243	SS-20s
128	GLCMs	130	Other (SS-4s)
209	U.S. INF missiles (with one warhead each = 209 warheads)	373	Medium-range nuclear missiles
178	Other European INF (British and French submarines and French land-based missiles	*Aircraft*	
		477	Medium-range nuclear-capable aircraft
387	NATO nuclear missiles (with 739 warheads)	*Total*	
		850	Total medium-range delivery systems (with about 2000 weapons)
Aircraft			
628	NATO medium-range nuclear-capable aircraft		
Total			
1015	Total NATO medium-range delivery systems (with 3000 weapons)		

Source: Interview with Marshal Sergei Akromeyev, *New York Times,* October 18, 1985.
Note: Soviet figures include British and French systems and give the Soviet count of both NATO and Soviet systems for Europe to the Urals; they exclude deployments in Asia.

given the mobility and reload capability of SS-20s, although U.S. negotiators advanced a specific verification approach only in the spring of 1986. The Soviets were more reticent on the subject: they customarily argued either that national technical means (satellite photography and sensors) would be sufficient for verification or, as in other negotiations, that it was premature to deal with the subject until the outlines of a specific verification agreement had emerged.

By early 1986, the Soviets had made several major concessions:

1. They finally accepted that any initial INF agreement would be based on some deployment of U.S. INF, dropping their effort to eliminate any deployment whatever.

2. They indicated willingness to focus on reduction and limitation of missiles, leaving aside aircraft for later treatment.

3. They indicated willingness to make deep cuts in SS-20s targeted on Europe and to destroy withdrawn missiles.

4. They indicated willingness to freeze Soviet SS-20s deployed in Asia and possibly make a slight reduction in them.

5. They have repeatedly shown some flexibility on the issue of including the British and French nuclear forces, leading to the conclusion that some mutually acceptable way of dealing with the issue is feasible.

Demonstrations of U.S. flexibility have been less numerous; however, the United States has offered flexibility on the level of Pershing II deployment and has offered not to exercise its claimed right of global equality by not deploying in Europe U.S. INF to equal the global total of Soviet SS-20s. (As a consequence, apart from deployment in the United States, a possibility probably of limited concern to the Soviet Union, U.S. matching of Soviet global totals would have to involve U.S. deployment in Asia, for which neither the United States nor Japan has as yet shown any inclination.)

Taken together, these moves could form the basis for an initial INF reduction within the next several years. This possible outcome might be close to the U.S. proposal of February 1986 described later in this chapter.

INF Negotiations: 1981–1983

After President Ronald Reagan assumed office in 1981, European NATO governments, worried by his militantly anti-Soviet presidential campaign and by the emerging sentiment in their publics against INF deployment, brought great pressure on the new administration to resume the INF negotiations. Finally, at the end of November 1981, the talks resumed; two years had elapsed of the four years provided for negotiation results in NATO's 1979 decision to deploy by the end of 1983.

President Reagan inaugurated the public diplomacy character of the renewed INF talks in mid-November 1981 by publicly announcing the U.S. negotiating position, the zero option. Under this approach, adopted with strong European support, NATO would relinquish its decision to deploy new U.S. INF missiles, deploying none, if the Soviet Union would eliminate all its existing INF missiles (SS-4s, SS-5s, and SS-20s), wherever stationed in the Soviet Union—that is, in both European and Asian portions of the Soviet Union. In a draft treaty presented in February 1982, the United States proposed in addition a freeze on the shorter-range Soviet SS-21, SS-22, and SS-23 missiles. Comparable U.S. missiles were not covered in the U.S. position until 1983. Aircraft were left to later negotiation, and British and French forces were not taken into account.

Only a week after President Reagan's announcement, General Secretary Brezhnev also went public with a Soviet proposal for a bilateral freeze on INF missiles in Europe. He offered unilateral reduction of a "certain portion" of Soviet INF in European Russia (west of the Urals). He presented his own zero option, saying the eventual negotiating goal after interim reductions would be elimination of all nuclear weapons, both INF and tactical, from Europe. Deployment in Asia was not covered. In a draft proposal presented in Geneva in February 1982, the Soviet Union proposed a staged reduction of INF, including some aircraft of both countries, to 600 delivery systems on each side in a first phase and 300 in a second phase. In May 1982, the Soviets publicly proclaimed a freeze on the level of Soviet INF capable of reaching Western Europe. In practice, the freeze seems to have covered only the creation of new SS-20 bases. Work continued on sites already under construction and further SS-20s were subsequently deployed there.

The U.S. proposal would have left untouched existing U.S. forward-based aircraft as well as British and French forces—to which these countries' plans to MIRV their submarine-launched missiles would add about 1000 warheads over the next decade. Specifically France intends to equip 6 submarines with 96 missiles, each carrying 6 warheads; to deploy a land-based INF missile with increased range; and to deploy Mirage 2000 jets equipped with standoff nuclear missiles. The United Kingdom is constructing 4 new submarines, each to be equipped with 16 U.S. Trident II (D-5) missiles, probably with 8 warheads each, and it plans to deploy Tornado jets with nuclear bombs.

Taken together, the U.S. and Soviet positions excluded the most logical potential compromises on the INF issue. The global Western position made it difficult to compromise on elimination of Soviet INF capable of reaching Europe in return for relinquishment of U.S. INF deployment while freezing Soviet INF in the Far East. Soviet proposals were equally nonnegotiable. Designed to prevent the deployment of any new U.S. INF missiles in Europe, the Soviet position made it impossible to compromise on an outcome with some U.S. INF deployment and some Soviet INF reductions. Instead the whole thrust of the Soviet negotiating and public diplomacy effort was aimed at preventing any U.S. deployment—and Soviet leaders persisted in this position all the way to withdrawal from the talks in 1983, showing the significance they attached to the possible deployments. The parallel with their strong reaction in 1958 to U.S. medium-range ballistic missile deployment is clear.

In a series of informal discussions in June and July 1982, U.S. INF negotiator Paul Nitze and Soviet negotiator Yuli Kvitsinsky worked out what became known as the "walk in the woods" compromise. This compromise would have permitted the United States to deploy 75 cruise missile launchers, each with four single-warhead missiles, while the Soviets would reduce their INF forces in Europe, and places capable of reaching Europe, to 75 SS-20s with three warheads each. Soviet INF forces in Asia would be frozen. The United States would not deploy any Pershing IIs; no account would be taken of French or British forces in this interim agreement. There is disagreement about which country first indicated a negative reaction to this proposal. In any event, both rejected it, although it probably would have been acceptable to the European NATO governments had the United States backed it and made it known to them. The Reagan administration was not willing to relinquish all Pershing deployment, and the Soviet authorities, although they feared the Pershing IIs more than the GLCMs, were not then prepared to accept any deployment of U.S. INF missiles in Europe.

In the period remaining before the collapse of the INF talks in

November 1983 the Soviet Union made one concession after another in the effort to block any U.S. deployment. In December 1982, Yuri Andropov, the new general secretary of the Soviet Communist party, publicly offered to cut Soviet INF in Europe to the combined level of British and French missiles and indicated readiness to postpone treatment of aircraft. British and French missiles, however, were single-warhead missiles as compared to the three-warhead SS-20, and Andropov said nothing about destroying withdrawn Soviet armaments, nor were Soviet INF in Asia to be reduced. But there was to be no U.S. INF deployment.

The European governments, whose publics, under the impact of Soviet criticism, had come to consider the original U.S. zero option position inequitable and nonnegotiable, now pressed the Reagan administration to adopt a more realistic negotiating position. In March 1983, President Reagan publicly offered the Soviets a second possible outcome in addition to the zero option, which remained valid. Under the new proposal, the United States would limit its Pershing and GLCM deployments in Europe—both types of missile would be deployed—to a specific number of warheads between 50 and 450, provided that the Soviet Union reduced the total of all its INF warheads on a global basis to the same level. As before, British and French forces were not included.

In May 1983, Andropov publicly announced Soviet willingness to limit Soviet INF warheads in Europe to the level of British and French warheads. Again no mention was made of destroying withdrawn Soviet missiles; Soviet INF in Asia would not be included; and no new U.S. INF missiles would be permitted. By this time, Japan, the United States's major ally in Asia, had insisted to the United States that Soviet INF in Asia must also be reduced in any agreement, and China had made known similar interests. Under pressure of its allies in Europe and Asia, the United States, while insisting on U.S. equality with the Soviet Union in INF as in strategic weapons and rejecting Soviet claims that other nuclear forces must be taken into account, was pressing for reductions on behalf of its allies, including the other nuclear powers against whose forces the Soviet Union was asking equal security.

In August 1983, Andropov offered to destroy Soviet INF withdrawn from Europe. Countering, in his speech to the UN General

Assembly in September 1983, President Reagan announced that if the Soviet Union would agree to reductions and limitations on a global basis (including Asia), the United States would continue to insist on being allowed an equal total number but would not deploy in Europe its entire quota of INF, although retaining the right to deploy the remainder elsewhere. U.S. negotiators did not specify what this cryptic formula meant, but many experts interpreted it as meaning that the United States would match Soviet INF in Europe and keep the remainder of its equal global quota in the United States, since there were no plans for, and no apparent interest in, Asian deployment. The president also announced that reductions in the planned U.S. INF deployment would include reductions in the number of Pershings, implying a willingness to negotiate the mix of Pershings and GLCMs, and that limits on bombers could also be negotiated outside the framework of the INF negotiations. In order to counter negative trends in European public opinion, NATO defense ministers meeting at Montebello, Canada, in October 1983, announced the unilateral withdrawal of a further 1400 U.S. tactical nuclear warheads from Europe. Also in October 1983, Andropov offered to freeze Soviet INF in Asia and to reduce Soviet INF launchers in Europe to about 140 SS-20 launchers, each with 3 warheads, so that the level of Soviet INF warheads, 420, would be equal to the British and French warheads if there were no U.S. INF deployment. The United States countered with a proposal that Soviet INF launchers in both Europe and Asia be reduced to 140—with a total of 420 warheads—which the United States would match with some mix of Pershings and GLCMs.

In informal discussion in October and November 1983, Soviet negotiator Kvitsinsky appeared ready to go even lower. He offered to go down to about 120 SS-20s in Europe with zero U.S. deployment, roughly equivalent to making equal warhead reductions from existing Soviet levels and from planned U.S. levels. British and French forces would not be limited in INF. Instead, they would be credited to the U.S. total of strategic weapons in START, the U.S.-Soviet talks on reducing strategic systems. Moreover, the total of British and French weapons included in START would be reduced by subtracting the warheads of the 120 Soviet SS-20s deployed in INF. (At this stage, Soviet negotiators indicated they were counting British Chevaline multiple reentry vehicles, not independently targetable, which were being fitted to the United Kingdom's Polaris missiles, at six per missile.) The Soviets had shown considerable flexibility: an agreement on this basis would have meant a 50 percent cut in Soviet INF warheads aimed at Europe from their level when the INF talks began in 1980, a result far beyond realistic Western expectations at that time and one that would have fully met the original German desire to reduce Soviet INF.

But it was too late. The issue was no longer a negotiation over INF levels, but a very public contest of wills between the United States and the Soviet Union as to whether the Soviet Union could stop all U.S. deployment. The last day of the negotiations was November 23, 1983, the day after the Bundestag confirmed the Pershing II deployment and the same day the first nine Pershing IIs reached a U.S. unit in southern Germany. The Soviet negotiators walked out of the INF negotiation and subsequently out of the START talks and, in less categorical terms, out of the MBFR talks.

The reason for the breakdown was quite clear: most U.S. and NATO officials were unwilling to accept any outcome that did not entail some deployment of U.S. INF. For its part, the Soviet Union took the categorical position of not agreeing even to a minimal U.S. deployment that of itself would have had limited military consequence. By the time the INF talks broke down in November 1983, the issue had long since ceased to be one of East-West force balance, intra-alliance coupling, or negotiation. It was a question of whether the European NATO governments, primarily the United Kingdom and Federal Germany, where the first deployments were to take place, had sufficient political strength and determination to carry out the initial deployments. Most Western officials felt that whether the original NATO decision to deploy had been right or wrong and whether the projected deployment of U.S. INF would bring additional security, giving in to Soviet pressure against deployment would be a serious political defeat for NATO, one that would leave it in dangerous disarray.

Who Won? Who Lost?

As deployment began, NATO officials proclaimed victory: the contest of wills with the Soviet Union had been won. But in fact everyone lost from the events of late 1983. NATO lost the consensus on defense issues that had been the foundation of the Atlantic alliance for decades. True, some German officials were pleased by the U.S. deployment because they considered that with U.S. weapons in position in Germany that could reach Soviet territory, the Soviet Union could no longer believe that it could launch a conventional or nuclear attack on Western Europe without the risk of strategic nuclear warfare with the United States.

But with nearly every major move in the INF negotiations announced publicly by the United States and the Soviet Union before it was officially introduced into the negotiations and an enormous effort of public diplomacy on both sides, European public opinion was mobilized at its highest level of activity in the postwar period. As the INF negotiations and the Soviet propaganda campaign wore on, large segments of the Western European public became increasingly worried that a U.S. administration headed by a former actor who had specialized in hip-shooting cowboy roles might engage in actions triggering conflict in the Third World that would result in nuclear war in Europe. An unprecedented series of public demonstrations began, of which church, trade union, and Social Democratic groups were the main instigators but which also attracted communist support. The first, in Brussels in April 1981, was on a small scale, but demonstrators numbered over 100,000 in Hamburg in June, 250,000 in Bonn, 200,000 in Rome, 150,000 in London, and 200,000 in Brussels, with other demonstrations in Oslo, Paris, and East Berlin. In November 1981, there was a demonstration of over 300,000 in Amsterdam and in December a demonstration of the same size in Bucharest calling for removal of all nuclear weapons from Europe.[2] Even larger antinuclear demonstrations took place in 1982 and 1983, including a mammoth demonstration of over 700,000 in New York's Central Park.

The Danish government maintained its decision to refuse to contribute to INF infrastructure, and the Belgian and Netherlands governments were repeatedly obliged to postpone their final decisions on deployment, which the Belgians finally took only in 1985 and the Netherlands in a hard-fought seventy-nine to seventy vote only in February 1986. In Federal Germany, in a development that may have been decisive in bringing about the ultimate deployment of U.S. INF, in October 1982 the Free Democrat party in the Federal German Bundestag defected from its coalition with the Social Democrats, deposed Chancellor Schmidt, and entered a new coalition with the Christian Democrats under Helmut Kohl. Had the German Social Democrats remained in government, there is some question that Chancellor Schmidt would have managed to maintain the unity of the party, although a majority composed of right-wing Social Democrats and Christian Democrats might still have maintained the 1979 NATO decision.

The antinuclear movement collapsed after the U.S. INF deployments took place, but its approach was incorporated in the programs of the major social democratic parties of Western Europe. In September 1982, the British Labour party voted overwhelmingly to abolish the United Kingdom's nuclear weapons and to bring about the withdrawal of all U.S. nuclear weapons from British soil when and if it assumes power. And in November 1983, the German Social Democratic party, meeting in special convention, decided to withdraw its earlier support for the 1979 two-track decision, and its Bundestag deputies voted against deployment. The consensus on defense in Germany, dating at least from 1960 when the German Social Democrats had abandoned their opposition to Federal German membership in NATO, had foundered on the issue of extended deterrence. Some of the practical results of the loss of consensus, however, were positive: there was a healthy new skepticism about the real nature and extent of the Soviet threat to Western Europe and about the East-West military balance and an increased desire to explore unorthodox means of defending Western Europe.

What was the residue of the INF controversy for the Warsaw Pact? The Soviet Union took the retaliatory actions it had threatened in the event of U.S. INF deployment. It placed additional Delta-class nuclear missile submarines on patrol off the U.S. coasts and moved forward into Czechoslovakia and East Germany the modernized version of its 900 kilometer Scaleboard SS-12 missile, the rough equivalent of Pershing I. The missile was now in position to reach targets in most of Western Europe.

But for the Soviet Union, too, the result was a defeat. The Soviet Union's withdrawal from the two sets of U.S.-Soviet nuclear reduction talks at Geneva was carried out as Brezhnev's successor,

Andropov, lay on his deathbed. After the mammoth protest rallies of 1981–1983 in Western Europe, it was not irrational for the Soviet leadership to seek to ascertain whether the shock effect of their walkout would mobilize sufficient public opposition to prevent initial deployment of the U.S. Euromissiles or at least to bring about a freeze in the early stages of deployment. Success in blocking deployment might also affect the 1984 presidential race in the United States to the detriment of President Reagan. But the Soviet leadership miscalculated the effects of its walkout in blocking deployment. It miscalculated still more the effects of the walkout on public opinion—in the Soviet Union itself, in Eastern and Western Europe, and in the United States. The public could not understand why the Soviet Union, since its establishment the most consistent public proponent of arms control and disarmament, was sulking like Achilles in his tent, while the conservative president of the United States smilingly proclaimed his willingness to negotiate further. In the West, the Soviet Union was threatened with the loss of its influence over public opinion and over European governments.

The Soviets did not take long to analyze their problem. Within weeks of his designation in February 1984, Andropov's equally short-term successor, Konstantin Chernenko, was describing a list of possible unilateral U.S. actions, such as agreeing to no first use of nuclear weapons and a freeze on nuclear tests, which would be the signal for resumption of Soviet participation in nuclear negotiations with the United States. The Reagan administration, however, refused to make any one-sided concessions.

After some Soviet fumbling in the summer of 1984 on the issue of negotiation on space weapons, Foreign Minister Gromyko was received by President Reagan in September 1984, and in January 1985, after President Reagan's reelection, Secretary of State George Schultz and Foreign Minister Gromyko agreed that the United States and the Soviet Union would resume negotiations in March 1985 on space weapons, strategic weapons, and INF. As they put it in their Geneva communiqué of January 8, 1985, the two ministers agreed that "the objective of the subject of the negotiations will be a complex of questions concerning space and nuclear arms, both strategic and intermediate range [the Soviet designation for INF] with all the questions considered and resolved in their interrelationship. The objective of the negotiations will be to work out effective agreements aimed at preventing an arms race in space and terminating it on earth, at limiting and reducing nuclear arms and at strengthening strategic stability." Yet it was not the prospect of President Reagan's program for ballistic missile defense that had brought the Soviets back to the negotiating table but the negative consequences for their international standing of their 1983 withdrawal from the INF negotiations.

INF Negotiations Resumed

When the Geneva talks resumed in March 1985, they had been reorganized at Soviet insistence into a single negotiation covering the three topics of space weapons, strategic weapons, and INF. In the INF discussions, the United States put forward substantially the same position it had been urging when the talks collapsed in November 1983: equal global limits for the INF missiles of both countries, preferably zero, but if not, then 140 launchers for each side. (Each GLCM launcher, with four missiles, was counted as one launcher.) The United States indicated flexibility on the mix of its Pershings and cruise missiles and willingness to negotiate on aircraft of INF range (over 1800 kilometers). Soviet negotiators insisted that the negotiations should be considered completely new because the Soviet Union, in breaking off the INF talks in 1983, had insisted it would not return to them; previous Soviet positions and concessions were no longer valid. But in practice, the Soviets too largely presented their earlier position: U.S. deployments would have to be reduced to zero, and then the Soviets would reduce to the level of the British and French. As they had from the outset, the data released by each country on the INF forces of the other in the resumed talks showed a wide discrepancy both in coverage of delivery systems and in actual numbers (see tables 6–1 and 6–2). The only point on which the data of the two countries coincide is in their count of U.S. INF missiles deployed in Western Europe; the divergences in what is counted and what is omitted, as well as in absolute numbers, illustrate the divergence in negotiating positions.

In April 1985, less than a month after his designation as general secretary of the Soviet Communist party, Mikhail Gorbachev publicly announced a unilateral freeze on further deployment of Soviet SS-20s and urged that the United States too freeze the level of INF deployments. Washington rapidly rejected the proposal, but Soviet negotiators at Geneva pointed out that its significance lay in implied Soviet acceptance that, henceforth, any INF agreement to be reached would have to be based on some deployment of U.S. INF. The Soviets at Geneva continued to insist that British and French systems be included in the U.S. count of INF delivery systems and warheads.

Relatively early on, however, Soviet negotiators hinted that it might be possible to envisage an interim INF agreement separate from conclusion of agreements on space and strategic weapons and not, despite the agreed language of the January 1985 communiqué, linked to space weapons. But these hints were not definitive, and some Soviet negotiators continued to insist that INF must remain linked with space weapons. In October 1985 on a visit to France, Gorbachev announced that a sufficient number of SS-20s would be taken off "operational" status to bring the SS-20 level in Europe to the level (243) at which they had been when the Soviets broke off the Geneva talks in November 1983. Soviet officials suggested that the removed missiles would be moved to a central location where they could be observed by the United States, but this was not done. Gorbachev also suggested separate negotiations between the Soviet Union and the United Kingdom and France about British and French nuclear forces, a clear indication that the Soviet Union would no longer insist that they be included in the U.S. INF total, or even in START. Despite rejection of the proposal by the British and French governments, Gorbachev's concept was one logical way of handling the issue of their nuclear forces.

Two New Zero Options

After much negotiation, the two governments agreed in July 1985 to hold a summit meeting between President Reagan and General Secretary Gorbachev in November. Clearly motivated by the approaching summit meeting, in early October 1985, the Soviet Union presented new reduction proposals for strategic and INF delivery systems. On INF, the Soviet Union proposed as a first step a moratorium on further deployment of Soviet and U.S. INF missiles in Europe. According to Soviet figures made public at the time, this would have meant 243 SS-20s for the Soviet Union—and 209 U.S. INF delivery systems. (The Soviet figure is disputed by the United States, which credits the Soviet Union with 270 SS-20 missiles in Europe and states that it does not have adequate evidence to credit the Soviet Union with having reduced the level of SS-20s in Europe to the 243 claimed by Gorbachev in October during his visit to France.) In a second step, all Pershing II missiles would be withdrawn; U.S. GLCMs would be held to their approximate level at the time of the proposal (about 130 missiles). Also in this second phase, the Soviet Union would reduce the number of its SS-20 warheads to the level of the combined total of U.S., British, and French missile warheads—about 300 if the Soviet figures are used—or approximately 100 SS-20s with 3 warheads each. There would be a freeze on missiles of 1000 kilometer range and under. Nuclear-capable aircraft and missiles would be removed from quick action alert status, which permits their rapid use in conflict. Withdrawn Soviet missiles would be destroyed. Finally, the Soviet proposal provided that the level of Soviet missiles in Asia would be frozen. There was also an alternate Soviet interim proposal which corresponded roughly to the first-phase freeze described above.

The most important aspect of this new Soviet proposal was the fact that it was clearly and formally based on Soviet acceptance that any U.S.-Soviet agreement on INF would have to be based on some INF deployment. A second innovative aspect of the proposal was the omission of aircraft from the first stage, an important move toward the U.S. position. This concession, however, was not as great as it appeared because the new Soviet program for reduction of strategic missiles presented in Geneva at the same time made clear that the Soviets had simply moved U.S. medium-range and carrier-based aircraft to the strategic count. Third, the Soviets agreed to freeze SS-20s in Asia.

In early November 1985, the United States, also with its eye on the pending Reagan-Gorbachev summit meeting, made a new INF proposal of its own. The U.S. proposal provided an equal ceiling of 140 launchers for both countries in Europe, the estimated

U.S. deployment level at the end of 1985 (108 Pershing IIs plus 32 GLCM launchers with 4 missiles each for a total of 140 launchers), with 420 to 450 warheads for each country. To reduce to the proposed warhead level, the Soviets would have had to reduce from the level of 810 warheads in Europe (270 SS-20s with 3 warheads each) with which the United States credited them, to 420, a reduction of about 50 percent. For its part, the United States would be prepared to discuss reducing its Pershings to a minimum level. If that level were 36, the size of a minimum self-contained U.S. Pershing unit, the resultant U.S. warhead total would be 452 (36 Pershings each with one warhead plus 104 GLCM launchers each with 4 missiles).

Using the U.S. figure of 270 for Soviet SS-20 missiles, this meant in practice that the United States would freeze its INF missiles, while the Soviets would have to reduce by about 190 SS-20s in Europe. In addition, the U.S. proposal stipulated that the approximately 170 Soviet SS-20s in Asia would be reduced by the same proportion as those in Europe—about 50 percent, or 85 missiles. No account would be taken of British and French systems. The United States reserved the right to match the Soviet global total of SS-20 warheads deployed in Europe and in Asia. There would be constraints on Soviet deployment of GLCMs and constraints on shorter-range systems.

Despite Washington publicity claiming a far-reaching U.S. move on INF, there was no concession to the Soviet Union in this proposal. In fact, under pressure from Japan and also from China, the United States had moved from its implied willingness to accept a freeze on Soviet SS-20s deployed in Asia, a requirement that the Soviet Union had moved to meet, to a requirement for a proportional 50 percent reduction of SS-20s in Asia.

At the November 1985 Reagan-Gorbachev summit, discussion of the specifics of reduction of strategic arms and of INF arms was limited. The main focus was on the opposing views of space weapons. But the two leaders agreed on a communiqué calling for early progress toward "an interim agreement on intermediate range missiles in Europe." The interim agreement was not further defined, but its minimum significance was that a first agreement on INF would not be complete and would omit some aspect of the issue to be dealt with at a later time (for example, aircraft, but possibly other aspects as well). General Secretary Gorbachev's acceptance of this language was considered further evidence of Soviet willingness to agree to a separate INF agreement, divorced from the question of space weapons, and administration experts began to focus on this possibility as a major item for the next Reagan-Gorbachev summit meeting.

In his postsummit press conference in Geneva and in subsequent statements, Gorbachev made clear that the Soviet leadership was not satisfied with the progress on arms control issues at the Geneva summit, though he also characterized the meeting as important for the political relationship between the United States and Soviet Union. In mid-January 1986, he sent President Reagan a comprehensive arms control proposal covering the items discussed at the summit and publicized the text in a television conference on January 15. In this proposal, Gorbachev suggested a three-stage program for the elimination of all nuclear weapons by the year 2000—a goal as ambitious and, unfortunately, as distant as President Reagan's dream of eliminating nuclear weapons through impervious ballistic missile defenses. Gorbachev proposed that in the first stage, the United States and the Soviet Union would decide to eliminate completely their INF ballistic and cruise missiles in Europe and would begin to implement this decision, as well as the reduction of their intercontinental nuclear forces. The United States would commit itself not to supply strategic or INF missiles to other countries. What is meant here is the U.S. commitment to sell Trident II (D-5) missiles to the United Kingdom for use on its submarines. In addition, the United Kingdom and France would commit themselves not to increase their strategic and medium-range weapons. In the second stage, the other nuclear powers—France, the United Kingdom, and China—would join in the reduction process. The United States and the Soviet Union would move further toward elimination of their INF weapons and would freeze their tactical nuclear weapons with a range below 1000 kilometers. Then after the United States and the Soviet Union had completed reduction of 50 percent of their strategic weapons, all nuclear-armed countries would eliminate their tactical nuclear weapons. In the third stage, all remaining nuclear weapons would be destroyed.[3]

For INF, the significance of this new Soviet proposal was that the Soviet Union had now formally dropped its requirement that British and French nuclear weapons would have to be included in the United States total of INF weapons. Once again, the Gorbachev proposal dealt with Soviet INF in Europe; no mention was made of Asia, though Foreign Minister Edvard Sheverdnadze was reported on a trip to Japan in early 1985 to have implied to the Japanese that the Soviet Union might be prepared to make some reductions in its SS-20s in Asia.

The weight of dealing with Soviet requirements regarding British and French forces was for the first time placed directly on their governments. French rejection came rapidly, followed by negative signals from the United Kingdom, where Prime Minister Margaret Thatcher has been under increasing pressure on the $20 billion plan to purchase Trident D-5 missiles from the United States. The Labour and Liberal parties already oppose the purchase as destabilizing and far too expensive, at the cost of further running down British conventional forces. And now the Soviet Union was suggesting that, by forgoing the controversial Trident project, Britain could contribute to an INF agreement that would radically reduce Soviet INF weapons aimed at Europe. It is probable that, in the long run, this Soviet proposal will contribute to mobilizing antinuclear sentiment in the United Kingdom and increase opposition to the Trident project. Even in self-centered France, where there is little public discussion about the national nuclear deterrent but where public opinion is in fact nearly as divided on the issue as in the United Kingdom, the Soviet offer will in time generate doubts and questions.[4]

During a visit to Moscow early in February 1986, Senator Edward Kennedy talked with Gorbachev, who gave explicit confirmation that the Soviet Union was prepared for a separate INF agreement, one not linked to progress on space weapons. Senator Kennedy also repeated that Gorbachev was beginning to question the value of a further Reagan-Gorbachev summit unless there was clearer evidence in advance that the summit would lead to progress in arms control.

In February 1986, President Reagan approved a new U.S. move on INF to be advanced in Geneva in response to Gorbachev's move of January. The proposal outdid the Soviet proposal to eliminate INF weapons by the year 2000 by suggesting reduction of U.S. and Soviet INF to zero over a three-year period starting in 1987. In the first year, which was in substance the same as the November 1985 U.S. proposal, each side would be permitted only 140 INF launchers in Europe, a 50 percent cut for the Soviets with no reduction for the United States, and the Soviets would also have to make a proportionate cut of 50 percent of their INF forces in Asia. These cuts would create a global ceiling in INF warheads for both countries. In the second year, remaining INF forces would be cut by a further 50 percent to 70 launchers in Europe and about 40 Soviet SS-20s in Asia until the second stage. In the third year, both countries would eliminate their remaining INF. (Under the February 1986 U.S. proposal, in the second stage, prior to destruction of all INF systems by both countries in stage 3, withdrawn Soviet systems would have to be destroyed while about 40 U.S. INF systems would instead be withdrawn from Europe to the United States to balance Soviet systems still deployed in Asia.) The U.S. proposal also demanded a freeze on shorter-range missiles. The U.S. proposal rejected both conditions raised by Gorbachev in his January 1986 arms control program; the United States would neither urge a freeze of their nuclear weapons on Britain and France nor commit itself not to transfer nuclear weapons to these countries.

At the beginning of March 1986, the United States finally presented in Geneva the INF verification proposal on which administration officials had been working for five years. The U.S. requirements were high:

1. An on-site inspection by field inspectors of the other country to establish the starting count of each side's INF missiles as a basis for agreed reductions. The background for this proposal was the U.S.-Soviet data dispute over whether the Soviets had 270 or 243 SS-20 missiles deployed within range of Europe and other uncertainties about SS-20 reloads.

2. In connection with the inspection, initial data exchange on deployed missiles to be followed by subsequent exchanges of updated data.

3. No encryption of telemetry for tests.

4. Restriction of missile deployment to designated areas around their operational bases. Missiles would be limited to these areas to aid verification. Because an agreement would be formulated in terms of limiting the number of warheads deployed on missiles of both sides, but verification of the agreement would be largely in terms of launchers deployed, any missile seen outside the designated area, unless in a designated production or maintenance facility, would be classed as a violation.

5. Supervised destruction of withdrawn missiles.

6. Follow-on on-site inspection on a random basis of certain facilities or suspected deployment sites. U.S. authorities were still considering various alternatives for this, including inspection of production plants, and did not advance a specific proposal on this topic.

Above and beyond difficulties over verification, which decrease its chances of acceptance, there is little chance of Soviet acceptance of the February 1986 U.S. proposal in its present form. It gives the Soviets no satisfaction on the issue of British and French nuclear weapons and in addition suggests the total elimination of Soviet SS-20s facing China and Japan, an outcome nearly unthinkable in the current state of Sino-Soviet relations. Not surprisingly, the initial Soviet reaction to the proposal was quite sour, with Gorbachev again questioning whether a second summit meeting would be feasible.

Western European reaction to both proposals for reduction to zero of U.S. INF weapons in Europe was one of concern. Even the theoretical possibility of eliminating the U.S. INF missiles for whose deployment they had fought so hard shook the British, German, Belgian, and Netherlands governments—the same governments that had originally urged the zero option on Washington in 1981. They asked what would happen to intra-alliance coupling in the event of such reductions and were fearful of the added importance that Soviet conventional preponderance would assume. French Foreign

Minister Roland Dumas stated that it was unacceptable that conventional weapons be given lower priority than nuclear negotiations, and a top adviser of President François Mitterand stated flatly that France would not accept a freeze on its nuclear arms. Chancellor Kohl said the zero option was a dream; one of his advisers said that the Federal Republic could not accept an agreement on INF unless something was done to limit conventional armaments and tactical nuclear weapons.[5]

In fact, European leaders need not have worried so about the possibility of reducing U.S. INF to zero. The prospects of U.S.-Soviet agreement within the next few years on a complete and detailed program for reduction of INF to zero is very small. We shall all be fortunate to see in that period an initial agreement with some reductions on both sides.

Alternative Approaches to INF

A compromise first-stage partial outcome for INF is possible within the next several years. It would consist of agreement on reductions of Soviet SS-20s aimed at Europe, probably less radical than the 50 percent now proposed by the United States, plus a small reduction of Soviet SS-20s in Asia to meet Japanese claims for equal reductions in Asia, which appear excessive; some commensurate freeze or reduction of U.S. INF; postponement or symbolic resolution of the British-French issue, on which the Soviets have repeatedly shown flexibility; and some verification appropriate for a first-stage agreement more modest than present U.S. requirements. The United States could commit itself to press for convening a four-power conference of the United States, the Soviet Union, the United Kingdom, and France to discuss reduction and control of nuclear weapons, to be held as soon as the U.S.-Soviet INF agreement and an agreement on reduction of U.S. and Soviet strategic weapons go into effect. In a pinch, if the United Kingdom agreed, the United States could include British nuclear weapons in the U.S. strategic total on the grounds that these weapons are committed to NATO. French nuclear weapons, which are not assigned to NATO, would not be included. If the British government was prepared to agree, the United States could also sell it Trident C-4 warheads, continuing its production line to do so, instead of more expensive D-5 warheads, thus making a useful if limited move toward the Soviet effort to restrict transfer of U.S. weapons to the United Kingdom.

This approach would give the Soviet Union and the United States an equal ceiling in Europe at a somewhat higher level than that now proposed by the United States, require a symbolic SS-20 reduction in the Far East, and bring a partial solution of the British-French problem. It is improbable that more can be accomplished at this time than a partial reduction of INF. Deeper reductions, plus reductions of nuclear-capable aircraft, will probably have to await further negotiations.

One institutional change might in time move the INF talks beyond the outcome of a limited reduction that now appears the maximum achievable and also have a continuing constructive effect on Western European coupling anxieties. This would be for the United States to eradicate the distinction between strategic and INF nuclear weapons and to follow the approach that all Soviet or U.S. nuclear delivery systems that can strike any part of the territory of either alliance should be considered strategic. This definition would cover in a single negotiation all U.S. forward-based systems and tactical nuclear weapons, as well as U.S. INF and strategic weapons, and it would include all Soviet and Warsaw Pact missiles, aircraft, or nuclear artillery capable of striking the territory of any member of the NATO alliance. This comprehensive approach would end the continual bickering with the Soviet Union over noninclusion of weapons systems that can strike Soviet territory and also the practice of focusing on segments of the spectrum of nuclear weapons, while other segments left untouched can increase. And it would deal with continual European worries about the United States's protecting itself through arms control negotiations with the Soviets while ignoring European interests, Chancellor Schmidt's complaint of 1977 and the European complaint of today when faced with the theoretical prospect of reduction of U.S. INF forces to zero. This concept, recommended by Raymond Garthoff and other experts, would permit an integrated approach to nuclear arms control and meet European desires to have "indivisible security" in the alliance.[6]

In practical terms, this approach would mean putting all nuclear warheads of the United States and the Soviet Union into a single pot from which reductions would be made. The United States has a very large number not only of gravity nuclear bombs for long- and short-range aircraft but also of other tactical nuclear weapons in Europe, which in its view could skew the count of strategic weapons to the advantage of the Soviet Union. But there is no reason why, though everything is in the same pot, subceilings on such weapons would not be possible. This approach would also make possible a further desirable organizational reform, with beneficial psychological results for U.S.-European relations: the direct participation of the NATO deployment countries in the U.S-Soviet talks on INF, in a working group together with Warsaw Pact countries that have Soviet nuclear weapons on their territory.

Treating the Coupling Sickness: Diplomacy or Deployment?

The U.S. reversion in 1986 to the 1981 zero option in the INF negotiations for evident if understandable propaganda purposes underlines what was clear from the outset about the entire INF project: whatever importance U.S. INF had for the Soviet Union, its military significance for the West was limited. The program was mainly a poultice for European coupling malaise. If the entire U.S. INF deployment can be dispensed with, then NATO's rationale that there was a need to introduce U.S. nuclear weapons in Europe independent of SS-20 deployment by the Soviets in order to establish a better chain of coupling with U.S. strategic weapons has no foundation. In 1986 as in 1978, U.S. officials were reassuring European leaders that 572 INF warheads were not many in a strategic confrontation of over 9000 strategic warheads in each country and that the INF deployment was not crucial to the U.S. commitment to Europe. In practical terms, this means that any first-stage cut should be feasible as long as it is politically acceptable to both sides. Nor will this first stage of limited reduction have much military significance. Therefore, whether it is reached will be mainly an issue of internal politics within the United States and the Soviet Union.

However, the worried West European reactions to the 1986

Soviet and U.S. proposals to reduce INF to zero illustrate once again that there is no good or lasting solution to the problems of extended deterrence, especially in the nonnuclear NATO countries. It is important that U.S. officials realize that it is a fundamental error to think, as have successive administrations, that this recurrent problem can be resolved by any given policy; the best that can be done is to manage it.

It is not a coincidence that the coupling problem has welled up in its most acute form in periods of poor relationships between U.S. political leaders and European, especially German, political leaders. President John F. Kennedy was far from pro-German or patient about recurrent German concerns over coupling; he instigated the recall of a Federal German ambassador who spoke to him insistently about German nuclear concerns. The relationship between President Jimmy Carter and Chancellor Helmut Schmidt was exceptionally poor. Characteristically, U.S. officials sought the same type of solution in each case: deployment of new U.S. nuclear weapons in Europe. Under Kennedy, it was the multilateral force; under Carter, the INF deployment. But the basic mistake was to believe in a hardware fix.

The logic of this brand of coupling is very weak. As Soviet leaders are aware, the presence or absence of U.S. nuclear weapons in Europe would at best be only a secondary factor in a U.S. president's decision to use U.S. nuclear weapons in the event of Soviet attack on Western Europe. That decision would be made by the president on the basis of all factors known to him at the time, the chief of which would be whether he believed that a Soviet attack on Europe sooner or later portended Soviet attack on the United States. The new U.S. INF missiles are no more and no less likely to be used in the event of Soviet attack on Europe than existing U.S. forward-based systems in Europe or Poseidon missiles assigned to SACEUR. Indeed, if U.S. leadership was as poor as it was considered by Europeans in the Carter administration and in the first Reagan administration, the deployment of new U.S. weapons would have been of no help at all in reaching the right decision.

To the contrary, the real basis for transatlantic coupling is the continued maintenance of U.S. equality with the Soviet Union in strategic nuclear forces, the maintenance of a close political relationship between U.S. and European leaders, and the retention of U.S. ground forces in Europe. The consequent automatic involvement of these forces in conflict in the event of a Soviet attack on Europe means for the Soviet leadership that the probable result will be a worldwide war with the United States. The INF deployment, a poor substitute for more direct measures to repair a strained personal relationship between European and U.S. leaders, brought intra-alliance controversy far more serious than the original problem of transatlantic confidence that gave rise to the INF decisions, controversy that threatens the continuation of these real U.S. guarantees for European security.

Because European worries about coupling are to some extent beyond their control and to some extent the unavoidable product of their dependent status, the larger responsibility for both the overall situation and the INF crisis is on the U.S. side. The proposal to adopt in arms control talks a definition of *strategic* as covering weapons that can strike the territory of either alliance and to enable direct participation of NATO countries where U.S. INF missiles are deployed in the Geneva talks could help. Beyond this, in the future, U.S. officials must have the courage to tell their president what the real nature of the problem is and help him to improve personal relationships with European leaders when they are poor. And U.S. officials, since they do have greater responsibility, need the courage to speak firmly to European leaders coming back for a new round of U.S. nuclear assurance—the courage to say a firm no.

The INF decision was made at a time when official opinion in both the United States and Europe saw no significant increase in the possibility of aggressive Soviet attack on Western Europe. It was made because of U.S. and European concerns about possible future Soviet political pressures on Europe based on SS-20 deployment; in fact, it did elicit massive pressures of this kind from the Soviets, pressures the Europeans withstood. Problems over intra-alliance coupling are the reverse side of that other intra-alliance problem: presumed European vulnerability to Soviet intimidation. Both are problems of confidence: the first, the lack of confidence of European leaders in the resoluteness of U.S. leaders in the face of Soviet pressure; the second, the lack of confidence of U.S. leaders in the resoluteness of European leaders in the face of Soviet pressures.

The cure for both problems is not more weapons; it is a better political relationship, with all the attention on the part of senior officials needed to maintain such relationships. We should go back to diplomacy in the earlier sense of the term: of relationships among leaders of states. This remedy will increase already heavy demands on the time, patience, and resourcefulness of senior U.S. officials who have to deal with European leaders who display exasperating imagination in finding some falling away of U.S. loyalty to Europe even in the most improbable circumstances. Even so, this approach is cheaper in the long run than the expenditure of resources and time involved in dealing with the problems arising from deployment of new U.S. weapons.

Notes

1. In writing this chapter, I have drawn particularly on four excellent books: Lawrence Freedman, *The Evolution of Nuclear Strategy* (New York: St. Martin's Press, 1981); David N. Schwartz, *NATO's Nuclear Dilemmas* (Washington, D.C.: Brookings Institution, 1983); Strobe Talbott, *Deadly Gambits* (New York: Alfred Knopf, 1984); and Raymond L. Garthoff, *Detente and Confrontation* (Washington, D.C.: Brookings Institution, 1985), chaps. 25, 28, as well as on numerous personal discussions with officials of both countries.
2. A chronology of some of these protest demonstrations can be found in Stanley Sloan, "NATO Nuclear Forces: Modernization and Arms Control," Congressional Research Service Issue Brief Number 1B8 1128 (Washington, D.C., August 2, 1983).
3. Text is in Foreign Broadcast Information Service (FBIS) report for Soviet Union (January 16, 1986), pp. AA1–AA9.
4. See Stephen F. Szabo, "European Opinion after the Missiles," *Survival* 27:6 (November–December 1985).
5. Jeanne Kirkpatrick, "SS-20 and Europe," *Washington Post*, February 23, 1986; James Markhan, "Europe Cool to Removal of US Medium Range Missiles," *New York Times*, February 25, 1986.
6. See, for example, Raymond G. Garthoff, testimony in Joint Hearing, "Overview of Nuclear Arms Control and Defense Strategy in NATO," Subcommittees on International Security and Scientific Affairs, and on Europe and the Middle East, 97th Congress, Second Session, March 18, 1982.

7

The MBFR Marathon

I n chapter 5, we discussed the earlier history of the European arms control negotiations, describing in particular how the decision was reached to begin the NATO–Warsaw Pact Mutual and Balanced Force Reduction negotiations in Vienna on October 31, 1973. This chapter describes the course of the MBFR negotiations, their main open issues, and their prospects for culminating in an agreement.[1]

Negotiating Concepts of the Two Alliances

NATO's Fundamental Negotiating Approach

Prior to the beginning of the MBFR talks, NATO's negotiating approach for MBFR, completed in the summer of 1973, had two important components. First, although the two alliances had agreed in the preparatory talks to discuss reductions in armaments as well as military manpower, NATO chose in its initial position to focus on military manpower. European NATO members did not want to reduce their armaments. No approach could readily be found to deal in a negotiable way with the fact of large Warsaw Pact numerical superiority in most major armaments. NATO was not willing to contractualize Warsaw Pact superiority in armaments by accepting it in an agreement, yet Pact reductions to parity would have been so great for most major armaments as to be unacceptable to the Pact. NATO's insistence on parity with the Warsaw Pact in arms control was borrowed from the U.S.-Soviet nuclear arms control talks and was designed to avoid a situation where NATO's inferiority would become even more important. This might occur, for example, if reductions were proportional. A 50 percent reduction of main battle tanks, using NATO data, would have meant reducing NATO's main battle tanks to under 7000, no longer enough to provide cover for NATO's 800 kilometer frontier with the Warsaw Pact, while the Warsaw Pact would still have over 13,000, a fully sufficient number for an attack on NATO forces.

Other NATO objections were that reduced armaments of Western countries whose home territory was in the MBFR reduction area (the Benelux countries and the Federal Republic of Germany) might have to be destroyed, making it impossible to use this equipment for reserve forces, as would have been logical. Equipment withdrawn by U.S. forces reduced through agreement would have to be taken 3000 miles across the Atlantic and could be returned only slowly—far more slowly than withdrawn Soviet equipment could return to Central Europe in the event of crisis, unless it could be agreed to store in Europe the equipment of withdrawn U.S. units. Moreover—and here we have a major drawback of the MBFR concept in the eyes even of its adherents—the Soviet Union, whose western territories are only 600 kilometers from the dividing line between the two alliances but outside the Central European area of reductions agreed for MBFR, would not be reducing its armaments in those territories and might well increase them. It is fair to say, however, that NATO never expended great effort in trying to think out ways of dealing with this key problem although there are potential solutions to it.

Having decided to aim at manpower reductions, NATO's original negotiation proposal focused specifically on reducing active-duty ground force personnel. It sought an equal 700,000-man ceiling for the ground force manpower of each alliance, with an overall ceiling of 900,000 men for the combined ground and air forces of each alliance. In the preparatory talks for the MBFR negotiations, East and West had agreed to exclude naval forces from discussion to avoid further complicating the already complex set of issues under consideration, and in NATO's view, rough equality already existed between the totals of air force personnel of the two alliances. In fact, at the time when NATO leaders had selected the concept of reducing the ground force manpower of both alliances to an equal ceiling, they estimated that the Pact had a manpower superiority of only some 30,000 active-duty ground force personnel in the Central European reduction area. They considered that it would not be unreasonable to expect the Pact to eliminate this limited superiority in moving to equal manpower ceilings with NATO.

NATO, then as now, considered the greatest danger in Central Europe to be a surprise attack by the Warsaw Pact, an attack with minimal preparation of four to five days, exploiting its numerical conventional superiority on the scene. NATO military experts reasoned that if parity in ground force manpower could be achieved through negotiation, the Warsaw Pact would no longer have the advantage in the critical first few days of a conventional attack. Therefore the likelihood of the feared surprise attack would be substantially reduced.

But before the NATO position was presented to Pact negotiators, painstaking review of its intelligence information brought a new estimate with the view that the Warsaw Pact's superiority in ground force manpower was far larger, perhaps by 100,000 men, than it had been considered at the outset. If true, the new information meant it would be far more difficult to achieve NATO's negotiating goal in the talks.

Before finally deciding on its negotiating objective, NATO studied at least two other reduction concepts, which represented some effort to cope with the problem of armament reductions. One of these, the concept of reducing by standardized brigade equivalents, foundered on the difficulty of reducing diversely organized NATO and Pact forces to equivalent reduction blocks, as well as on the antipathy of the Western Europeans to armament reductions. The remaining approach, Option III, called for reduction of some U.S. nuclear weapons to obtain withdrawal of a Soviet armored corps from East Germany. U.S. officials pointed out that to gain Soviet agreement to this objective and in addition to the large Pact manpower reductions now estimated as necessary to reduce to a common ceiling, some reasonable quid pro quo would be needed, but it was decided to hold action on the U.S. nuclear reduction in reserve. NATO officials believed that the Soviet Union might be willing to pay a stiff price to establish the genuineness of its frequent appeals for force reductions. In other words, some

NATO officials thought the Soviet Union was then prepared to make a serious effort to dismantle the East-West military confrontation. They were to be disappointed.

NATO also proposed that the equal manpower ceilings be alliance-wide ceilings rather than ceilings on the forces of individual nations so that other NATO members could compensate for and maintain the overall alliance total if one alliance member were to reduce its forces unilaterally, for domestic reasons, subsequent to a reduction agreement. European NATO members were especially apprehensive in this context over the long-term possibility of U.S. troop withdrawals from Europe. Moreover, with painful memories of the imposed Versailles peace settlement after World War I, Federal Germany resisted the political implications of a limitation on its forces in an international agreement with the Soviet Union. It feared the Soviet Union might misuse such an obligation to achieve a *droit de regard* ("right of oversight") over the Federal German armed forces, a concern also shared in a more general sense by other Western European NATO states, which, in their preoccupation with a possible Soviet *droit de regard* tended to ignore the at least equal opportunity NATO would have to establish a *droit de regard* over Soviet and other Warsaw Pact forces.

In the original NATO concept, the residual (postreduction) alliance-wide ceilings on the active-duty ground and air force personnel of the two alliances in the reduction area, called common collective ceilings, were to be attained in two separate phases, embodied in two separate, consecutively negotiated agreements, a concept to which NATO would return twelve years later. U.S. and Soviet forces would be reduced under the first agreement and Western European and Eastern European forces in the second agreement, which would also provide for further U.S. and Soviet reductions.

This plan satisfied two different demands within the Western coalition. First, some Western European governments, still immensely distrustful of the Soviet Union, wished to see Soviet withdrawals carried out first as a sign of Soviet good faith before making their own reductions. And in the United States, domestic political pressure for the unilateral withdrawal of U.S. forces from Europe was mounting. Under the détente-minded Brandt government, Federal Germany had wanted to reduce its Bundeswehr forces in the first phase of MBFR along with the United States. But before the NATO negotiating concept was advanced to the Soviets, U.S. defense officials managed to convince the German government that it should relinquish the idea of early German reductions. They argued that the sight of European governments hastening to reduce their forces from the outset would have a negative impact on members of Congress interested in burden sharing.

So the phased approach was retained, and the first specific result of the MBFR talks was to prevent unilateral reductions by NATO direct participants, including the United States, Great Britain, Federal Germany, and the Netherlands. In fact, U.S. forces, drawn down considerably from Europe in the Vietnam War, actually went up 40,000 men in the first decade of the MBFR talks without any Soviet increase.

An additional objective of the NATO reduction approach was that the Soviet Union should take at least 50 percent of total Warsaw Pact reductions in both phases, corresponding to the proportion of its troops in the overall manpower strength of the Pact. From the outset, the NATO participants were interested in maximum withdrawals of Soviet forces to the Soviet Union, showing their lower evaluation of the military capability of non-Soviet Warsaw Pact states by the far lower priority they placed on their reduction.

The second major component of NATO's initial position in the MBFR talks, in addition to manpower reductions, was a program of associated measures, some related to verification of manpower reductions and residual manpower levels and others measures of warning against surprise attack, designed to help both sides recognize when military activities departed from the norm. These measures included prior notification of large troop movements, as well as the presence of observers at those movements who could confirm by direct observation the accuracy of the earlier information as to nature and size of the activity. An initial proposal was presented by NATO participants in the spring of 1973 as measures that would be undertaken by U.S. and Soviet forces alone. It rapidly became apparent that the Soviet Union would accept only measures that would apply to all direct participants, including Federal Germany.

Despite their declared interest in this project, it took NATO participants six years to present new proposals for associated measures covering all direct participants. They did so in the same session in which they withdrew their nuclear reduction offer of 1975, thus decreasing what they were prepared to offer the Soviets while increasing their requirements in terms of associated measures.

Warsaw Pact's Initial Negotiating Position

The Warsaw Pact's initial position differed from NATO's in ways that reflected its own view of the Central European situation. The Pact proposed a single agreement, to be implemented in stages: a symbolic reduction of 20,000 men for each alliance, to be followed by a freeze on the forces of individual nations, to be followed by reductions in manpower and armaments of 15 percent in the existing strength of each national component, and finally by individual ceilings on the manpower and armaments of national forces. With the initial 20,000-man reduction, total reductions would be about 17 percent. Thus the Warsaw Pact's initial approach differed from NATO's in four important respects: reductions were to be proportional rather than to equal numerical levels; force limits were to apply to individual nations rather than to alliances as a whole; there would be a single agreement, implemented in phases, rather than two separate agreements; and armaments as well as manpower were to be reduced.

The Pact proposal for proportional reductions would, like the NATO proposal for reduction to a common ceiling, have required mutual agreement on the current manpower levels of both alliances. Moreover, the proposal embodied the Warsaw Pact's contention that rough numerical parity already existed between the ground forces of the two alliances. Thus, from the outset of the MBFR talks, there arose the long-standing and still unresolved disagreement over the number of Warsaw Pact active-duty ground and air force personnel in Central Europe, as well as over the number of Pact armaments. NATO's own figures have changed from time to time on the basis of new information and new computation. At various times, NATO has estimated Warsaw Pact manpower at as much as 180,000 ground force personnel and 40,000 air force personnel more than shown in figures later provided by Warsaw

Pact representatives. (In the last officially exchanged figures, those of 1980, NATO counted its ground force manpower at just over 744,000 [50,000 French forces deployed in Federal Germany are not included in official NATO figures], and its air force manpower at just over 198,000. It counted Warsaw Pact ground force personnel at just over 956,000 and air force personnel at just over 224,000, while the Pact claimed it had only a little over 815,000 ground force personnel and 182,000 air force personnel, for a total discrepancy between NATO and Pact figures on Warsaw Pact ground and air force manpower of about 183,000 men.) The proposal for individual national limits rather than alliance limits reflected the Warsaw Pact's determination to limit the forces of Federal Germany. Under an alliance-wide common ceiling, the Soviet Union feared that Federal Germany would build up its forces. The proposal for a single agreement reflected the same concern: under the Western plan for two separate agreements, the Warsaw Pact considered that there would be no binding obligation on Western European states, including Federal Germany, to come to agreement actually to reduce their forces. Under the Western concept, Soviet forces would have been reduced and limited without any certainty that a Federal German reduction would actually take place. The Warsaw Pact wanted armament reductions on the commonsense ground that reduction of military personnel without reduction of armaments would not result in a real reduction of destructive power in possible conflict. At the same time, the Pact did little to meet NATO's more specific objections to armament reductions based mainly on the geographic proximity of the Soviet Union and the fact that there would be no reductions or limitations on its territory.

NATO rejected the Warsaw Pact's overall approach on the grounds that a percentage reduction in men and arms would lock in the Warsaw Pact's claimed numerical superiority and that individual national ceilings for residual forces would not permit NATO to make force adjustments within the alliance.

Additional MBFR Negotiating Concepts

At the end of 1975, NATO deviated from its focus on manpower to present the nuclear reduction proposal that European NATO participants had been unwilling to use at the outset of the negotiations. NATO participants offered to withdraw 36 U.S. Pershing I ballistic missiles, 54 U.S. nuclear-capable F-4 aircraft, and 1000 U.S. nuclear warheads in exchange for Soviet counterreduction of an armored corps consisting of 5 divisions, about 70,000 personnel and 1,700 tanks. This proposal was based on the "mixed package" reduction concept, whereby each side would be called on to make a reduction of different composition—in this case, U.S. nuclear weapons versus a Soviet tank corps—but considered of equal military significance. In effect, the concept proposed withdrawal of elements each alliance found most threatening in the military posture of the other; the West found Soviet tank units most threatening, and the Pact presumably found U.S. nuclear weapons most threatening. In addition to these phase I Soviet reductions, NATO demanded a Warsaw Pact commitment to reduce its personnel, in a second phase, to the proposed common collective ceiling of 700,000 men for ground forces and 900,000 men for ground and air force combined.

Pact negotiators never indicated agreement with the NATO conceptual approach. They made a counterproposal of Soviet nuclear reductions early in 1976 that offered equal percentage reductions of 2–3 percent of U.S. and Soviet manpower and withdrawal by each country of 300 tanks, 54 nuclear-capable aircraft, a "certain number" of Soviet Scud-B and U.S. Pershing launchers plus an equal number of warheads, and withdrawal of a corps headquarters. The NATO offer was withdrawn in 1979 when it was decided to remove the U.S. warheads unilaterally as part of NATO's decision to deploy Pershing IIs and cruise missiles in Western Europe. This outcome represented a failure on both sides to come to serious grips with the problem of reduction of nuclear weapons and of armaments in general.

The new set of confidence-building measures put forward by NATO in 1979 included prior notification of out-of-garrison activities and large force movements into the MBFR reduction area, required use of specific entry and exit points permanently manned by observers, periodic exchanges of data on forces, and an annual quota of inspections by each alliance of the other's forces.

Achievements and Obstacles

The long history of the MBFR talks shows slow but definite movement of the Warsaw Pact toward the Western position. By the summer of 1980, the Warsaw Pact and NATO had already agreed in principle to the following:

1. The long-term goal of reducing ground force personnel in the MBFR reduction area to a 700,000-man ceiling, equal for both alliances, with a 900,000-man common ceiling for combined ground and air force manpower of each alliance.

2. Initial small reductions of U.S. and Soviet personnel in the general range of 10,000 and 20,000, respectively.

3. A residual ceiling after phase I reductions on Soviet and U.S. ground force personnel and a collective freeze on the remaining personnel of each alliance.

4. Further reductions by all participants on a timetable to be agreed.

Given several Western changes of position in the interim, however, there no longer seems to be general agreement on these points.

Since 1979, the Warsaw Pact has also accepted in principle Western concepts of associated measures to verify residual ceilings and provide assurance against surprise attack, including some that Warsaw Pact negotiators in Stockholm have so far been unwilling to discuss. These are:

1. Prior notification of large-scale troop entry (20,000–25,000 men) into the Central European reduction area for rotation or training purposes.

2. Exit-entry points at airports and ports and on roads and railroads, to be used by forces entering and leaving the Central European area, and which would be permanently manned by military personnel of the opposing alliance. General Secretary Gorbachev announced formal agreement to this point in presenting his arms control program of January

15, 1986; this agreement had been foreshadowed in numerous informal statements by Pact negotiations at Vienna. The question of whether all military personnel entering or leaving the reduction area, including the semi-annual rotation of Soviet conscripts into East Germany, and the number of exit-entry points and the procedures to be used at them, however, remain to be agreed.

3. Prior notification of out-of-garrison activities by units of large size. Criteria for size and area of coverage are yet to be agreed, and this is an important divergence.

4. Exchange of data on forces remaining in the area after reductions. The degree of detail in the data to be exchanged has yet to be agreed.

5. Inspections of the forces of the two alliances by personnel of the opposing side. There is as yet no agreement as to the number of these inspections, under what circumstances they would take place, and how they would take place.

6. Noninterference with national technical means of verification.

7. Establishment of a consultative committee to discuss issues of compliance.

The Data Dispute

In spite of this considerable progress, there has been no MBFR agreement. The primary practical obstacle has been the East-West dispute over the number of Warsaw Pact active-duty ground and air force personnel in the reduction area, which has remained unresolved since the Pact first presented figures on its forces in 1976. Once both sides had agreed in principle to a 700,000-man common collective ceiling for ground force personnel, the implications of the data discrepancy for force reductions could be clearly seen. For NATO, a reduction of about 90,000 from its present level of approximately 790,000 men would be required. (French forces in Germany are included for the purpose of computing Western reductions.) But the reductions required of the Warsaw Pact vary dramatically according to whose data are used.

If, as the Warsaw Pact claimed in its 1980 figures, its own ground forces are about 815,000 men, a reduction of 115,000 men would be required. About half of the Pact's forces in the MBFR reduction area are Soviet, so this would mean in turn a Soviet reduction of about 57,000 men. But using NATO's estimates that the Warsaw Pact's ground forces number about 960,000, a total Warsaw Pact ground force reduction of 260,000 men would be required to reach the common collective ceiling of 700,000 for ground force personnel. About 130,000 of these ground force personnel would be Soviet—some 70,000 men more than the Soviet Union would be required to withdraw on the basis of the Pact's data.

The problems of obtaining accurate information on the military forces of the closed societies of the Warsaw Pact countries have been described in chapter 2. There are several possible explanations for the difference between the NATO and Warsaw Pact data. It may be caused by the deliberate omission by the Pact of certain categories of active-duty personnel from their count. This has already been established for certain categories of Polish personnel, mainly general-purpose construction units. Another possibility is errors in NATO estimates. Perhaps category 1 Pact forces are manned at lower levels than NATO estimates or NATO is double counting combat unit personnel also assigned to housekeeping duties on military posts.

Since 1976, Warsaw Pact representatives have produced two batches of figures on their forces, both disputed by NATO. But the Warsaw Pact, while unwilling to accept NATO's data, has also been unwilling to provide the further detailed information needed to resolve the discrepancies by detailed comparison of Warsaw Pact and NATO figures on the same Pact units. Pact negotiators state that divulging further figures, like the peacetime manning levels of the Soviet divisions deployed in the Soviet Group of Forces in East Germany, would—in a situation where they claim Western interest in proceeding to actual reductions is in question—merely reveal sensitive intelligence information on the readiness level of their forces for combat. Of course, if Soviet forces in East Germany are, as appears possible, manned in peacetime at a level below the high degree of readiness with which they have been credited, it would be to the mutual benefit that this fact become known in the West. This information would reduce remaining concerns about possible Soviet attack on Western Europe, especially attack with minimum preparation, and contribute to a different perspective on the confrontation.

The Warsaw Pact argued early on that such specific figures represented security information that could be made available only after the Western participants had shown themselves ready to conclude a reduction agreement. Later, Pact negotiators argued that it was not in fact necessary for the two alliances to agree on the current size of their forces before making a force reduction agreement or even to agree to reductions of specified size. Instead, the two alliances could reduce to the agreed-upon ceilings of 700,000 and 900,000 and then verify the residual force levels. Pact negotiators failed, however, to indicate agreement to the specific details of inspections that would have made this approach more convincing.

Up to 1985, NATO insisted that agreement be reached on force data before any reduction took place. This was partly because the mere existence of the disagreement over data made it desirable to clear up the discrepancy as a matter of mutual trust. But it was also NATO's belief that the size of reductions needed by both alliances should be calculated from an agreed base before those reductions are made because this information would assist in fixing postreduction levels and would provide a baseline for testing compliance with manpower ceilings once reductions had taken place.

The determined withholding by the Warsaw Pact of practical cooperation on the data issue indicates that important interests underlie their position. These doubtless include reluctance for military reasons to accept reductions as large and as unequal as those called for by the Western figures and a fear of discrediting the Soviet Union, which compiled the original figures presented by the Warsaw Pact in Vienna, through accepting conflicting Western figures. Another possibility is purposeful use of the data dispute by some group within the Soviet Union to block an MBFR agreement. It is, for example, no secret that the Soviet Defense Ministry has the final say on release of data on Warsaw Pact military forces and that these data are considered security information. Perhaps the Soviet military establishment does not wish Soviet military forces reduced by agreement with the West, fearing the impact of such an agreement on its efforts to obtain a continuing high share of Soviet defense resources. As noted, it is also possible that Western figures themselves may not be fully accurate because they must be compiled from fragmentary evidence and that Soviet or other Warsaw Pact units are in fact manned at lower levels than Western intelligence agencies believe.

Other Stumbling Blocks

Aside from the data dispute, there are other major negotiating problems in the MBFR talks. First, it has not been agreed how many on-site inspections should take place and under what conditions. Up to December 1985, when it considerably increased the number, NATO had asked for a quota of eighteen inspections a year to take place on NATO demand at short notice—that is, the Pact could neither object to the area or the unit selected for inspection nor interpose delay. Under the different Warsaw Pact concept of inspection in both MBFR and CDE, a complaint would first be discussed among signatories, and only if this discussion does not resolve the issue would an inspection take place. The chances here of delay and obfuscation are considerable.

In addition, the operation of inspections, including what inspectors would want to see, has not been agreed. Despite Soviet agreement in principle to on-site inspections and NATO's own emphasis on verification, in 1986, six years after presenting its inspection proposals, NATO had still not presented detailed suggestions to Pact negotiators as to how these inspections would actually operate. How much would inspectors be permitted to see of the garrisons of Soviet forces? NATO governments are likely to want to carry out intrusive inspections of sleeping and messing quarters and to see enough of major equipment like tanks and artillery to be able to count them in order to be able to make a founded evaluation of the manpower of Warsaw Pact units. These Western desires will conflict with ingrained Soviet secretiveness on military matters even though the Soviets would have mutual rights with regard to Western forces.

Another major area of controversy is the degree of detail of the data on forces to be exchanged by the two alliances following the initial reductions. NATO participants are asking for a list of all units down to the battalion level with their official designation, location, actual strength on the date of the report, and their subordination. In connection with inspections, these kinds of data could provide a good basis for assurance as to compliance with force limitations. The data provided must add up to no more than the permitted level. Sampling inspections of arbitrarily selected units could, when compared with information on the strength of the same units provided by each alliance, result in a reassuring compliance test. But obtaining Soviet agreement to provide information of this level of detail will be difficult.

Still to be resolved at Vienna is the Western proposal that out-of-garrison activities be prenotified and that observers of the other side be invited to these activities in an area that covers not only the area agreed for the Vienna talks, as this measure did in its original form, but also much of the western Soviet Union. As already noted, NATO made this proposal in response to the desires of NATO flank participants to have some portion of an agreement to which they could adhere directly. There is a related Warsaw Pact proposal that the size of these out-of-garrison activities be limited. Although there are difficulties, it would be logical to seek a trade-off here, aimed at agreement on both measures but for the MBFR area only. There is some sentiment in NATO, however, to drop these measures in MBFR if they are agreed in CDE.

A further question for resolution is overcoming Pact insistence that most associated measures should enter into effect only after participants have completed reductions to the agreed common ceilings. The Pact's present concept is that the United States and the Soviet Union would make small reductions in a first phase, follow that by negotiated reductions to the 700,000-man common collective ceiling, and only then implement the associated measures. This would mean NATO would have to reduce about 90,000 men before associated measures were in effect—clearly an unsatisfactory arrangement. It may be possible to incorporate solutions for these associated measures into a compromise agreement for resolving the data dispute.

Another problem arises from the West's December 1985 proposal to be described below. Over the years, Western negotiators had moved to meet Soviet criticisms that the West's original concept of two successive but unconnected negotiations would leave the Soviet Union having reduced and limited its forces in a first negotiation, without any assurances as to West European, specifically German, reduction at a later point. In the interim, the West had developed a plan for Western European commitments for later reductions to be made as part of an initial agreement. In December 1985, Western participants reverted to the two-negotiation concept.

If an agreement is to be reached in Vienna, there will also ultimately have to be some trade-off between the Western desire to have a specific sublimit on Soviet forces and the Soviet desire to have a specific sublimit on German forces. This issue has been left in abeyance during recent years as the negotiations have marched in place. The Western proposal is to freeze overall NATO and Pact forces collectively but to limit specifically the forces of both superpowers because of their superpower status and because both are reducing in a first stage. If there are binding assurances on later European reductions, the Soviet Union might be willing to accept sublimits on the superpowers' forces for the purposes of a first agreement on the understanding that this step would not prejudice treatment of the issue in later phases of reduction. A second possibility would be to institute a modified version of the 50 percent rule. Under such a rule, originally proposed by Chancellor Helmut Schmidt, no single country would have more than 50 percent of the total ground force manpower of its alliance. Such a rule, without singling out the Soviet Union or Federal Germany, would in practice have imposed sublimits only on Soviet and Federal German forces in the reduction area. Provisions could be made for flexibility for these two forces to increase if their allies made unilateral reductions. A third approach would be to drop formal sublimits but to accept a solution proposed informally by the Warsaw Pact at an earlier stage in the talks. Under this approach, no participant in either alliance can make good more than 50 percent of reductions made unilaterally by another member of its alliance, unless maintaining this restriction would require the overall strength of that side to decline; in that case, the rule would be suspended until the full permitted strength was reached again. Finally, it might be enough to report levels of national forces after reductions under the postreduction exchange of data; it is quite unlikely that the force relationships among members of the respective alliances will change to any large degree since they reflect enduring political relationships. For example, under a collective ceiling, the Soviet Union, intent on further burden sharing, is unlikely to permit the Poles to decrease so it can increase.

A further stumbling block is obtaining Pact agreement that, to simplify things, armaments should not be reduced in a first agreement but in subsequent negotiations.

MBFR's Failings, Real and Alleged

In looking back over the MBFR negotiations, one must ask why these negotiations have continued for more than a decade without yielding any outcome more substantial than tantalizing agreements in principle. What has gone wrong in Vienna?

A Failure of Political Will

The foremost reason that no agreement has been achieved in the MBFR talks is the failure of both the United States and the Soviet Union to accord them sustained high-level interest. In any negotiation, the strength of political interest in bringing about an actual outcome, sometimes called political will, is the decisive element. No bilateral or alliance-to-alliance negotiation on the sensitive topics of national security that form the subject matter of arms control negotiations like MBFR can be successfully concluded without receiving priority interest at some point from at least one of the two sides. If both sides have only moderate but not urgent interest, this usually proves inadequate to motivate an outcome. Negotiations where it is a matter of indifference to one side or the other whether there is an outcome, or where no outcome is desired, are conducted mainly for the sake of being seen to negotiate; a positive outcome is unlikely even if the other side has shown priority interest in an outcome. For the United States, and probably for the Soviet Union, multilateral arms control negotiations like MBFR, CDE, and the chemical and biological warfare negotiations at the UN Commission on Disarmament have failed to achieve top-priority interest because they are not considered, rightly or wrongly, to involve issues of national survival.

The record of U.S.-Soviet arms control negotiations over the past decade also suggests that neither government is capable of providing top-level interest and supervision for more than one arms control negotiation at a time. In this sense, one obvious reason the MBFR talks have not received consistent attention is that the first priority for both superpowers has always been their nuclear relationship. In the 1970s, presentation of the Western proposal for U.S. nuclear reductions in MBFR was delayed for at least two years until the time was right in SALT (after the Vladivostok accords), where the MBFR move was apparently seen as useful in coping with the Soviet interest in restricting U.S. forward-based systems. More than once the superpowers have withdrawn their negotiating chips from the MBFR talks to use them in the U.S.-Soviet nuclear context. As already noted, NATO's 1975 proposal in MBFR to reduce U.S. Pershing I missiles, nuclear-capable aircraft, and nuclear warheads in return for Soviet tank and personnel reductions was withdrawn in 1979; the United States then agreed to withdraw the same 1000 nuclear warheads from Europe unilaterally to smooth the way for the Benelux states' decision to allow deployment of new INF weapons. NATO offered at the same time to negotiate with the Soviet Union on U.S. Pershing IIs, the follow-on model of the Pershing I, which would have been restricted had the Soviet Union agreed to NATO's 1975 proposal for reduction of Pershing I and its follow-on models. Similarly, the Soviets unilaterally withdrew 20,000 Soviet troops from East Germany in 1979 as part of their effort to convince Western European governments to reject the planned deployment of U.S. Pershing IIs and cruise missiles; earlier, the same troops had been offered as part of the Soviet reduction proposal in MBFR. The Soviet Union showed the low priority it assigned to MBFR when it pushed its proposal for a follow-on conference of Helsinki Accord signatories on European security despite its knowledge that this rival conference, which ultimately took the form of the Stockholm CDE, would undermine the authority of the MBFR forum. As we will discuss subsequently,

Soviet leader Mikhail Gorbachev dealt the MBFR negotiations a further and possibly fatal blow when, in April 1986, he proposed reduction of conventional armaments and tactical nuclear weapons in the area from the Atlantic to the Urals.

Moreover, ever since domestic pressures for U.S. troop withdrawals from overseas subsided in the mid-1970s following U.S. withdrawal from Vietnam, U.S. political leaders have seemed to consider the MBFR talks as primarily a Western European interest. Some senior military officers have shown an awareness of the talks' potential for stabilizing the confrontation in Central Europe, but the absence of consistent political interest at the top level in achieving an agreement has often left the field to interests of one military service or another (or to the parochial interests of one ally or another), with resultant damage to the realism of the Western negotiating position. For example, though East and West had long agreed that first-stage Soviet and U.S. force reductions should be preceded by exchanging lists of the units to be reduced by each side, it was not possible for a decade to bring the U.S. Army to present even an illustrative list of the types of units it would withdraw from Europe if a first-stage agreement were concluded.

In the face of neglect by the superpowers, the European participants in MBFR have failed to provide impetus of their own to propel the talks to a conclusion. Experience with the INF and CDE talks shows that U.S. administrations have been prepared to be highly responsive to Western European desires and suggestions when presented forcefully, with specific details, in parallel by several allies. The Western allies prevailed on the United States to enter separate talks on the INF issue, and their views have been dominant in the formulation of the U.S. negotiating position in INF from the zero option to subsequent proposals. Yet this did not happen in MBFR—and for a reason.

Federal Germany, militarily the most important European member of NATO, was originally the moving force behind MBFR, but it became far less active as divisions of opinion emerged within its own government on the subject matter of the talks. In the mid-1970s, for example, Chancellor Helmut Schmidt tried to resolve the impasse in MBFR over the question of possible subceilings under the collective alliance-wide ceilings, an issue that, as we have just seen, remains unresolved to the present, by suggesting in a speech in the German Bundestag the "50 percent rule": that after reductions no single member of an alliance should have more than 50 percent of the alliance's manpower. But the proposal was dropped because of opposition from Schmidt's own foreign minister, Hans Dietrich Genscher, whose support as chairman of the Free Democratic party was essential to continuation of the Schmidt government. Personal feelings on the subject between the two leaders ran high, and in practice the German leadership role in the alliance on MBFR went into a state of suspended animation.

Inflated Expectations

Some of the criticisms leveled at the MBFR talks over the years, especially criticisms of its design and concept, are important enough for discussion here for the light they may throw on the future of arms control in Europe.

One frequent criticism, originally from French officials and now mainly from German officials, especially in the Foreign Ministry, has been that the MBFR reduction area is too small, constituting a special area around Germany. On the one hand, this reflects concern about subjecting Federal Germany to possible limitations and controls over its forces that would not be applied to its major Western European partners, Britain and France. On the other, it reflects the view that the MBFR concept is defective because the reduction area does not include the western military districts of the Soviet Union, where a large number of forces are stationed that could be used against NATO forces in the event of conflict. It is true that under the approach agreed for MBFR, Soviet troops stationed in the western Soviet Union would not be subject to the reductions, limitations, and inspections applied to those within the MBFR area. It is also true that Soviet troops withdrawn from the MBFR area can remain close at hand in the western Soviet Union, whereas U.S. troops reduced under an agreement must withdraw 3000 miles across the ocean. These are genuine defects in the MBFR concept, but the question that must be asked is whether anything better was or is feasible.

True, as the result of pressure from West Europeans, especially

France and Federal Germany, the CDE area now covers the whole of the western Soviet Union to the Urals. Securing Soviet agreement to this wider area was an impressive achievement. But, despite Gorbachev's proposal of April 1986 of armament reductions in the same area, it is doubtful whether the Soviet Union will engage itself in future phases of CDE to measures with real bite—real restrictions, reductions, limitations, and intrusive inspection on its own territory. It is more likely that it will prove feasible to obtain Soviet agreement to measures like this if they are to apply to Soviet forces outside the Soviet Union.

Another line of criticism of MBFR has been that the focus of the negotiations is wrong and that MBFR's emphasis on reducing individual servicemen rather than combat units or armaments is misplaced. It is believed that manpower reductions, even if implemented, would be ineffective in reducing the level of confrontation. Yet soldiers are ultimately the agents of military conflict and also are more comparable than other negotiable force components. Moreover, reduction by units, even if equivalent units can be identified, does not eliminate the need to establish a limit on the manpower of the remaining units, which could otherwise be increased. This criticism also overlooks the actual history of MBFR and the efforts made to work out other reduction approaches—against the adamant opposition of Western European MBFR participants to any form of armament reduction because it would mean destruction of their equipment. Nonetheless, it is a defect in MBFR that no adequate arms reduction concept has yet been developed.

A more general criticism of the focus of the MBFR negotiations is that force reductions and limitations as such are no longer a useful vehicle of arms control and that emphasis should properly be placed on confidence-building measures and crisis stability. During a period of increased U.S.-Soviet tensions that has slowed the pace of arms control negotiations, support in Europe and the United States for reduction and limitation of armed forces has greatly decreased. Controversy over SALT II has emphasized the fact that although strategic launchers were limited in number, warhead levels increased dramatically. The Reagan administration has challenged the value of the still-unratified SALT II agreement on grounds of noncompliance by the Soviet Union. As a consequence, reduction agreements are in disfavor as difficult to achieve, ineffective because they are not comprehensive in coverage, and inadequately verifiable. For their part, left-wing and liberal critics criticize force reduction negotiations for acting as a motor of force increases because of pressures in the negotiating process to equal the rival in all respects and for creation of bargaining chip weapons, which then acquire support as militarily indispensable.

Yet reductions as a means of bringing nuclear weapons under control continue to have plausibility. If deep cuts could be made in nuclear launchers and warheads, this could effectively eliminate the possibility of a first strike. In part, the critical trend reflects frustration with the lack of progress in U.S.-Soviet nuclear reduction talks as well as in MBFR. If the United States and the Soviet Union can in the future conclude a new reduction agreement, this action would validate the arms control approach, and much of the criticism directed at it would fade away. Moreover, supporters of confidence-building and crisis stability measures as an alternative to reductions overlook the fact that confidence-building measures and force reduction and limitation are not only complementary and mutually enhancing; they form part of a single spectrum of measures, ranging from exchange of information on one end, through restrictions on activity to deep cuts at the other extreme. For example, are proposals for zones of prohibited or reduced armaments confidence-building measures, or reductions in a specified area?

A more general comment must be made in response to current criticism of classic arms control, consisting of reductions and limitations: progress in the whole range of arms control is so difficult, so limited, and so fragmentary that it should be seized wherever the opportunity to conclude an intrinsically acceptable agreement, however partial, presents itself. There is no perfect form of arms control that with one incisive approach can resolve the entire problem of the East-West military confrontation. Moreover, as they are seen and used by the two superpowers and by the NATO and Warsaw Pact alliances, reductions, confidence-building measures, and other agreed steps of arms control are not intended—not yet—as means of dismantling the East-West confrontation but only of controlling or managing it. NATO's proposed reduction in MBFR, for example, was only 10 percent of NATO manpower; the Warsaw Pact proposed a reduction of only about 15 percent. Arms control as an approach for management of the military confrontation is in fact more part of the political East-West relationship than of the military one. It is a form of mutual psychological reassurance between the leaderships of East and West as to their intentions. It is a distortion to apply to it, as is frequently done, the criterion of whether it is militarily significant. Arms control, however partial, is useful; it should not be criticized for not being disarmament, though it should ultimately lead to disarmament.

Vienna: Strong Promise, Elusive Accord

A first MBFR agreement could make conventional war in Europe less likely and increase security for both sides. A first agreement would also open the way to further reductions, which would increase the benefits. Yet until recently, it has appeared less likely each year that the MBFR talks would actually culminate in an agreement. The new Western proposals of December 1985, which emphasize on-site inspection, and the subsequent, surprisingly positive statement in General Secretary Gorbachev's January 15, 1986, arms control program that the outlines of a first agreement in Vienna appear to be emerging, may have increased prospects for progress.

What could an MBFR agreement achieve? A first agreement along the lines now under consideration in Vienna would be modest in scope, but it would result in withdrawal of a Soviet division from Central Europe. Like the Soviet division unilaterally withdrawn from East Germany in 1980, such a unit would probably revert to category 3 and a low state of readiness. A first agreement would freeze remaining NATO and Pact military manpower at its present level and institute a regime of verification measures that would offer more precision, accuracy, and control than the like product of CDE, albeit in a smaller area.

Several of the associated measures proposed by the West in MBFR—prenotification of troop movements inside or into the reduction area, use of entry-exit points permanently staffed by personnel of the opposing alliance for military personnel entering or leaving the area, and periodic exchange of data on forces—would help in verifying that manpower ceilings were being respected and would provide early warning of troop movements or concentrations departing from the normal preannounced pattern. The information gained through these associated measures could be checked. Observers at out-of-garrison activities could report on the nature of those activities. Inspection on a sampling basis could ensure compliance with manpower ceilings. Low-flying air inspections could give all-weather capability to check for unannounced force movements and concentrations. This capability would be an important addition to satellite photography of the type in service up to now, which is partially blinded by the clouds that cover Central Europe for 60 percent of the year.

Taken together with information gathered by national intelligence collection, implementation of these measures would provide considerable assurance that neither side was preparing for conflict. It would insulate the military confrontation in Central Europe against the destabilizing effects of accidental, unauthorized, or mistaken actions by individual units or personnel that might otherwise be misinterpreted and set in train a sequence of actions leading to conflict. The East-West consultative commission for MBFR, whose main job would be to discuss compliance issues, could have its mandate expanded to aid in deflecting or managing incipient crises or take on this function pragmatically.

With a first agreement of this type to administer, MBFR or a similar agreement could become a practical and eminently usable forum for the management of the military confrontation in Europe, entailing not only the possibility for further reductions but of a still tighter regime of advance notification, observation, and inspection that would further reduce the possibility of surprise attack by either alliance. A first MBFR agreement on the Western model would not prevent force improvements on either side; however, successful experience with a first agreement might convince Soviet leaders that they can afford to cut back on force modernization, allowing NATO to follow suit, damping down the competitive spiral of force improvements.

A first MBFR accord would confer some benefit even if its provisions were violated. Significant violations of the terms of the treaty, such as entry into the area by units of personnel without preannouncement, would be detected and would provide unambiguous evidence of hostile intention. Such clarity would be useful to both sides. It would address an oft-cited weakness of Western defense: the slowness of NATO political authorities, acting on the basis of ambiguous intelligence indications regarding possible Pact attack, to make timely decisions to move NATO forces into forward defensive positions. The measures would have similar benefits for Warsaw Pact leaders, who, if faced with conflicting information and signals from the NATO countries, might otherwise make hasty decisions based on misperceptions.

A series of agreements in MBFR or another forum reducing the level of military manpower and then tackling armament reductions could in theory provide the rudiments of an East-West security system that could make it a little easier for the Soviet Union to permit social and economic change in Eastern Europe without fearing so much that such change would adversely affect its own security. Again in theory, such an East-West security system might be an acceptable vehicle in the long term for a situation where the states of Eastern Europe, although remaining members of the Warsaw Pact, were permitted increasing latitude by the Soviet Union to develop their own domestic political and economic systems. More specifically, the reduction and limitation of the forces of both sides, together with the additional clarity as to military intentions provided by associated measures, would give the Soviet leadership assurance that the NATO powers would not attempt to take advantage of possible change in Eastern Europe. The alliance-to-alliance nature of an MBFR agreement would make clear that the West accepted the continuing membership of the Eastern European states in the Warsaw Pact.

Today, we are a long way from these benefits of force reduction agreements, although it is worth keeping them in mind. There is still concern in administration circles in Washington and in some European governments that conclusion of an MBFR agreement would so reassure Western European publics that their willingness to support large defense establishments would begin to unravel. This worry underrates the capacity of Western governments, already evident with past U.S.-Soviet arms control agreements, to put in perspective for their publics the limited change that a first MBFR agreement would make in the continuing massive East-West military confrontation. It also leaves out of account the consideration that even a first MBFR agreement could, at no cost, insulate Western European decision making against Soviet efforts to translate military power into political pressure and could do so more effectively than NATO force increases of many divisions. This is the reverse side of the coin of concerns about the unraveling of Western European public support for defense expenditures. Given the central nature of the intimidation possibility for U.S. policymakers, it is the more significant one.

Most important, concern about the negative effects of actually achieving East-West arms control agreements, as distinguished from merely negotiating on them, underrates the seriousness of the ongoing attrition of European public support for defense (and especially for the role of nuclear weapons in defense) and the long-term abrasive effects of this attrition on U.S.-European relations. Even for opponents of arms control, judging on a basis of strict national interest of the United States, the evident costs of continuing without arms control outweigh the putative losses from concluding agreements.

In sum, there can be little doubt that an MBFR agreement would be a valuable first step in the long task of dismantling the East-West confrontation in Europe. Yet significant obstacles—both practical difficulties in negotiating an agreement acceptable to all participants and underlying political barriers to the achievement of any agreement—remain in the path to success in Vienna. The most intractable of these obstacles has been the dispute over the number of Warsaw Pact troops in the reduction area; resolution of this dispute could open the way to a first MBFR agreement.

Paths toward Resolution of MBFR's Problems

The orthodox and objective way to resolve the data dispute in MBFR would be to compare detailed, updated data of both sides for the same units—in the present case, mainly Soviet units—at the current level of forces, thus identifying for more detailed discussion those specific units, or types of units, on which the differences between the figures of both sides are largest. This information, of course, is exactly what the Soviets have so far refused to give, and there is little indication that future efforts along these lines will meet with more success than past ones.

On the other hand, the Warsaw Pact's preferred approach to the data dispute, under which the two sides would not agree on prereduction force levels or the size of reductions but simply on the postreduction force levels of 700,000 men, entails serious problems. The real test of such an agreement would come only after both sides had made sizable reductions to a common ceiling of 700,000 men. If inspections at that time did not produce agreement between the two sides' figures, this would lead to a very difficult situation indeed.

The Western proposal of December 1985 takes an intermediate approach that should be more fruitful: suspend the requirement to agree on data before reductions, make an initial small reduction of U.S. and Soviet forces, and try to solve the data issue on the ground through on-site inspection on the basis of figures provided in the postreduction exchange of data to which the Pact has agreed in principle. In their proposals of December 1985, NATO participants in Vienna dropped the requirement of prior agreement on data, proposed a reduction of 5000 U.S. and 11,500 Soviet ground force personnel, and a proposed series of ninety on-site inspections (thirty per year over a three-year period) to verify the Soviet reduction level and clarify data issues concerning other Pact forces. If agreement is not reached on data in that period, the agreement would expire.

The new Western proposal rests on the consideration that it should be possible to resolve the counting dispute more easily and more effectively on the ground, through giving priority to field verification, than at the negotiating table, where any data agreement achieved will in any event only be on paper until it is verified in the field. In return, before reductions take place, the Soviet Union would have to be willing to agree to two things in connection with verification: first, to exchange fairly detailed information on its postreduction forces (information it has not been willing to provide on its forces as they now stand) and, second, to agree to workable procedures for an agreed number of inspections that could be used to check the number of Soviet soldiers in the area—again, measures the Soviet Union has so far refused to agree to until after reductions have taken place. The verification measures would be put into effect as soon as the first limited U.S.-Soviet reductions had taken place rather than waiting until both sides had made much larger reductions, as the Soviets now propose.

This approach might succeed in reaching data agreement. If it were implemented, it might be that the West would discover that the total of Pact forces in the area is less than it has been calculating, placing a common ceiling within practical reach. If the approach did not succeed, there would be no risk to the security of either side through reductions of a limited size under an arrangement that would automatically expire after a three-year period.

Under the suggested approach, NATO countries could use their quota of inspections to inspect at short notice (of twelve hours or so) specified Soviet or other Warsaw Pact units that the NATO countries had themselves selected. Inspection findings would be compared with data supplied by the Warsaw Pact on these same units and with NATO's own holdings of information on these units. If the inspections took place promptly and covered a reasonable proportion of Pact units and if the results conformed with information supplied by the Pact as well as NATO holdings, NATO would have reasonable satisfaction as to Pact figures and Pact compliance with reductions and postreduction ceilings. Further assurance would be given by continued periodic exchange of data, prior announcement of entry or departure of troops from the reduction area, and use of the exit-entry posts by personnel of each alliance entering and leaving the area.

The new Western proposals have two drawbacks. First, they reintroduce the concept of two successive negotiations, withdrawing assurances on subsequent European reductions that Western negotiators earlier advanced. Significantly, the commitment for further reductions to a common ceiling appears to have dropped out of the Western proposal. Second, the number of proposed inspections—ninety over a three-year period—is very high. It would permit three inspections of each of the twenty-six Soviet divisions in Eastern Europe in the three-year period. In February 1986, the Pact tabled a new draft agreement that recapitulated earlier points, including agreement in principle to on-site inspections but only after initial discussion of the complaint leading to the request for inspection. Their initial detailed reaction to the West's December 1985 proposal was negative. Only if Pact negotiators start discussing the possible number and implementation details of the Western inspection proposal will serious negotiation begin.

Will MBFR Yield an Outcome?

With the latest Western proposal to use on-site inspection to resolve the data dispute, the conceptual basis for a first agreement in Vienna is on hand. The remaining obstacles to a negotiated agreement in MBFR are not insuperable; for some time, the talks have been in a position where a political push from participating governments in East and West could quickly bring practical results. With sufficient high-level political interest in an outcome on both sides, the Vienna talks could produce a first agreement within a year.

It is quite uncertain, however, whether there will be a positive outcome in Vienna. Thus far, many political leaders on both sides appear to consider that East-West agreement to reduce military forces in an initial MBFR accord, however modest in scope, could constitute a serious blow to the rationale for maintaining large standing forces in Europe. They seem to prefer the more cautious route of the CDE, where agreement on confidence-building measures of evidently limited significance would place less strain on this rationale. Political leaders are not the only problem. The resistence of military establishments in East and West to force reductions is far greater than to confidence-building measures, for reductions strike at the very rationale for the forces. For political leaders, agreement of one's own military establishment is often more important for concluding arms control agreements than the positions taken by the other side. Quite aside from all specific suggestions, proposals, and timetables, no result will be achieved in Vienna unless the heavy inertia of the institutional military interests that the confrontation has created on both sides can be counterbalanced by sustained top-level political interest in an outcome.

There are many more specific reasons for this situation on the Western side, among them the pessimistic conclusion that the Vienna talks after twelve years are incapable of culminating in agreement, the persistent U.S. inclination to view the MBFR talks as a matter of interest primarily to European NATO states, and the ambivalence in Federal Germany about the value of an MBFR agreement, an ambivalence that for years has prevented that country, militarily the most important of the European NATO countries, from taking the lead in the implementation of the MBFR negotiations as it had done in pressing for their initiation.

For its part, the Soviet leadership has been prepared over the years to make a small reduction of forces in an MBFR agreement. It has moved quite far over the past five years toward acceptance of tougher verification controls: on-site inspection in the (still unratified) Peaceful Nuclear Explosions Treaty; on-site supervision of destruction of chemical weapons stocks in the Geneva Committee on Disarmament; proposed on-site inspection for a moratorium on nuclear testing; and agreement in principle to inspection in MBFR. But the December 1985 Western MBFR proposals for on-site inspections entail a degree of frequency and intrusiveness that the Soviets have not yet found acceptable. They may not be willing to move so far at this time even if Western requirements are reduced in further negotiation. Soviet officials assert that Gorbachev's proposal of April 1986 for a new negotiation on armament reductions in a wider area does not mean that the Soviet Union has lost interest in MBFR and that they continue to want a first agreement in Vienna. But the Gorbachev proposal is a bad sign.

These factors make it questionable whether a first limited reduction agreement can be reached in MBFR. They make it even more questionable whether, if a limited first agreement is in fact achieved, either side is ready for more sizable reductions thereafter.

We have already summarized some reasons for general decrease in the West of support for reduction and limitations as an arms control approach. But there are more specific reasons for pessimism over the proposal of large NATO-Pact negotiated reductions. In 1973, NATO's senior military officers agreed only with reluctance to a limited reduction of NATO active-duty military manpower in MBFR. Their reasoning was that NATO standing forces were barely numerous enough to cover the 1000 kilometer border with the Warsaw Pact, especially the 800 kilometers of the Central Front in

Germany, where crack Soviet units could suddenly mass against NATO's thin line of defense. In recent years this reluctance has returned full force. For the moment at least, NATO has cold feet on active-duty manpower reductions; proposed initial U.S. reductions have progressively shrunk over the years from 29,000 to 5000, and the commitment to reduce to a common ceiling has been dropped from the Western position on MBFR. The reasons for this shift are various. The U.S. Army has always been skeptical about negotiated withdrawal of U.S. ground force personnel from Europe, believing that the Congress will strike these personnel from the budgeted overall strength of the Army. Paradoxically, the Netherlands and Belgium, once strong advocates of ground force reductions, have been moved by degrees of strong public antinuclear sentiment to advocate expanded conventional forces. NATO commanders are considering the manpower requirements of improving conventional forces through emerging technologies, of countering new Soviet tactics, and of establishing new missile defenses. SDI is already throwing a long shadow over the idea of force reductions in Europe. If both superpowers deploy some form of missile defense and their allies do so as well, this is likely to spur rivalry in further buildup of conventional forces on both sides. Even if these changes take shape only to a limited degree, the prospect of increased NATO manpower requirements is enough to eliminate the already weak support of senior NATO military officers for further force reductions in MBFR.

These are powerful obstacles to any MBFR reductions going beyond a symbolic initial reduction. But the main obstacle to success of any ambitious approach to force reductions in Europe is the Soviet interest in maintaining the status quo in Eastern Europe. It is a near certainty that the Soviet Union will continue to insist on keeping large forces in forward position in Eastern Europe, largely, although not exclusively, because of the failure of the Soviet Union and the communist governments of Eastern Europe to solve the problem of making these governments self-sustaining. It is improbable that these Soviet forces will be used to attack Western Europe, but they will also not be moved back. It would be difficult indeed for the Soviet leadership to admit to itself that the threat from NATO was not a serious threat, that the attempt to transplant the Soviet system to Eastern Europe had failed, that the system had been maintained only by the physical presence of Soviet forces, or to consider dispassionately whether these political purposes could be met by fewer Soviet soldiers.

Powerful institutional interests will continue to support this essentially political motivation for keeping Soviet troops in Central Europe. The ostensible raison d'être of the Soviet ground forces, and the basis for their own claim on important allocations of Soviet resources, is the Western military threat as they perceive and present it. This means in practical terms that the Soviet Union will not only insist that large Soviet forces remain in Eastern Europe but that these forces will be well equipped. This in turn will continue to create a requirement for a balancing NATO force. For the foreseeable future, these factors appear to establish narrow limits to the possible scope of reductions in Soviet personnel or armaments to which the Soviet Union would be prepared to agree. Reductions of up to 50,000 men remain theoretically possible.

In sum, then, the long-term outlook for the MBFR talks is not very good, despite their potential for damping down the East-West confrontation. The CDE now taking place in Stockholm is likely to produce some agreement on confidence-building measures in the next year or so, possibly before the November 1986 CSCE review conference in Vienna. And if the CDE does succeed, it is almost a forgone conclusion that it will be followed by further phases of CDE negotiations, in which force reductions may be considered in some form. Although dealing with the problem of force reductions in a negotiation with thirty-five participants including neutral states will surely prove even more difficult than it has in the MBFR talks, this development will probably cause the MBFR talks to go under or to be subsumed in some way if they have not yielded results by that time. If this should occur, the result may well be that there is no effective forum in which to negotiate East-West force reductions.

This fact gives added importance to a first MBFR agreement. Moreover, as described below, it may be possible to find ways of dealing with some of the obstacles to force reductions that have emerged in MBFR. In any case, it would not be wise to apply a perfectionist standard. Even a modest first MBFR agreement would be an advance, and its achievement could improve the general prospects for future progress in negotiated reductions.

Notes

1. Two useful sources for the early phases of the MBFR negotiations are John G. Keliher, *The Negotiations on Mutual and Balanced Force Reductions* (New York: Pergamon Press, 1980), and William Prendergast, *Mutual and Balanced Force Reduction* (Washington, D.C.: American Enterprise Institute, 1978).

    For the most part, in writing this chapter, I have relied on my personal notes of service with the MBFR talks, from the preparatory talks in January 1973 until October 1981, when I left Vienna, and on my discussions with officials of both the NATO and Warsaw Pact alliances.

8
The Conference on Disarmament in Europe: A Lasting Institution

T he thirty-five-nation Conference on Confidence- and Security-
Building Measures and Disarmament in Europe (for short, the
Conference on Disarmament in Europe, or CDE) has been meeting
in Stockholm since January 1984. The conference, which is taking
place within the CSCE framework described in chapter 5, owes its
existence mainly to the efforts of France and the Soviet Union.

From Helsinki to Stockholm

The Helsinki Final Act provided for review conferences at five-year
intervals to assess past implementation of the Act and to develop
the CSCE process. The first review conference began in Belgrade
in October 1977 and lasted until March 1978. It was an unpro-
ductive and sterile session, with no new agreements adopted. The
Carter administration held to its aim of furthering human rights, a
desirable objective made ridiculous by its excessive pretensions of
punishing all transgressors the world over. The administration saw
an opportunity to use the Belgrade review conference to hold up
for inspection the poor record of the Soviet Union and Eastern
Europe in the human rights field and persuaded the NATO allies
to follow this approach. Although the conference clearly made the
Soviet Union realize the ongoing problem it had created for itself
in the recurrent CSCE reviews of human rights, all the European

NATO governments thought the United States and its chief representative, former Supreme Court justice Arthur Goldberg, had overdone the emphasis on human rights.

In the field of confidence building and security, NATO participants at Belgrade proposed increasing the notification period for major maneuvers from twenty-one to thirty days, lowering the threshold from 25,000 to 10,000 troops, providing more detailed information on maneuvers, and more frequent exchange of observers and improved access for observers to the maneuvers they were witnessing. The neutral and nonaligned states proposed prenotification of related smaller maneuvers when they totaled more than 25,000 men and expanding the obligatory notification of major troop maneuvers to cover all out-of-garrison movements. Sweden proposed publication of defense expenditures. The Soviets proposed a treaty on no first use of nuclear weapons; freezing military alliances at their present membership (aimed at blocking Spanish membership in NATO); and limitation of the size of maneuvers to 40,000 men. Romania proposed a ban on new military bases and a freeze on military budgets; and East Germany proposed a ban on neutron warheads. Clearly, many of the proposals advanced were becoming more specific.

With considerable hypocrisy but also with some basis in the insufficiently binding legal status of obligations undertaken under the Helsinki Final Act, the Soviet Union proposed a measure calling for more consistent application of the Helsinki confidence-building measures. In fact, from 1975 to 1977, NATO had prenotified seven major maneuvers, with observers invited to five, and twelve smaller maneuvers, with observers invited to five. The Warsaw Pact had prenotified five major maneuvers and invited some observers to four of them. The Soviet Union had invited U.S. observers to only one exercise in this period, in 1977. (From the conclusion of the Helsinki Final Act until the CDE began in 1984, NATO and the neutral and nonaligned states notified thirty-nine major maneuvers and invited observers to thirty-one; the Pact notified twenty-two major maneuvers but invited observers to only seven.)[1]

Despite the larger number of proposals presented at the Belgrade Review Conference, it produced no tangible outcomes. But before the next review conference in late 1980 in Madrid, two important developments imparted new life to the CSCE process. Two months after the close of the Belgrade Review Conference, a new active player appeared in East-West arms control. On May 25, 1978, the President of France, Valéry Giscard D'Estaing, made a major speech at the meeting of the UN Special Session on Disarmament in New York. His two main proposals were for an international satellite verification agency and for a conference on disarmament in Europe to be held in the framework of the CSCE. After the return to power in 1959 of General Charles de Gaulle, who disdained arms control, and the inception of the French program to develop nuclear weapons, France had not played a major role in arms control. But President Giscard was already beginning to feel the pressures from the French Socialists, which resulted in his defeat by François Mitterand in 1981. In December 1977, Mitterand had written a series of articles in *Le Monde* proposing a thirty-five-nation conference on disarmament in Europe.

The conference on disarmament proposed by President Giscard was to be divided into two phases. In the first, a number of separate confidence-building measures would provide for information exchange, notification of military activities, and verification. In the second phase, conventional armaments that could be used in attack would be reduced on a country-by-country basis. President Giscard said nuclear weapons should not be dealt with in this conference, but through negotiation among nuclear powers, in which France would be prepared to associate following major reductions by the two superpowers. Naval forces would also be excluded, as in MBFR, as a complicating factor. The phase one confidence-building measures were to be legally binding and applied to the whole of Europe "from the Atlantic to the Urals" to end the dangerous practice of making most Soviet territory a sanctuary from arms control restrictions. The confidence-building measures proposed by France built on those of the Final Act and on the Belgrade discussion. They also contained many features of the MBFR associated measures we described in chapter 7, which were being discussed in NATO just as the French proposal was being prepared.

The French proposal for a conference was welcomed by the members of the European Community, and in the communiqué of the December 1979 NATO Ministerial Council, it was said to provide a basis for continued development of a NATO position on this subject. This was polite language, but the United States was in fact negative toward the French idea. It did not want an additional conference on European security at a time when NATO was already engaged in the MBFR talks and the United States was about to undertake the obligation to negotiate with the Soviet Union on reducing intermediate-range nuclear weapons. It believed the French proposal was aimed deliberately at undermining the MBFR talks, for which the Carter administration still had some hopes, a suspicion that was justified. U.S. enthusiasm for a new European security conference with the Soviet Union diminished still further with the Soviet invasion of Afghanistan in December 1979.

In May 1979, a year after the French proposal, the Warsaw Pact countered it with a proposal for a "Conference on Military Détente and Disarmament in Europe," to consist of a phase of confidence-building measures to be followed by a phase of force reduction. The confidence-building measures were to cover air and naval maneuvers and extended to include military activities in the Mediterranean (but not to the Urals in the Soviet Union). The reduction component included not only general references to force reductions in Europe, but also such concepts—familiar from the Belgrade Review Conference—as nonexpansion of alliances and their eventual dissolution; zones free of nuclear weapons; and commitments on nonuse of force and on no first use of nuclear weapons.

The French and Soviet proposals provided the main material for discussion of security issues at the second review conference for the Helsinki Final Act in Madrid, which began in November 1980 and ended in September 1983 after three years of polemical discussion of the Soviet invasion of Afghanistan and suppression of the Solidarity movement in Poland. Nevertheless, the conference did agree on a mandate or agenda for a European security conference that combined the main elements of the original French and Soviet approaches.

As the Madrid talks proceeded, the Reagan administration gave reluctant support to the idea of a European security conference, but specified four conditions for U.S. support. First, the conference would have to remain an integral part of the CSCE and be part of a balanced outcome of the Madrid conference (meaning an outcome that showed some progress in human rights). This position ensured more generally that discussion of security issues would remain connected with the CSCE human rights issue, frustrating the efforts of the Soviet Union to rid itself of this embarrassing theme. This condition also conflicted with the desire of France and the neutral and nonaligned nations, with many tacit sympathizers in NATO, to divorce the conference from the insoluble human rights issue, with the aim of making possible more serious progress in the security field. Washington's second condition was that the conference must deal only with confidence-building measures rather than also with force reductions as specified in the original French proposal; in addition, it should result in "politically binding" measures, an effort to increase the degree of commitment over that of the CSCE measures. Third, the conference should not conflict with other arms control negotiations, such as MBFR.

The second and the third points were related. The Reagan administration did not have great enthusiasm for force reductions in Europe and considered MBFR an increasingly questionable enterprise; it certainly did not want two such negotiations. The administration therefore took the position that MBFR should not be undermined and that the new conference should restrict itself to confidence-building measures until their effects could be assessed in practical application.

The fourth U.S. condition was that the conference should cover ground force activities in the whole of Europe and should cover only those naval and air activities occurring in adjacent sea and air space that were directly related to ground activities. Washington's objective here was to seal off the geographic coverage of the conference to Europe and to block Soviet efforts to extend its coverage to the United States. Washington explicitly made its acceptance of the conference dependent on acceptance of these criteria by the European NATO states and their subsequent energetic support of these criteria. NATO countries, strongly interested in holding a European security conference but not at the cost of a breach with Washington, accepted the conditions.

Since the Soviet Union, its Warsaw Pact allies, and the neutral and nonaligned nations also wanted a European security conference, the operative question was whether the Soviets could bring themselves at Madrid to accept these U.S. conditions. The main Soviet objections concerned the functional and geographic coverage of the conference. The Soviets wanted coverage of nuclear weapons and air and naval forces, all resisted by the NATO countries. They also wanted geographic coverage to include the United States, and they resisted inclusion of the Soviet Union to the Urals until this was agreed.

Yet once again, President Brezhnev came to the rescue of his favorite European security conference project, just as he had earlier made the CSCE possible by accepting U.S. participation in CSCE and Soviet participation in the MBFR talks. In a speech to the Twenty-sixth Congress of the Soviet Communist party in February 1981, Brezhnev accepted extension of the geographic area to the entire European part of the Soviet Union west of the Urals provided that the Western states were willing "to extend the confidence zone accordingly." This statement was the key move at Madrid. It was tantamount to conceding to the Western position on geographic coverage because it agreed in principle that the coverage of the conference could extend to the Urals without establishing a specific price to be paid by the West for this concession. Soviet negotiators at Madrid were downcast. After seeking in vain to obtain a Western offer to requite this Soviet concession, the Soviet negotiators indicated that they did have in mind extension of the area to the United States and Canada, or at least to large areas of the Atlantic Ocean and thus to coverage of naval forces. Although it was possible to reach agreement two years later on a mandate for the CDE, the ocean issue remained alive in CDE itself until it was resolved by a further unilateral Soviet concession when the new Soviet leader, Mikhail Gorbachev, dropped the requirement for coverage of naval exercises in his arms control presentation of January 15, 1986.

In September 1983, the Madrid Review Conference concluded with an agreement on the mandate for the Conference on Disarmament in Europe, to be held in Stockholm beginning in 1984. The mandate said that the first stage of the conference would aim for the adoption of a set of confidence- and security-building measures designed to reduce the risk of military confrontation in Europe, to cover the whole of Europe as well as the adjoining sea area and air space; the measures were to be of military significance, politically binding, and must have adequate verification.[2]

Progress at Stockholm

As is customary in arms control negotiations, the early months of the CDE were spent in presentation and justification of proposals. At the outset, the NATO states proposed a program of confidence-building measures that in essence represented an expansion and tightening of the Helsinki Final Act provisions on prenotification of military exercises. It will be recollected that the Final Act entails an obligation to give twenty-one-day advance notice of maneuvers by forces greater than 25,000 men and also provides for voluntary invitation of observers to those maneuvers as well as voluntary notification of smaller maneuvers. (NATO exercises are far larger than Pact exercises, going up to 300,000 men for larger annual maneuvers. Most Warsaw Pact exercises consist of only a division at a time or less.) Three of the six measures proposed by NATO participants deal directly with these force activities.

The West's proposals in Stockholm provided that, first, ground force military activities for which advance notice would be presented would include not only large maneuvers (that is, force movements whose explicit purpose is training) but all out-of-garrison movements of any combination of units composing the majority of combat elements of one division (that is, two regiments plus command and control) moving either inside the zone of Europe or entering the zone. This combat element definition, also used in MBFR, was developed to equate the generally much larger NATO divisions, stripped of their logistics elements, with much smaller Warsaw Pact divisions that do not have as many support elements, such as combat engineers, directly incorporated in them. In practice, it would establish a minimum level of about 7000 men. Expansion of the definition to cover all out-of-garrison movements rather than only maneuvers is designed to decrease the possibility of deception. The logic is that prenotification of maneuvers can create a false sense of security if a would-be aggressor could concentrate forces under some pretext other than maneuver, such as a change of station, and not be required to give advance notice of this activity. The Western proposal also extended the advance notice requirement to reservists for mobilization activities involving call-up of more than 25,000 men or the majority of combat units of three divisions and to amphibious activities with three or more battalions. The Helsinki requirement for advance notification is increased from twenty-one to forty-five days; information is to be provided on designation, purpose, duration, and participants and the location, number, and types of forces involved. Alerts are exempted from the advance notice requirements; notice of alerts is to be given as they begin.

Second, invitation of observers is required rather than voluntary. Two observers per signatory state are to be invited to these activities to confirm their nature, including alert exercises lasting more than forty-eight hours. The rationale is that a ground force attack would require a considerable concentration of forces, as well as certain activities, such as full loading of live ammunition and strengthening of medical units, that would be observable. Observers would watch to ensure that the activity remains within the advertised limits and does not include activities that could indicate aggressive intent. The value of the observers, of course, depends on the degree of their access to the information needed.

Third, NATO also called for exchange of annual forecasts of out-of-garrison activities (the Helsinki Act contained no parallel provision), which would add all new out-of-garrison activities scheduled since submission of the last annual calendar. The requirement of a calendar of advance notification requires each force to delineate its normal scope of activity in advance and makes it far easier to detect deviations.

The Western states also proposed three other measures for which no parallel provision was made in the Helsinki Final Act: annual exchange of information among participants on their military forces, providing unit designation, command subordination, headquarters location, and composition of units down to brigade or regiment level; verification measures, intended to test compliance with the proposed confidence-building measures and consisting of noninterference with national technical means and a limited number of inspections per year on the territory in Europe of participants (no more than two inspections per year for each participating state); and improved communications—bilateral visits, dedicated communication links (hot lines), and the like—to be agreed among conference participants on a bilateral basis.

Several of the proposals put forward by the Soviet Union and

Warsaw Pact participants in their draft treaty of May 1984 were of different character from these specific, rather limited Western confidence-building measures. These Pact proposals called for:

1. A treaty on the nonuse of force by participants against each other and the maintenance of peaceful relations among them. This treaty was to include a commitment for nonuse of force, no first use of nuclear weapons, and a mechanism for crisis consultation, inquiry, and information exchange.

2. Mutual freeze and reduction of military budgets.

3. Establishing zones free of nuclear weapons.

4. A ban on chemical weapons in Europe.

In addition, the Warsaw Pact proposed confidence-building measures, in general more modest than the Western proposals:

1. A limit of 40,000 men on the size of ground force maneuvers.

2. An expansion of the Helsinki Final Act's measure on prenotification of exercises to require thirty-day notice of ground, air, and naval maneuvers with more than 20,000 personnel, 200 aircraft in the air at the same time, or 30 combat ships plus 100 aircraft in southern, northern, and Central Europe.

3. Thirty-day notice of major movements of land and air forces of over 20,000 personnel within Europe, or into or out of Europe, and of movements of more than 100 aircraft into Europe. This measure accepted the idea of notifying movements but also covered transit of outside troops through Europe, which the United States has tried to have excluded from the scope of CDE.

4. Improvement of observer exchanges at major maneuvers (but not at other movements).

5. Adequate verification (unspecified).

During the first months of the Stockholm CDE, NATO participants criticized the Warsaw Pact program of political commitments as purely declaratory, potentially misleading to Western publics, and lacking real substance in the form of specific commitments. They urged participants instead to focus on their own more specific confidence-building measures. The Soviet negotiators criticized NATO proposals as efforts to obtain license for espionage. They also gave clear priority to their proposal on nonuse of force over all other Soviet proposals, arguing that Western moves, and especially U.S. moves, toward acceptance of this measure would be a sign of real interest in arms control results following Soviet withdrawal in late 1983 from the bilateral U.S.-Soviet negotiations at Geneva. Soviet negotiators hinted that Western acceptance of this concept could lead to resumption of the U.S.-Soviet nuclear negotiations.

At the end of the spring 1984 round at Stockholm, the neutral and nonaligned states presented some generally worded concepts calling for constraints on military activities, including limiting the size of maneuvers and establishing zones of restricted military activities, such as border areas. NATO participants, however, especially the United States, have held that proposals placing restrictions on military activities—as distinguished from measures providing merely for broader exchange of information through prenotification or use of observers—should be considered only in a follow-on conference, CDE 2, after there has been full opportunity to evaluate the actual operation of the more limited confidence-building measures embodied in a first CDE agreement.

A First CDE Agreement

What sort of agreement could emerge from such a diversity of proposals? European NATO participants, strongly interested in a positive outcome of the CDE talks, urged Western acceptance of the East's concept of nonuse of force. In part, their motive was to send a signal to the Soviet Union of Western desire to resume collapsed U.S.-Soviet talks at Geneva. But they also appear to have had in mind a potential compromise for Stockholm itself, with the NATO participants agreeing to include in an agreement a commitment on nonuse of force in return for Warsaw Pact agreement to specific confidence-building measures proposed by the NATO participants. In their Washington Declaration of May 31, 1984, the NATO participants hinted at this possibility. In his speech in Dublin a few days later, President Reagan offered inclusion of a commitment on nonuse of force as part of an otherwise satisfactory agreement at Stockholm. The president's speech in a European forum was designed to demonstrate administration interest in arms control given the fact that many elements of European opinion were highly skeptical of U.S. motives on arms control at this juncture, following the beginning of U.S. INF deployments and the collapse of the Geneva talks. It was also intended to signal to the Soviets U.S. readiness to resume the Geneva talks. Chernenko, shortly after his designation as general secretary, had mentioned U.S. agreement to nonuse of force as one of the steps that could bring the Soviets back to the negotiating table at Geneva. Yet soon after, Chernenko himself became mortally ill. The Soviet government, confused by its succession problems, did not respond to the Reagan signal. By the summer of 1984, however, the essential elements of a trade-off were on the table in Stockholm: the substance of NATO's confidence-building measures in return for some version of the Soviet nonuse of force concept.

One constraint measure that may not be included in a first CDE agreement should be given active consideration for the future: a numerical limitation on the size of maneuvers by ground forces. Such a measure, proposed by both Warsaw Pact participants and the neutral and nonaligned states, is also acceptable to some NATO participants, including France and Norway. This measure would make it difficult to concentrate forces prior to attack and would do so more directly than prenotification. If CDE signatories accepted the 40,000-man limit on maneuvers suggested by the Warsaw Pact, this would make it very difficult, in the context of the NATO–Warsaw Pact confrontation, to mount a successful attack. Violation of the measure, like violation of other confidence-building measures, is feasible, but violation would be an important warning of pending attack. By producing clearer evidence of hostile intention than would be available without it, such a measure could help the NATO coalition to reach timely decisions to react.

Nonetheless, several NATO nations, especially the United States, were reluctant to include meaningful restraints on military activities in a first CDE agreement. NATO maneuvers are usually larger than Pact maneuvers: from 1975 to 1983, twenty-one of twenty-seven NATO exercises exceeded 40,000 personnel, but only four of eighteen Pact exercises did so. A second reason NATO commanders have been unwilling to accept these limits is that they could inhibit large-scale alert exercises moving NATO forces to their readiness positions for a possible conflict. As a result of considerations like these, it is likely that any initial limitation on the size of out-of-garrison activities on which agreement can be reached at CDE phase 1 will be so high as to have limited value as a constraint.

The prohibition of maneuvers in border areas, proposed by the neutral and nonaligned states, is another specific proposal worth future consideration. Such a measure would be beneficial as an obstacle to threatening maneuvers of the kind carried out by the Soviet Union along the Polish border in September 1981 in connection with the Solidarity development, when 100,000 Soviet and Warsaw Pact troops sought to intimidate Solidarity supporters through demonstrative troop movements. It could also be useful by introducing in a general sense the concept of zones of restricted activity or deployment. Nevertheless, such a measure would pose special problems for NATO. Like the limit on the size of maneuvers, it would prevent NATO forces, configured for largely static defense, from moving forward into preparedness positions. In addition, this measure runs afoul of one of the fundamental problems of NATO defense: the relative shallowness (the lack of defensive depth) of NATO territory as compared to the Warsaw Pact. A potential answer is to have a wider belt on the Warsaw Pact side than on the NATO side, but such a possibility could be negotiated, if at all, only in a configuration like MFBR that permits alliance-to-alliance negotiation rather than in a forum that argues for equal treatment for all thirty-five signatories of the Helsinki Final Act, regardless of great differences in their geographic situation and the size and importance of their armed forces.

The provisions for inspection in a first CDE agreement will be limited. The proposal for obligatory invitation of observers at all out-of-garrison activities, not just maneuvers, has encountered strong resistance from the Soviet Union and other Pact members. Even Western proposals suspend the requirement for prenotification of alerts and for the presence of observers in the initial stages of alerts—exceptions that presumably will be insisted on by commanders on both sides who wish to continue testing the state of readiness of their own forces. Additional exceptions may be requested by Western participants for troops in transit from other areas via Europe to a third area. In theory, on-site inspections could be used to confirm the existence of a force concentration that has not been prenotified, and, similarly, if there are limits to the permitted size of out-of-garrison activities, observers could note movements and concentrations larger than those permitted. In addition to NATO countries, a group of neutral and nonaligned countries headed by Austria, Sweden, Switzerland, and Yugoslavia has given this idea strong support, and in 1985 there were some signs of Warsaw Pact receptivity.

Some provision for consultation among participants should be included in CDE agreements. Ideally this would be some arrangement for a consultative commission meeting periodically and at the very least would provide for consultation in the event of suspicion of noncompliance, as suggested by some neutral states, including Switzerland. Some NATO participants have opposed a standing commission, fearing it could provide a podium for Soviet propaganda on the entire field of NATO defense activities in Europe. But there is no reason why the Soviet Union should have one-sided use of such a body for propaganda purposes. Western participants could make equally good use of it to comment on defense developments in the Soviet Union and Eastern Europe.

By mid-1985, the pace of CDE had picked up. Warsaw Pact participants had ceased to press vigorously for most items of their more general program and even began to drop these topics from their presentations without asking for some Western concession in return, as is customary in most negotiation. In October 1985, on his presummit visit to Paris, General Secretary Gorbachev gave a clear signal of Soviet interest in reaching CDE agreement; he publicly announced agreement to the idea of an annual calendar of prenotified activities, something Warsaw Pact negotiators had hitherto declined to accept so formally. In drafting the communiqué for the November 1985 Reagan-Gorbachev summit, Soviet officials agreed to positive treatment of the prospects for a CDE outcome, and on January 15, 1986, Gorbachev announced that the Soviets were relinquishing their efforts to include naval exercises under a first CDE agreement, though they would raise the issue in later negotiations. Efforts of Soviet negotiators to obtain explicit assurances to this effect for CDE phase 2 slowed the negotiations in the summer of 1986. Nonetheless, in taking these actions, Gorbachev was following the precedent of Brezhnev's high priority for CDE and Brezhnev's willingness to toss the ballast of earlier positions overboard as unilateral concessions. There is no doubt the Soviets wish to use the CDE as a device to impress Western Europe with their cooperative attitude, but the costs of doing so in terms of Soviet agreement to specific measures are beginning to transcend cosmetics. Perhaps the Soviets are gaining some interest in the substance of confidence-building measures as conceived by Western participants.

Stockholm: Modest Goals, Probable Success

The young CDE talks are likely to culminate in agreement before the marathon MBFR negotiations, probably by the time of the third review conference for the Helsinki Final Act to be held in Vienna in November 1986. In this regard, CDE has been the beneficiary of two important differences between the two negotiating forums: the arms control measures being discussed in Stockholm are far more modest in scope than even the limited force reductions and associated measures being debated in Vienna, and the CDE from the outset faced a firm deadline in the form of the November 1986 CSCE review conference to which the conferees were obligated to report. Such deadlines are highly advantageous for moving negotiation along. It is quite likely that a first CDE agreement will be reached, containing a commitment on the nonuse of force and many of the confidence-building measures proposed by the NATO participants, plus some loose consultation mechanism and possibly a numerical limitation on the size of land maneuvers.

The stage would then be set for endorsement of CDE results

by the CSCE review conference beginning in November 1986 and eventually for the approval of a mandate for CDE phase 2. Last-minute disputes could cause CDE 1 to miss the Vienna CSCE deadline, but even if that happens, CDE participants will continue to negotiate during the CSCE review, and the outcome is likely to be much as described. At Vienna, more than CDE 1, CDE 2 will be in the balance. Western governments, especially the U.S. government, are insistent on keeping the main elements of the Helsinki Accords—security and human rights—moving forward together. This means a requirement for some progress on this subject at Vienna before there can be agreement on the mandate for CDE 2.

Weighing CDE's Impact

What would be the military significance of a first CDE agreement along the lines discussed here? Let us begin with a description of the things the agreement will not do. Such an agreement would do nothing to dampen the NATO–Warsaw Pact competition in modernized armaments. With the possible exception of a limitation on the size of out-of-garrison activities, an agreement would place no restrictions on military activities, and it would neither limit nor reduce the size of the military forces kept by NATO or Warsaw Pact nations. Indeed, the great success of the Madrid Review Conference—obtaining Soviet agreement to expand the area of application of the CDE conference to include the Soviet Union west of the Urals—is at the same time the greatest weakness of the CDE format. For a long time to come, it is improbable that the Soviet Union will agree to measures of real stringency on its own territory, whatever the chances for agreement on reductions in the MBFR talks.

The requirement to give advance notice of military activity is the main content of CDE. Such a requirement gains significance as it becomes comprehensive. If all sizable military activities are covered by a requirement for prenotification and the presence of observers, there would be an important increase in each country's knowledge of the normal pattern of military activities of other participants. In terms of our main focus of interest, the NATO Central Front, if all force movements were covered by prenotification and attended by observers, it would be much more difficult to carry out the necessary preparations for a standing-start attack.

Conversely, the more exceptions in coverage of force movements there are in CDE measures, the weaker will be the effects. If the requirements for prenotification and for observers are suspended for the initial stages of alerts or for troops in transit, as proposed by the West, these exceptions would create big loopholes. In the case of alerts, the time period for suspension of coverage may be limited to forty-eight hours or so; yet a good deal of preparation for surprise attack could take place during one of these unannounced alerts. The potential damage could be limited if the numerical size of alerts fell under a general limitation on the size of out-of-garrison ground force activities, or if the number of alerts individual countries could call were limited.

It also appears that the CDE prenotification measures will be drafted so that in practice they will not cover mobilization exercises. The measure has been opposed by the Swiss and the Swedes, who attach great significance to mobilization as an effective means of defending their neutral status, as well as by the Soviets. This is an important shortcoming since mobilization activity, essential to bring low-manned units to combat strength, is a major warning indicator. Adherence to a requirement to prenotify mobilization would contribute to confidence, and violation of it would be a clear warning.

A further shortcoming of CDE is that air force activity is covered only when it is part of a ground activity. It is extremely difficult to set up systems for advance notification of air force maneuvers since air forces train continually. But because ground force attack would be accompanied by a struggle for control of the air, this omission could be significant. Some way of limiting the number of aircraft each country is permitted to have in the air at a given time could be useful.

Nearly all confidence-building measures can be deliberately exploited by a would-be aggressor to increase surprise. Soviet forces mobilized, concentrated, and exercised in so many maneuvers just prior to the invasion of Czechoslovakia that many Western observers were convinced that their activities were limited to exercises and that invasion was increasingly impossible. Egyptian forces lulled even the hypersuspicious Israelis by breaking out of an exercise pattern to launch their 1973 attacks on Israeli forces in the Sinai. But it is fair to say that, on balance, CDE's package of confidence-building measures with prenotification and observers adds considerably more to information and warning than it creates potential for camouflaging aggressive intention.

If it contains a consultation provision, a first CDE agreement would have some possibilities for future growth. A center to coordinate information could develop into some form of East-West crisis reduction center. The impact of a first CDE agreement on Western public opinion is likely to be limited, but it will provide at least a partial answer to public desires in Europe for progress in arms control.

Phase 2 and Beyond

Perhaps the most important aspect of the first CDE is that it will almost automatically (depending on progress in human rights) be followed by a second CDE. In fact, given the interests involved, it probably will be followed by a series of future conferences on European security lasting over coming decades.

The view of the United States is that there should be no automatic commitment to a second phase of CDE and that there should be time to evaluate actual experience under a first agreement before deciding on a second one. Yet the Madrid agreement that established the Stockholm conference already contains a partial commitment to continue in a second phase of negotiation. Moreover, it is already quite clear that both Western and Eastern European governments, as well as the neutral and nonaligned states, wish to continue in a second phase of negotiation. These nations are interested in pressing forward with negotiated détente, and each wishes to play an active role in East-West negotiation. Moreover, it is good domestic politics to be seen to be actively engaged in the effort to improve East-West relations.

It is evident from its actions thus far that the Soviet Union too will support continuation of CDE negotiations. It will do so mainly because it is in the interest of its own Western European policy to present itself as conciliatory and because the CDE negotiations provide a useful forum to assess and to influence the military policy of the European states, especially the European NATO states. The characteristic dynamic of the CDE negotiation has in the past been that, when the majority of other participants have supported some move on CDE, whether continuation of the forum or some specific measure, the United States has not found it politic to be the sole standout and has been brought along, however reluctantly. This is why the CDE process will continue, probably indefinitely, in phase after phase, and this is how many decisions will be reached in each phase.

But there is no one-sided advantage here for the Soviet Union. As the European superpower, it is the object, whether explicit or implicit, of most of the concerns of European states and of the restrictive measures they have proposed and will continue to propose in CDE. Pressures from Western European nations and the neutral and nonaligned states have not been without effect on the Soviet Union, which responded by increasing the coverage of CDE measures from the 200 kilometer strip provided for in the Helsinki Final Act to the entire western part of the Soviet Union up to the Urals, and which appears willing to give advance notification of its maneuvers and possibly even to accept some rudimentary form of inspection on its territory. The same dynamic operates on the Soviet Union as on the United States, although to a lesser extent: neither superpower finds it comfortable to assume a wholly isolated position at a multilateral conference, though the Soviet Union's isolation is nearly always camouflaged by superficial support from Warsaw Pact states.

If, as is probable, agreement is ultimately reached to hold a second phase of CDE, what should its content and subject matter be? It can be assumed that in CDE 2, the Soviet Union would attempt to gain more serious consideration for the general points of its program in CDE phase 1, such as reduction of military budgets and no first use of nuclear weapons. It is also probable that the Gorbachev proposal of April 1986 for force reductions from the Atlantic to the Urals, which will be discussed in the next chapter, will provide a major focus of Soviet efforts at the Vienna CSCE review conference to shape the agenda for CDE phase 2. Ultimately, some version of this proposal may be adopted. But whatever the fate of the Soviet proposal, the most logical priority for CDE phase 2 is a continuation and intensification of the content of phase 1: more confidence-building measures.

The first task of CDE phase 2 should be to fill in the gaps in prenotification of out-of-garrison activities under the phase 1 agreement, making it as comprehensive as possible and narrowing, if not eliminating, exceptions for alert, mobilization, and air exercises. A comprehensive prenotification measure, especially if combined with the presence of observers in all but the most exceptional circumstances, would be valuable.

Yet it is already possible to forecast that it will not be as easy to reach agreement in CDE phase 2 as in CDE 1. If measures are to have more bite, there will also be more resistance to them. This resistance will come above all from military commanders whose freedom of decision and flexibility will be increasingly limited by measures with real bite. Faced by a choice between equal restrictions on one's own forces and on the forces of a possible adversary and no restrictions on either, military commanders almost always prefer the state of no restriction. The resistance will be strong in CDE phase 2 against agreed constraints or limitations on military activities.

The first such constraint, if not already agreed in CDE 1, would be to limit the permitted size of out-of-garrison activities. Beyond that there could be restrictions on areas in which large exercises are permitted—perhaps frontier areas—on their geographic extent, limitations on the number of exercises permitted simultaneously, perhaps on the absolute number permitted per year, or in the weapons and equipment they are permitted to exercise or have with them while engaged in maneuvers. For example, there could be prohibitions on simultaneous exercise of self-propelled artillery and tanks, taking bridging equipment out of storage sites to the field, or loading live ammunition for field exercises.

Measures of this kind shade into a category of measures providing for permanent zones or areas from which certain types of equipment are forbidden, such as zones of limited armaments on border areas, a topic we shall be exploring later. Zones from which certain weapons would be eliminated or their number limited are in turn close on the spectrum of possible measures to the classic arms control concept of reductions and limitations. Moreover, according to the tentative agreement reached at the Madrid conference, CDE phase 2 is to be devoted to reduction of arms, and, as we have seen, the Soviet Union has made a proposal to this effect.

Yet it is already clear that this will be difficult. We have already discussed the difficulties involved in reduction of armaments in the MBFR talks and the difficulty there of finding a negotiable and practical reduction concept for this purpose. The problem of finding a reduction scheme that will not fix in treaty form the existing disparities of scale—say between Luxembourg's 600-man army and the armed forces of the Soviet Union—becomes more acute when, as in CDE, participants are treated as individual states. True, it is theoretically possible to restrict the number of weapons in relationship to total population, but if countries are to be handled individually, the Soviet Union as the most populous country in Europe would be permitted a huge number of armaments. It would seem that where reductions are concerned, the alliance-to-alliance format of MBFR is the more workable. The Gorbachev proposal of April 1986 appears to acknowledge this point by suggesting that the first round of armament reductions be between the two alliances.

A further area for CDE to investigate is that of conflict containment measures for use once hostilities have broken out. Confidence-building measures are of little use once conflict has started; indeed, they can be exploited for the purpose of misleading. Once conflict has broken out, a new set of measures is needed to try to limit the duration of the conflict and possible misperceptions about the objectives of participants. This subject, too, would be appropriate for CDE phase 2.

As we have been emphasizing, there is a direct relationship between confidence-building measures and force reductions as two points on a single spectrum of arms control. Confidence-building measures will at some point lose their support, though not their rationale, if they are accompanied by important increases in force capabilities in both alliances. On the other hand, although the capacity of the CDE process to reduce directly the level of the East-West military confrontation in Europe is limited, even a first CDE agreement will increase mutual confidence and set the stage for other measures of dismantling or attrition outside CDE. Looking ahead over the next decades, with possibly two or more further follow-on CDE negotiations, one can see an increasingly effective system of measures against surprise attack and reducing the risk of conflict by misperception. In consequence, there will be broader recognition in Western Europe that the possibility of attack by the Warsaw Pact is very low and wider if not explicit recognition in the Warsaw Pact leadership of the improbability of attack by NATO forces. It is unclear whether this increased confidence will result in unilateral force decreases by mutual example, abstention from force improvements on both sides, or negotiated reductions, but such developments will be a possible consequence.

Notes

1. For background on the CSCE review conferences, see John Borawski, Lynn M. Hansen, and Suzanne Parry, *From the Atlantic to the Urals* (McLean, Va.: Pergamon-Brassey's, forthcoming 1987). For background on the CDE, see James E. Goodby, "The Stockholm Conference," *Arms Control Today* (September 1985). John Borawski, "The Stockholm Conference on Confidence and Security Building in Europe," *Arms Control* 6:2 (September 1985).
2. Text in David Barton, "The Conference on Confidence- and Security-Building Measures and Disarmament in Europe," Chapter 15 in *World Armaments and Disarmament: SIPRI Yearbook 1984* (London: Taylor and Francis, 1984). See also Edward Killham, "The Madrid CSCE Conference" in *World Affairs* 146:4 (Spring 1984) and Congressional Research Service, "The Conference on Disarmament in Europe," issue brief IB84060 (June 1, 1984).

9
The Limited Promise of Arms Control in Europe

Large segments of the European public continue to expect arms control negotiations in Europe to fulfill the classical functions of disarmament with regard to the huge NATO–Warsaw Pact military confrontation in Europe. They not only expect arms control to make war, especially nuclear war, less likely; they also expect it to arrest the upward creep of armed forces under the impetus of new technology and to take decisive steps toward dismantling the confrontation. This is exactly what arms control in Europe should be doing. Now that the watershed of the East-West confrontation has been reached, arms control should continually push its level downward.

If arms control is coordinated with defense, as would be logical, then it could also increase security and reduce the risk of surprise attack. It could contribute to a credible conventional defense against Soviet behavior in Europe. Arms control can bring European and U.S. governments closer in their assessment of the Soviet threat and can maintain continual pressure on the Soviet Union to translate cooperative statements into specific actions with regard to its armed forces. If organized according to an overall concept, arms control could in addition maximize the possibility for the West of negotiating trade-offs among the various component elements.

Hopes like these are not unrealistic because they conform to the overall status of the East-West confrontation at this point. We know what we want arms control in Europe to achieve: to make real progress toward dismantling the military confrontation. But we have to look dispassionately at the actual prospects. These hopes are premature. The road to arms control in Europe has been a long one. It took twenty years of confrontation and posturing before serious negotiation could begin. Today, with good luck, we may be on the verge of the first results, and they will be very welcome. They will start the confrontation on its move down the downward slope. But these results will be limited and modest, and although achievement of the first results will reinforce determination to continue, it will take a long time before decisive progress can be made.

The preceding chapters have described the three arms control negotiations dealing with the confrontation in Europe: the bilateral U.S.-Soviet INF negotiations at Geneva, the Vienna negotiations on mutual and balanced reductions of conventional forces, and the CDE negotiations on confidence-building and security measures at Stockholm. Although these negotiations are in a position to make specific contributions fairly soon to reducing the risk of war, they appear unlikely in the next decade to make a decisive contribution to dismantling the NATO–Warsaw Pact military confrontation. The MBFR talks could bring a modest reduction of U.S. and Soviet ground forces and some useful associated measures. But in their present configuration, they are unlikely to bring deep reductions of men or equipment. A first CDE agreement will bring useful agreement on prenotification of out-of-garrison activities, which will almost certainly increase confidence between East and West. Successive CDE conferences may devise new confidence-building measures that generate more information on normal patterns of military activity and more effective ways of questioning departure from them. They can gradually introduce restrictions on those types of military activities that have the greatest potential for launching a surprise attack or for misperception. But they appear unlikely in their present format rapidly to develop workable methods for force reductions. The INF talks may make a first modest reduction in INF in Europe, but this will leave many INF weapons deployed, and the talks show no signs as yet of the capacity to deal with the thousands of nuclear delivery systems under the 1000 kilometer range.

Before looking at the prospects for a more integrated approach to European arms control that might overcome the limitations of these individual negotiations, it will be useful to review some aspects of the East-West confrontation that are not now being dealt with in any arms control talks. Reductions of conventional and tactical nuclear armaments, although they fall within the purview of MBFR and perhaps a coming phase of CDE, have not been grappled with in either forum to date. Other important issues—a permanent European risk reduction center and chemical weapons—do not fall within the scope of any current European negotiation, although a worldwide ban on chemical weapons is under negotiation at the UN Conference on Disarmament in Geneva.

Tackling Armaments in MBFR

Chapter 7 described the failure of NATO and the Warsaw Pact to develop in MBFR any workable concept for the mutual reduction of armaments, especially the increasingly expensive major conventional armaments like tanks and aircraft that eat up Western and Eastern defense budgets. There is a possible solution for this problem, one worth looking into in the future. In the early discussion of armaments reductions in MBFR, Soviet representatives suggested that arms reduced by countries whose territory was inside the Central European reduction area (in particular, Federal Germany) would have to be destroyed. Soviet weapons, on the other hand, would merely be withdrawn to Soviet territory, where they could be stored or deployed in an active-duty unit with their overall level perhaps increased. The disparity of treatment made this approach unacceptable.

Western experts, however, anticipate that the Soviet Union may reduce any unit withdrawn from Central Europe pursuant to an MBFR agreement from category 1 to category 3, in practice a holding unit for the withdrawn armaments of the category 1 unit. This was the case with the Soviet division withdrawn from East Germany to the western Soviet Union during 1980. This circumstance suggests a way to make the method of reducing conventional and tactical nuclear armaments comparable for the Soviet Union and for NATO countries located in the MBFR reduction area or, indeed, in a wider area: in effect, by transferring the armaments from active-duty units to reserve units. Soviet forces withdrawn from the

MBFR reduction area, along with their heavy equipment, would be placed in category 3 reserves rather than maintained as active-duty units. On the NATO side, specified active-duty units of countries whose territory is inside the MBFR reduction area, along with their heavy armaments, would be transferred to the reserves. In the case of the Soviet Union, reduction in status to category 3 appears to be verifiable by satellite photography. This approach would not of itself limit the level of armaments in active-duty units in either alliance, nor would it limit the level of armaments in storage in the Soviet Union, but under this approach, U.S. armaments in prepositioned storage in Europe would also not be limited. In view of the distance of their home territory from the reduction area, withdrawn U.S. units would not be required to shift to reserve status and could leave their equipment stored in the MBFR reduction area.

This scheme would apply only to Soviet units withdrawn from Central Europe or possibly to category 1 and 2 Soviet divisions stationed in the western Soviet Union. It would not apply to those Soviet divisions that remain stationed in Eastern Europe; and it is a central point of our analysis that the Soviet Union will not be prepared to reduce large numbers of its forces in Eastern Europe because of their political function. Consequently, this approach might not bring a decisive reduction of armaments from active-duty units of both alliances. But there is a limit to the number of major armaments that can be assigned to active-duty units if their overall manpower is limited by agreement.

We should also try to visualize for MBFR a negotiating concept that would take into account the political obstacles to force reductions as such and still bring some progress toward increased stabilization of the NATO–Warsaw Pact confrontation. For example, if large-scale withdrawals of Soviet forces in Central Europe are infeasible at this time and further reductions of NATO forces are difficult, perhaps some degree of reorganization could give an answer. Could we bring the Soviet Union to restructure its forces in East Germany to be somewhat less threatening? Its resistance to restructuring may be less than to large withdrawals. On the NATO side, the declining German birthrate and the high cost of military forces argue for some sort of belt of static defenses along the Federal German border with East Germany in order to take the first impact of possible Soviet attack. German political opinion has thus far steadfastly rejected any such belt as deepening the division of Germany. But perhaps instead a belt could be part of an arms control agreement with the Warsaw Pact intended to reduce the risk of conflict and to improve East-West and inner-German relations.

In seeking to meet arms control objectives and take account of political realities, elements from various already formulated approaches might be combined rather eclectically into a single concept. Using the MBFR reduction area, the first element would be a zone of restricted armaments on both sides of the Federal German border with East Germany and Czechoslovakia. Mobile heavy weapons—tanks, self-propelled artillery, helicopters, bridging equipment—and all nuclear warheads and nuclear delivery systems, as well as dual-capable systems, and static conventional weapons of more then 50 kilometers range would be prohibited in this zone. To avoid large-scale disruptions, the zone should be no more than 50 kilometers wide on the NATO side. It should be 100 kilometers wide on the Pact side because of the greater depth of Warsaw Pact territory and because the Soviet Union is so much closer to the German border than is the United States. There would be no restriction on the number of military personnel in the zone, on the construction of antitank obstacles or light field fortifications, or on deploying fixed-position artillery, antiaircraft weapons, antitank weapons, or multiple rocket launchers of limited range. However, again borrowing from MBFR, there would be a freeze on the military personnel of both sides in the overall MBFR reduction area, and there would be on-site verification by inspectors of the other alliance.

Under this approach, both NATO and Warsaw Pact commanders would face a choice between separating the personnel of armored units from their equipment and storing the latter outside the restricted zone or restructuring the forces inside the zone to operate static defenses. (A third possibility—withdrawing armored units from the zone and constructing new facilities for them, leaving the zone substantially without forces—would be expensive and disadvantageous.)

In effect, acceptance of this scheme would induce the Soviets to modify somewhat their tank-heavy forward position. Most Soviet divisions in East Germany are stationed in a belt between Berlin and the Federal German border; the deeper the zone of reduced armaments, the more restructuring of these forces would be required. Yet these changes would not affect Soviet capacity to maintain political control, their primary interest.

On the Western side, manpower-poor NATO could emphasize high-tech defenses in the restricted zones, manned by restructured units of allied forces in their present sectors, maintaining the important deterrent effect of this stationing pattern. The fact that both sides were permitted obstacles and barriers as part of an arms control agreement agreed to by East Germany as well as other Pact states might overcome Federal German objections to erecting barriers and antitank defenses, at least at the most vulnerable points, where, for example, pipes for liquid explosives can be placed in series to form tank barriers. Restricted zones of this kind should increase NATO warning time by one to two days and also create a heavily defended zone to take the first impact of possible Pact conventional attack, with present NATO standing forces acting as operational reserves.

This approach would not have decisive effect in making conflict in Europe impossible, but it would make it less likely. It would be especially useful in lowering the risk of war through crisis escalation, and it would improve NATO's capability of dealing with a conventional Warsaw Pact attack by conventional means. Indeed the establishment of static defenses would give some genuine content to the concept of no early use of nuclear weapons by creating one additional barrier, in this case a literal one, which would have to be broken through before resort to nuclear weapons must be considered.

Creation of a zone of static defense and obstacles as a screen in front of NATO's mobile armored forces could also be pursued unilaterally by NATO. Or NATO could institute such a zone while simultaneously proposing to the Warsaw Pact an agreement prohibiting heavy mobile weapons from a belt on both sides of the Federal German border. There are two possible moves less complicated than the zones of prohibited armaments. The first would be for both sides to eliminate heavy bridging equipment in the MBFR reduction area, inhibiting their capability for rapid forward movement. The second would be for both sides to lower the active-duty manning level of their units in the MBFR reduction area (or a wider area) instead of reducing by units. This approach would leave it to each alliance to decide whether to reduce its manning level across the board, preserving organizational structure, as the Soviet Union and United States would presumably wish to do, or to convert specified active-duty units within deployed divisions to reserve status, as NATO countries in the reduction area might wish to do. If reducing manpower levels of units in the MBFR reduction area were combined with Soviet action to reduce category 1 and 2 units in the western Soviet Union to category 3 status, this approach might ultimately prove a militarily meaningful and politically acceptable route to deeper NATO-Pact force reductions. It would of course entail the same verification difficulties as an MBFR agreement on the present basis.

Other Neglected Arms Control Issues

Among other aspects of arms control in Europe that are not now being adequately covered, one has a clear answer: there is a clear need for a NATO–Warsaw Pact risk reduction center, for which the logical location is MBFR. If a first MBFR agreement is achieved, a consultative commission will be needed to coordinate the exchange of information and the operation of associated measures. This group could be given the additional mission of prompt investigation of minor border clashes, border-crossing incidents by military personnel or aircraft, and unnotified troop movements. It would also be a suitable forum for informal discussion of strategic issues, including the rationale for major force improvements and technological change. On his visit to Paris in October 1985, Gorbachev proposed organized dialogue between the two alliances in some form. Given this statement, the Soviet Union might be prepared in principle to explore the possibility of such a risk reduction center in MBFR, which would be particularly useful if negotiation of reductions should be suspended in this forum in favor of some broader forum like CDE.

In the previous section, we discussed one possible approach to reducing tactical nuclear armaments in Central Europe, reducing them by converting the units equipped with them to reserve units. Unfortunately this told us nothing about an agreed basis for reductions. There is no easy answer to the problem of controlling tactical nuclear weapons because of their variety and large number—including thousands of dual-capable delivery systems, artillery, and aircraft, as well as missile launchers—and the relative ease with which they can be concealed. The nature of these weapons may be an argument for dealing with them separately from conventional armaments. If so, several steps could be taken now. The level of these weapons could be frozen in a first INF agreement. Exploratory East-West talks should be held to examine the range of agreed reduction possibilities. Their first task should be to develop confidence-building restraints, such as separate storage of warheads from delivery systems and perimeter inspection of storage sites by sensors and by inspectors from the opposing alliance. Limitations on dispersal of launchers from garrison and taking nuclear-capable aircraft and missile launchers off quick reaction alert would also be useful confidence-building measures. Each side should be free to make unilateral reductions.

Control of chemical weapons is an even more difficult problem. The United States stores chemical weapons in the Federal Republic of Germany and the Soviets in East Germany. The negotiations in the UN Conference on Disarmament in Geneva for a verifiable worldwide ban on production and deployment are unlikely to bring agreement for many years. In the interim, the Geneva participants should set up a separate subcommittee for verification of prohibition against deployment. If they can resolve the very knotty problem of usable verification procedures—and unofficial discussions between the Federal German Social Democratic party and the East German communist party have brought some progress here—then they should apply these results in a test area, logically the MBFR reduction area.

There are good reasons for the United States to consider this approach because current U.S. legislation provides that if the United States goes into production of the new binary chemical weapons, present stocks of chemical weapons, including those in Federal Germany, must be removed and destroyed by 1994. Since there is no current prospect that Federal German political opinion will allow deployment of new binary chemical weapons in the Federal Republic, this removal would leave a one-sided advantage to the Soviet Union, believed by some American intelligence agencies to have over thirty chemical weapon storage sites in Eastern Europe. In the circumstances, it would be worthwhile to follow up on the unofficial draft agreement and to see if it can be converted into a working agreement. Verified prohibition of storage of chemical weapons in Central Europe will not prevent use of these weapons in the event of conflict since the weapons can be rapidly brought into the area or delivered by aircraft or missile from outside the area, but their verified absence from the area will create greater East-West confidence from successful operation of inspection measures while making early use of chemical weapons somewhat less likely in the event of conflict.

The NATO-Warsaw Pact confrontation is on the verge of two new waves of modernization: development by both alliances of improved shorter-range missiles with greater accuracy which could be fitted with conventional or chemical warheads—and development of tactical antimissile defenses to cope with these new weapons. If both types of weapons are deployed by both alliances, as seems possible over time, neither will be more secure and both will be considerably poorer. Yet in the INF talks in Geneva, both the United States and the Soviet Union have in the past suggested what amounts to a freeze on shorter-range systems as a first step. This freeze could and should be made to explicitly cover shorter-range missiles with chemical or conventional warheads. As a first step, an initial INF reduction agreement could be formulated so as to cover conventional and chemical warheads for both cruise and ballistic missiles of any range under residual limitations or a freeze. If the overall number of missiles is constrained, neither alliance will be in a position to expand its capacity for missile delivery of conventional or chemical warheads on a large scale.

A Comprehensive Approach to European Arms Control?

The three forums for European arms control form a negotiating crazy-quilt—at best overlapping yet incomplete, at worst working at cross-purposes. Because no single forum of the three appears likely to reach an agreement soon that will contribute decisively to dismantling the East-West confrontation in Europe, it is worth considering whether some other approach integrating the work of existing forums could have more impact. Perhaps organizational unity could bring an integrated negotiating approach to all the fields of possible arms control in Europe: confidence building, including constraints on force activities and deployments; reduction of the possibility of surprise attack; and reduction of military manpower and armaments, including nuclear armaments and chemical weapons.

The CDE framework as it stands is not very usable for such a purpose. The extension of these negotiations' geographic coverage to include the western Soviet Union, while a positive achievement, also means that force reductions there will be difficult to achieve. Moreover, it is difficult to envisage a reduction concept that can be applied to thirty-five individual participants equally without two unpalatable results: acceptance, in treaty form, of the cumulative numerical superiority of the Warsaw Pact countries over the NATO states in most major armaments; and individual national ceilings on military forces that would prevent members of NATO from making up for unilateral reductions or shortfalls of other alliance members. A further limitation of CDE is that France has refused to date to negotiate nuclear weapons there.

MBFR too, despite the advantages of its alliance-to-alliance format, has problems, not the least of which is French nonparticipation. In addition, despite MBFR's capacity with regard to force reductions and associated measures and its experience with tactical nuclear weapons, its slow operational method could be disadvantageous in a forum for more comprehensive negotiations.

If neither the CDE nor MBFR forum is suitable for comprehensive European arms control negotiations, might it be possible to link or meld them in some way? Indeed if both negotiations should culminate in first agreements, practical considerations will make this issue much more pressing, for there will be a confusing overlap of similar measures. The obligation to report out-of-garrison activities in advance, for example, would be undertaken for two different areas, on two different schedules, and with different degrees of stringency and commitment. Perhaps the most rational way to deal with this outcome would be for the MBFR participants to add to an MBFR agreement, as binding obligations, those CDE measures that apply to the MBFR area and whose content goes beyond commitments already assumed in MBFR. Such action would result in two concentric zones: a single consistent set of more stringent obligations applying to the MBFR area and a second set of less binding measures applying to the CDE area outside the MBFR zone.

If, as seems more likely, CDE succeeds in a first agreement and MBFR, after twelve years of negotiations, does not, then MBFR's future appears dim. In this event, it might prove possible to amalgamate the two negotiations under the CDE umbrella in some way that preserves an alliance-to-alliance format for negotiating force reductions. This might be accomplished, for example, by disbanding the MBFR talks and establishing a working group in CDE phase 2, of which the participants would be the MBFR participants plus France. This possibility relies, however, on France's willingness to relax its objections to alliance-to-alliance negotiation if it took place in a forum subordinate to CDE, of which France was a major initiator. As to the reduction area, this could be the present MBFR reduction area but including French forces in Germany—again, if France would drop its objection to the MBFR reduction area on the strength of embedding the talks in the framework of negotiations dealing with a wider area. Since the MBFR area excludes the Soviet Union, Soviet agreement to measures with real bite is most plausible there. Alternatively the MBFR reduction area could be expanded to include both France and the western Soviet Union.

The April 1986 Gorbachev Proposal

A proposal by General Secretary Gorbachev appears to fit into this category. In April 1986, during a visit to East Berlin, Gorbachev made a proposal for substantial reductions in all components of land and tactical air forces, including both conventional and tactical nuclear weapons, in the entire area from the Atlantic to the Urals. Reduction would be by units, with reduced armaments to be destroyed or stored on national territory. Measures to prevent surprise attack would be agreed; a resulting agreement would be subject to full verification, including on-site inspection if needed. The negotiation process would begin with members of NATO and the Warsaw Pact, and then reach out to include neutrals and nonaligned.

Soviet officials have said they have no preference as to negotiating forum for this proposal, but that the MBFR talks are not suitable for reasons of geography and participants; this leaves the possibility of a separate working group in CDE phase 2 composed of the two alliances, or of a wholly new forum. In fact, this Gorbachev proposal seems likely to be the centerpiece of Soviet recommendations for CDE phase 2 at the CSCE review conference to take place beginning November 1986 in Vienna. The proposal speaks to the French interest in reducing armed forces in CDE phase 2, although the French do not wish to reduce nuclear armaments. It would also be attractive to Federal German officials, who have objected that an MBFR agreement could create a special zone in which Federal Germany would be subject to reductions and limitations to which France would not be subject, and would also not cover Soviet forces in the western Soviet Union that would be used against NATO forces in the event of conflict. The Soviet proposal also contains a useful feature in suggesting alliance-to-alliance negotiation at the outset, enabling a focus on the serious NATO–Warsaw Pact confrontation rather than forces of the small European neutral states. The initial NATO reaction to the Gorbachev proposal has been to ask for results in CDE and MBFR to demonstrate Soviet seriousness before going further on this new project. But the features just described will make the proposal attractive to the Western Europeans, and NATO may eventually accept negotiation on this basis, possibly in CDE phase 2, giving an excuse for allowing the MBFR negotiations to lapse, as may be one Soviet motive in proposing it.

The Gorbachev proposal of April 1986 has the merit of addressing directly the neglected question of armament reduction. Perhaps it is motivated by a desire to negotiate limits on the new generation of high-technology weapons which NATO is contemplating under the label of "emerging technology," which, Soviet Marshal Ogarkov has written, cause concern to Soviet military experts. However, given the great disparity in size of Warsaw Pact and NATO units (U.S. divisions of 18,000 men as compared with Soviet divisions of 12,000 men), the proposal that reductions be by units is not practical as a basis for negotiation without a good deal of further refinement. Reduction of armaments by equal amounts or by percentage would leave the Warsaw Pact with a very large numerical superiority in most major armaments, a superiority that NATO has hitherto refused to contractualize in a treaty—there is not much room for equal ceilings in this proposal. The practical effect of the proposal is to postpone still further first agreements on force reductions in Europe. It will probably be a long time before East and West agree to negotiate seriously on this proposal and a still longer time before some usable basis for reductions can be identified. Nonetheless, it is worth serious examination, and may in the long term prove to have productive possibilities.

Theoretically, it would be possible to deal with the problem of force components not covered in present negotiations in another organizational way that might provide an integrated approach and also ensure that these issues received high-level attention. This would be to add a fourth subnegotiation to the three concurrent ones— on space weapons, strategic nuclear weapons, and intermediate-range nuclear forces—now taking place in Geneva. This fourth subnegotiation would cover conventional and tactical nuclear forces in Europe, as well as confidence-building measures. European NATO and Warsaw Pact members would participate in at least this subnegotiation and the INF subnegotiation, allowing direct participation of those European countries on whose territory U.S. nuclear weapons are deployed (though France would probably refuse to participate).

Despite the practical costs of excluding the allies from arms control decisions, the United States would be reluctant to take actions like these. Indeed, the prospects for achieving agreement between East and West—or within the West alone—on any integrated approach to arms control and then of carrying that approach to actual fruition are, unfortunately, limited. Perhaps in the very long run, the CDE forum would be a possibility. But the two superpowers control the bulk of nuclear weapons deployed in Europe and prefer to negotiate separately and bilaterally on this subject matter; the United States continues disinclined to share control of its nuclear weapons or its national future with its European allies and remains prone to debilitating division over arms control within its political leadership. France, despite its aspirations to leadership in Europe, will probably not be able to leave behind its concept of autonomy in isolation in order to provide the needed forward impulse. In Federal Germany, sharply divided political opinion on defense and arms control issues will probably be unable to come to any internal consensus on this subject. Great Britain's Tory governments have taken a conservative position toward European arms control during the 1970s and 1980s and, in negotiations like MBFR, seem to have seen their role largely as stiffening NATO's negotiating position against possible German or U.S. weakness. On the Warsaw Pact side, the underlying problem remains the extreme unlikelihood that the Soviet Union will prove willing to withdraw large numbers of its forces from forward positions in Eastern Europe.

The Limits of Arms Control in Europe

Progress in ongoing negotiations, as well as success in incorporating neglected issues into European arms control, could help in making war less likely. But even so, the capacity of the existing negotiations decisively to diminish the scale of the East-West military confrontation in Europe would remain limited. Moreover, it appears that for the foreseeable future, no organizational change can overcome the cumulative effect of institutionalized interest and the numerous other built-in obstacles to major disarmament in Europe. There does not seem to exist a single encompassing arms control approach to the NATO-Pact confrontation that by its intrinsic effectiveness and broad appeal could dismantle the confrontation to a decisive degree.

This conclusion is not unexpected. As we have seen, the level of East-West distrust is so high that arms control negotiation polarizes leadership opinion within the countries of each alliance, leading to limited objectives and limited results. No government in East or West has thus far permitted arms control to become anything more than an occasionally useful tool for the management of a continuing military confrontation. Political leaders on both sides are still far from the level of mutual trust that would make possible serious discussion of disarmament and of dismantling the European military confrontation. Indeed, although it does not always work in the way intended, arms control on the present limited basis is in fact a confidence-building measure designed to improve the East-West political relationship and to create long-term conditions for more decisive action to dismantle the confrontation. As we have seen earlier in this book, growing segments of the European public are becoming impatient with this circumspect approach. They consider that it condones and even legitimizes a continually mounting but less justifiable confrontation. Their answer is unilateral abstention to break the competitive upward spiral of arms. Yet the unilateralist approach, although it gives some insights into the nature of the East-West problem, may not provide the impetus to real disarmament its adherents hope for. By the time it has run the gauntlet of stiff opposition from domestic groups and allies, the end product may itself be a limited confidence-building move that may not elicit much early or visible response from the Warsaw Pact.

The state of U.S.-Soviet relations remains a factor of central, although no longer wholly determinant, importance for East-West relations and arms control in Europe. It is possible in the twenty-year time span of this analysis that, in addition to an initial agreement on INF reductions, the United States and the Soviet Union will also reach one or more agreements to reduce their strategic nuclear forces, perhaps ultimately by as much as the 50 percent both have agreed should be their goal. Such a development would have great intrinsic significance; it might, through a combination of reductions with deployment of mobile missiles on both sides, eliminate the possibility of a successful first strike by either country.

Yet even if this outcome can be achieved, it is nearly certain that the significance of the agreements will be heavily disputed in both countries and that the U.S.-Soviet nuclear confrontation will continue. New U.S.-Soviet agreements would be welcomed in Europe and would give impetus to arms control negotiation there. Yet even with this productive ripple effect, the East-West military confrontation in Europe will also continue.

If this is so, perhaps more overtly political measures could have more effect in creating the preconditions needed for more far-reaching progress toward dismantling the East-West confrontation. In particular, if the largest single obstacle to far-reaching arms control in Europe is the Soviet role in propping up the communist regimes of Eastern Europe, perhaps future decades will bring some evolution in Eastern Europe toward more self-sustaining regimes and other political changes that will make military support by Soviet troops less central, or perhaps there is some prospect of a negotiated political settlement of the division of Europe that would enable major force reductions. In part III, we will look at the future development of the countries of Eastern Europe to see whether it may be possible to make more direct progress toward decreasing the military confrontation in Europe by this route.

Part III
Political Aspects of the European Confrontation

———

10
Political Change and East-West Solutions

For the foreseeable future, the prospects for far-reaching force reductions in Europe are blocked by Soviet military occupation of Eastern Europe for the main purpose of propping up individual communist governments. Any chance of large-scale withdrawal of Soviet forces, or perhaps eventually neutral military status for the Eastern European states, would depend on the governments of the Warsaw Pact becoming more self-sustaining or on an internal change in the Soviet Union that could bring a change in Soviet policy toward Eastern Europe. What are the chances that the NATO–Warsaw Pact military confrontation in Europe may be resolved, or at least mitigated, by such political change if arms control negotiation cannot now do the job? Could political change in the Soviet Union and other Warsaw Pact states make it possible to have more fruitful negotiation with them over the military confrontation?

A Political Solution to the Division of Europe?

Nine successive conferences of U.S., Soviet, British, and French foreign ministers in the late 1940s and 1950s failed completely in the effort to resolve the problem of divided Europe and divided Germany. But in the 1980s the antinuclear movement in Western Europe and opposition to deployment of INF missiles brought with them a renewal of hopes and fears in the West that the time may finally have come for some sort of major political settlement in the center of divided Europe which could bring a resolution of the East-West military confrontation. Some, like the German Greens, who have adopted this approach as their party program, believe that withdrawal of the two German states from their respective military alliances, the dissolution of NATO and of the Warsaw Pact, the withdrawal of U.S. and Soviet forces to their homelands, and a position of obligatory neutrality for all states of Europe would greatly increase security in Europe. Some Federal Germans—not the Greens, who claim they are too realistic to expect such an outcome—connect this notion with the hope of self-determination for the East German population that could result in some form of association between the two German states, a possibility we will examine more closely in the next chapter.

The possibility of a negotiated solution is implicit in the structure of the division of Europe itself. Its realization could in theory have many benefits: decisive strides toward dismantling the East-West military confrontation, the restoration in some form of the unity of the German people, and the return of some degree of autonomy to the individual states of Eastern Europe. The problem with this solution is that none of the participants, except possibly the populations of Eastern Europe, would find it acceptable.

In the European NATO states, public and governmental opinion would consider unacceptably risky the idea of a solution combining withdrawal of U.S. troops across the Atlantic with withdrawal of Soviet troops to the nearby border of the Soviet Union, only 600 kilometers from the NATO–Warsaw Pact dividing line. Most of the states of Western Europe would also have a negative attitude toward any form of German reunification. Foreign Minister Giulio Andreotti spoke for all of Europe, East and West, when he indiscreetly said in 1984 that he preferred the status quo of a divided Germany. Of all the NATO countries, only the more remote, larger United States might find the idea of some form of German unity relatively acceptable. But the United States would share Western European concerns about the emergence of a power vacuum in Western Europe through a situation of obligatory neutrality for Germany and the increased possibilities for the extension of Soviet political influence over the resources of Western Europe that this approach could create.

In the political sense, then, most of Western opinion prefers the continuation of the division of Europe, even at the cost of the East-West confrontation that has grown up around it, to the elimination of that confrontation by means of political negotiation—as long as there is not a prior, fundamental change in the nature of the Soviet system. Our brief review of possibilities for political solution to the problem of the East-West confrontation has led us instead to identify strong motivations for maintaining the status quo. The Western European governments and their people want neither the reunification of Germany as such nor its putative cost in security terms. When we add to these strong political forces in support of the East-West status quo those Western institutions—defense ministries, armed forces, arms manufacturers, and political parties—whose efforts, however motivated, also tend to maintain the East-West military confrontation, the result in the West alone is a very powerful constellation of forces making for the continuation of the confrontation.

The existence of a cohesive, united Western Europe with strong military forces of its own capable of deterring Soviet attack could change negative views about withdrawal of U.S. forces from Europe. But such a development, if indeed it ever takes place, is a generation or more away. And particularly if U.S. forces are to be withdrawn from Europe, the political independence of Western Europe cannot be ensured without the contribution of Federal Germany to common defense. This excludes German neutrality in any form.

The Eastern Europeans and Soviets would have their own reactions to political solutions of the kind we have been discussing. Eastern European governments would oppose any settlement based on withdrawal from Europe of Soviet and U.S. forces because departure of Soviet forces from their countries could well entail their own demise, perhaps in the literal sense. The populations of Eastern European countries might find the approach acceptable; their distaste for Soviet occupation is probably stronger than their fears of a united Germany.

The present leadership of the Soviet Union would, however, find such an approach wholly unacceptable. Residual fears of Germany remain too strong to contemplate any form of German unity.

And beyond that, any relaxation of Soviet control over East Germany would also imply the ultimate internal autonomy of all the Warsaw Pact states and a high risk of the eventual collapse of their communist regimes.

It is hard to discern whether, in the European context, the Soviet leadership considers that its hard-won achievement of nuclear parity with the United States is a net gain or loss for Soviet security. On the one hand, the Soviet Union possesses the ultimate deterrent to Western attack and the ultimate answer if successful conventional attack does take place. On the other hand, the Soviet leadership may consider that it faces the same potential problem NATO leaders see with the Soviets: a quick Western attack by conventional means below the nuclear threshold. For this reason and also for historical, emotional reasons and reasons of pure intellectual conservatism so ingrained in this autocratic society, holding the terrain of Eastern Europe for purposes of military defense continues to be important for them.

Even if the Soviet leadership came to consider the military cordon sanitaire in Eastern Europe less necessary because of the Soviet Union's enormous strength in nuclear weapons, the shattering disconfirmation of the legitimacy of the Soviet system itself that would result from elimination of communist regimes in Eastern Europe would make such a change unacceptable to the present Soviet leadership. This means that any radical change in the Soviet hold over Eastern Europe would have to be preceded by radical change in the Soviet system itself—either its collapse or its development into a totally different system of a pluralistic type.

The Prospects for Political Change in Eastern Europe and the Soviet Union

There is ample evidence that the Warsaw Pact system of communist states in Eastern Europe is far from a success. None of the governments of Eastern Europe has become self-sustaining in the sense that it could survive in its present form if Soviet armed forces were removed from its territory or could not easily intervene from Soviet territory. Without Soviet military support, each of the communist-dominated states of Eastern Europe would move toward some form of political pluralism and removal of the local communist party from its monopoly control over political power. In some Eastern European countries, the process would be gradual, in others abrupt and violent. In a sense, the citizens of the Western democracies when paying for NATO defense are paying for the built-in inefficiencies of the communist system in Eastern Europe and in the Soviet Union as well.

The historical record of the past forty years places this forecast beyond dispute. There were riots in East Germany and in Czechoslovakia in 1953; a nationwide uprising in Hungary in 1956; a radical movement for change in Czechoslovakia in 1967–1968; large-scale workers' riots in Poland in 1956, 1970, 1976, and 1980, culminating in the Solidarity movement; and repeated large-scale labor unrest in Romania in the 1970s. In each case, the development had to be repressed by force or the threat of force. Soviet troops had to be used directly in East Germany in 1953, in the bloody repression of the Hungarian uprising, and in the invasion of Czechoslovakia, as well as in the deliberately menacing maneuvers of Soviet forces on the borders of Poland in 1981 that preceded the institution of martial law in that country.

The political cost of these interventions has increased with each episode. They have discredited all claims of the communist system in Eastern Europe and of the individual Eastern European governments to legitimacy and popular acceptance, as well as the claims of the Soviet Union itself to represent a lofty political concept. They have dissolved the ideological bonds that united the Soviet Communist party with other communist parties the world over, especially those of Western Europe, and to a large degree destroyed the attraction of the Soviet system for the rising elites of developing countries. Because the costs of intervention are rising, as demonstrated in particular by the case of Poland, the Soviet leadership has become increasingly reluctant to intervene with military force. Yet no one in Eastern Europe or, for that matter in the West, doubts that, if faced by an extreme threat to an individual communist regime in Eastern Europe, the Soviet leadership would ultimately decide to intervene with military force. It is this belief on the part of the ruled and rulers alike that sustains individual Pact governments as well as the entire Warsaw Pact system.

With the limited exception of Hungary, whose Janos Kadar enjoys some respect as a national figure, none of the national leaderships of Eastern Europe have anything close to the degree of spontaneous, freely accorded public support that could ensure their political survival if Soviet military power were removed. Each of the Pact governments is obliged to spend uneconomically large sums to maintain control over information and censorship, a large apparatus of secret police and informers, and, with few exceptions, border guards, minefields, and barbed wire fences to keep their populations at home.

Economically, none of the Pact governments has achieved sufficient success to generate the political support needed to make it self-sustaining. Eastern European living standards, although in many cases higher than that of the Soviet Union, are in most cases lower than all but the poorest countries of Western Europe. Poland especially is kept alive economically by a Soviet subsidy. Even relatively prosperous East Germany owes its situation to the advantages of being able to trade freely with Federal Germany and of annual hard currency subsidies that approach 5 billion deutsche marks annually.

From the 1960s to the 1980s, the Soviet Union was obliged to subsidize the whole of Eastern Europe to a total of perhaps $65 billion, mainly through artificially low energy prices, favorable terms of trade, and acceptance of low-quality consumer products.[1] The price of Soviet oil and gas in Eastern Europe has now increased, and the era of subsidies has come to a close except for especially vulnerable cases like Poland. Each Eastern European economy suffers from lagging productivity, low-quality production, and an inability to sell enough products in Western and even in Third World markets to gain foreign currency for its own essential imports of modern machinery and raw materials. Widespread concealed unemployment, low worker morale, and resistance to change by workers and local trade union and party officials have kept unprofitable plants in production. In all but a few cases, ineffective central planning and Communist party centralism have frustrated timid experiments designed to give enterprise managers slightly greater freedom of decision. Governments have not been able to maintain a flow of consumer goods sufficient to meet consumer purchasing power or to induce higher production from workers. Black markets, graft, nepotism, and many other forms of social and economic corruption are widespread.

These are the present realities of Eastern Europe. Is there any real possibility of change inside Eastern Europe that could bring some movement toward resolution of the East-West military confrontation in Europe? One theoretical possibility, that of internal collapse of the Warsaw Pact system, can be ruled out. A new class of younger, better-educated functionaries and technicians has replaced less-educated, old-line communists of the earlier period. Their loyalty is maintained by economic privilege and by the knowledge that, in a freer system, they would not long survive politically and, in many cases, physically. For the general population, the Pact economies maintain costs of housing and basic necessities at low, subsidized prices. Although communist economists are becoming more open in discussing the possibility of unemployment through closing inefficient enterprises, if this occurs to a cautious experimental extent, Eastern European governments will be obliged to provide adequate economic and retraining support for workers whose jobs are closed down. Living standards in Eastern Europe are not advancing, but they are still at a level considerably higher than they were twenty years ago.

Nevertheless, goaded by continued low living standards and continued comparison in the coming decades with the more successful economies of Western Europe—and the word on this comes through to the remotest village in Bulgaria or Romania—popular discontent may erupt in one or more Pact countries. Perhaps Romania is the most likely place. There, an autocratic and nepotistic leadership has failed in economic leadership to an unusual degree, with real physical hardship for many as a result. And it is probable that worker discontent on a major scale will again flare up in Poland within the next decades. But national authorities have large forces of heavily armed riot police for just such contingencies. If they and their national armed forces cannot maintain control, then Soviet forces will intervene. In sum, there is at present no sign of collapse of the Soviet system in Eastern Europe.

Nor is there any sign of collapse of the system in the Soviet Union itself. Even under a regime with major built-in inefficiencies, the Soviet Union has become one of the world's two military superpowers. It is the world's largest country geographically, twice the size of the United States, with enormous natural resources. Its national economy is the world's third largest, after the United States and Japan. Development of the Soviet system toward pluralism, if it ever took place, would be an international development of such moment that the adjustments necessary to accommodate a unified Germany or withdrawal of U.S. forces from Europe would be secondary in importance and far more feasible, but there is now no sign whatever of such a development.

True, in the long term, there is scope for gradations and subtleties. If some Eastern European governments maintained the outer appearance of Marxist-Leninist systems and continued to insist that they were faithful adherents but slowly changed so that they were not so in substance, this might be tolerable to a Soviet leadership that had itself moved beyond militancy to lip-service to communist tenets. But there is also no sign that the Soviet leadership, always sensitive and alert to external threats, could move to this Laodicean muting of communist orthodoxy. One of many preconditions for such a development would have to be a thorough relaxation of U.S.-Soviet rivalry. But this in turn is improbable before radical changes in the Soviet outlook take place, so the vicious circle of rivalry and ideology remains. Another precondition is that the large and varied Soviet population would tolerate such a mellowing ancien regime of communism and not seek to sweep it away.

Nonetheless, there are many reasons why pressures for economic and political change in Eastern Europe will remain strong and why the worried leaders of Warsaw Pact governments will continually experiment with the economy and, in the long run, also with the political structure of their countries. Eastern European leaders are well aware of the built-in weakness of the command economy model they have taken over from the Soviet Union. They have the motivation to increase production, which their workers lack—not least in order to survive as governments and to retain their individual positions of privilege. They are under unremitting pressures from their own populations to improve their economies and from the Soviet Union itself to make these economies more viable. Experiments with the economy are a less risky way of coping with public discontent than change in political institutions.

Consequently, in coming decades, most Warsaw Pact governments will make piecemeal experimental changes—like the Hungarian New Economic Mechanism, introduced as early as 1968—
aimed at decentralizing economic decision making, improving
management skills and productivity, and eliciting stronger worker
motivation. These experiments will be cautious because of concern
over the potential adverse effects. They will be limited in effect
because of deep-rooted bureaucratic conservatism and because of
the deadening hand of the tacit alliance between party officials who
do not want their authority decreased and workers who want full
employment, total job security, and subsidized prices for food, util-
ities, and housing. Soviet approval will be needed for most such
changes. It will be forthcoming in many cases but slowly and
cautiously.

Many East European governments will continue to follow the
Hungarian example piecemeal, with more flexible prices and mar-
ket-oriented agricultural reforms. Slowly there may be a cumulative
increase in the role of privately owned enterprises and services. In
Poland, nearly 25 percent of the work force is already employed
in the private sector. Some inefficient plants will be closed and their
workers retrained and reassigned. More prices will be made open
to effects of supply and demand within controlled limits. These
changes will be too cautious to result in real economic break-
throughs. They are likely, however, to prevent further economic
decline and to move the Eastern European systems slowly toward
more mixed economies, combining state ownership and direction
of main sectors with some elements of a market economy.

On political matters, the populations of the Warsaw Pact countries show several characteristic attitudes. Most accept that major
change is improbable. But even the most apathetic share in a continuing desire for more personal scope, more freedom to travel
outside the communist system, more unbiased information and factual content in the public media, and more accountability of government authorities, as well as resentment of the privileges of the
new class of communist leaders and their ubiquitous, often blatant
nepotism and favoritism. All elements of the population, even pro-
communist elements, show increasing national feeling and a desire
to decrease visible Soviet preponderance, a desire that most Eastern
European governments share with each other and act on in a sub-

dued and careful way. Most ordinary Eastern Europeans also share considerable caution as to the limits to which their own governments and the Soviet Union can be pushed without sharp reaction.

Taken together, these attitudes produce moderate but unremitting pressure for change. In the next decades, a slow, gradual movement toward institutions and conditions of greater personal freedom will probably take place in Eastern Europe. It will be uneven and punctuated by repressions but cumulative in its long-term effects. The rubber-stamp parliaments of Eastern Europe will gain somewhat in authority and importance, including exercise of oversight over economic performance and the use of hearings. The public media will become more informative and a little more daring in their coverage. The judiciary, which in Poland has resisted actions of the martial law regime as not conforming to Polish law, will become somewhat more assertive. Cumulatively and over decades, while the Warsaw Pact continues to exist, these evolutionary pressures may slowly lead Eastern European countries to move closer to Western European models in the decentralization of the economy and in political life. In the interest of shoring up the economic and political viability of the individual Warsaw Pact states, the Soviet Union will have cautiously and reluctantly accepted piecemeal many individual changes that it would have rejected out of hand if presented as a single reform.

Among the most constant of the public pressures in Eastern European populations is a desire for better East-West relations, arms control, and decreased military expenditures. These desires are shared by Warsaw Pact governments, as is the universal view that better East-West relations decrease Soviet pressure for disciplined support of the Soviet Union and for more military spending by Pact governments. As a consequence, Eastern European governments have given strong support to East-West arms control negotiations and will continue to do so. In recent years, Eastern European governments have been reluctant to back the most militantly worded declarations on East-West relations urged by Moscow. They pressed Moscow to return to the negotiating table after the Soviet Union withdrew from the Geneva talks in 1983. In the CDE negotiations at Stockholm and the MBFR negotiations in Vienna, they have urged conciliation and compromise. Although in the early 1970s the East German government was so apprehensive about the consequences of possible East-West arms accords for its control over its own population that its arms control position was more rigid than that of Moscow, it has now also shifted to a more conciliatory approach. Of the Pact countries, only Romania has repeatedly dared to take an independent line in making its own proposals in Stockholm and Vienna without Soviet agreement. Others have done so occasionally and not found it politic to do so as a regular matter. But all support the East-West negotiating process and find it very good domestic politics to do so.

The Limited Prospects for Political Change

There appears to be little possibility of major political change in the important elements of the framework of the East-West military confrontation in Europe: the continued existence of the two rival alliances and of the Soviet political system in Eastern Europe as institutionalized in the Warsaw Pact. For decades to come, the prospect is for the continuation of both the Warsaw Pact, formally renewed in 1985, and of the NATO alliance, though both will be subject to continuing strains and continuing change and adjustment. Even major improvement in U.S.-Soviet relations is not likely to affect the deep-seated values that will maintain the rival military coalitions, although it could bring important movement in lowering the East-West military confrontation.

But we have also seen that an evolutionary process is underway in Eastern Europe, which has already contributed toward blunting the East-West military confrontation. Certainly it should be the objective of Western policy to promote this peaceful evolution. Most of the Western European states follow this objective in their policy toward Eastern Europe, none more consistently than the Federal Republic of Germany in its policy toward the second German state, the German Democratic Republic. In the next chapter, we analyze the inner-German relationship, seeking in particular to identify its potential to contribute toward dealing with the confrontation.

Note

1. M. Marrese and J. Vanous, *Implicit Subsidies and Non-Market Benefits in Soviet Trade with Eastern Europe* (Berkeley: University of California Press, 1983).

11
The Inner-German Relationship: Can It Change the Political Map of Europe?

Nowhere is the relationship between Eastern and Western Europe more important than in the relationship between the two German states. The Federal German government continues to be the most loyal ally of the United States on the European continent and the most important NATO partner of the United States in the military sense. But nowhere in the NATO alliance has there been such negative development in public attitudes on defense issues. And nowhere in the alliance is the gap in assessment of Soviet policy so great as that between political opinion in Federal Germany and in the United States. These related circumstances account for many past misunderstandings and will be the source of many in the future.

As in other Western European countries, Federal German public opinion and opposition political parties have increasingly expressed a European perspective on defense and East-West issues quite distinct from the U.S. view, and in this they are ahead of the more orthodox German government but strongly affect its actions and views. The Social Democrats want the new INF weapons removed from Germany; some of them believe this should be done unilaterally if necessary; the political Right wants the right of co-decision in the use of nuclear weapons; the left-wing Greens favor military neutrality for Federal Germany. In the early 1980s, German public opinion was brought vividly to life on U.S. television as hundreds of thousands of Federal German citizens demonstrated against the U.S. missiles their government had voted to deploy. Also disturbing to Germany's allies is the increasing pace of contacts between the two Germanies, a pace that Federal German Chancellor Helmut Kohl and East German leader Erich Honecker defiantly chose not to slacken even at the height of superpower tensions over the missile crisis in late 1983, when the Soviet Union withdrew from the U.S.-Soviet arms control talks in Geneva.

Germany is unique as a divided country on the boundary of East and West in Europe. Because of this division, the distrust generated by Germany's dark historical past, and the energy and power of German society, the recurrent nightmare of Germany's Western allies is that the Soviet Union will offer, or appear to offer, some version of reunification in exchange for the military neutrality of a united Germany and that the pressure of its public opinion would oblige the German government to accept. In less stark versions of this nightmare, Federal Germany's allies worry that it is becoming increasingly vulnerable to Soviet pressures because of its growing relationship with the German Democratic Republic (GDR). To a large extent, these visions reflect inflated Western fears of the Soviets' ability to play on public opinion trends in Federal Germany: the chafing resentment against NATO, the rising tide of neutralist sentiment, and the abiding interest in a close relationship with fellow Germans in the GDR.

The concerns are also rooted in the structure of the situation in Central Europe: the Soviet Union holds the GDR and could in theory give it up one day. And they are rooted in past experience. National feeling reached its greatest, most horrifying intensity in Germany a scant half-century ago. The Soviet Union in the early 1950s repeatedly held out offers of reunification in an attempt to head off the rearming of Federal Germany and its inclusion in NATO, offered confederation of the two German states in the late 1950s to stop deployment of intermediate-range Thor and Jupiter nuclear missiles, and seems to have hinted in 1983 at some form of reunification as a reward for rejecting the deployment of the U.S. INF missiles.

Given their deep-rooted fear of the massive shifts in Europe that would come with the military neutrality of Federal Germany—

in practical terms, it would mean the end of NATO—Federal Germany's allies tend to see any expression of antinuclear sentiment there as an ominous indication of neutralist sentiment, tend to see twin objectives of reunification and neutrality behind Federal Germany's policy of political engagement with the GDR, and tend to see every German shift out of lockstep with U.S. policy as a significant move toward the Soviet Union. As a result, in an alliance already racked by the INF controversy and disagreements over the larger questions of how to defend Europe and strategy toward the Soviets, the German unity question in all its aspects—the possible reunification of divided Germany, neutralism as a potential route to reunification, the deepening relationship of Federal Germany with the GDR, and Federal Germany's policy of political engagement with the Soviet Union—could become an increasingly divisive issue within NATO in the next decade unless some clearer understanding of its potential risks and gains can be achieved.

The German Question, Past and Present

The constitution of Federal Germany describes the restoration of German unity as the chief objective of the "provisional" West German state. In the first decades after the end of World War II, most Federal Germans, however, numbed by the shattering defeat of the Third Reich and preoccupied by the task of rebuilding their cities and their lives, were content to leave the unity issue to the combined efforts of Germany's new Western allies, above all the United States, and of the German government, whether by negotiation with the Soviet Union or by the application of superior power. Germans who wanted to do more to help their friends and relatives in the GDR—and they were many—were daunted by the certain knowledge that such efforts would be misunderstood in the West, undermining their own security and protection. And they saw no practical way to influence the policy of the Soviet behemoth that held fellow Germans in its power.

From the end of World War II until the mid-1960s, Federal Germans, political leaders and public alike, considered that they faced a stark, mutually exclusive choice between a closer relationship with the United States in NATO and with the states of the

European Community on the one side and some form of alignment with the Soviet Union on the other. Any middle ground, in which Federal Germany could be integrated into the Western alliance while at the same time mitigating the division of Germany by developing some relationship with the Soviet Union, the GDR, and the other countries of Eastern Europe, appeared quite impossible. Chancellor Konrad Adenauer, convinced that only through close ties to the United States and Western Europe could West Berlin be protected and Federal Germany enabled to recover from the Nazi era, tied Federal Germany's foreign policy closely to that of the United States. Indeed, motivated by fear of the Soviet Union resulting from the experiences of World War II and the Soviet takeover of the GDR and the rest of Eastern Europe, the vast majority of Germans saw close relations with the West as the sole guarantee of their security.

In the early years of Federal Germany, recurrent hopes that reunification could be brought about through negotiated agreement between the Soviet Union and its wartime allies in the West—France, the United Kingdom, and the United States—were disappointed by the repeated failure of four-power negotiation. Events of the 1950s and early 1960s—Soviet repression by military force of the 1953 uprising in East Berlin and the much more widespread 1956 Hungarian uprising and, above all, the construction in 1961 of the Berlin Wall—brought the final realization that the Soviet Union was willing and able to use force to maintain its hold over Eastern Europe and that the United States was not in a position to contest that hold. The division of Germany was finally perceived as an enduring if not permanent condition, a conclusion reinforced by the Soviet invasion of Czechoslovakia in 1968 to repress the drift away from the Czechoslovak Communist party's monopoly of power.

With this realization, Federal Germany's only practical course was to seek to improve on the status quo by first accepting it: to ameliorate the burden of division for individual East Germans through dealing with the Soviet and East German governments, while trying to retain some opening for possible change in the long-term future. In the United States, the Kennedy and Johnson administrations had also concluded that the Soviet system was a durable, if not permanent, feature of the international political situation and were following a policy of political engagement toward the Soviet Union. As a result, the barriers to a more active German policy of diplomatic relations with Eastern European states were lowered.

There were hesitant beginnings under the Christian Democrats in the 1960s. Chancellor Adenauer made a quiet offer to the Soviets before he left office in 1966: Federal German acceptance of the loss of former German territories to the Soviet Union and Poland in return for the military neutrality, not of Federal Germany, but of an independent GDR with internal political freedoms. In an influential memorandum of 1965, the Council of Evangelical Churches reminded Federal Germans of their moral obligation to help their fellow Germans in the GDR and to achieve reconciliation with the countries of the Warsaw Pact, including the GDR. And in 1966, the Erhard government proposed an agreement on nonuse of force to the states of the Warsaw Pact.

The Social Democratic–Free Democratic coalition of Chancellor Willy Brandt and Foreign Minister Walter Scheel that came to power in 1969 pressed its new *Ostpolitik* ("Eastern policy") with vigor and determination. Negotiating in the early 1970s through its main Western allies on Berlin and directly with the Soviet Union, Poland, Czechoslovakia, and other countries of the Warsaw Pact, Federal Germany accepted the loss of former German territories in the East absorbed by Soviet Union and Poland. In return, it achieved agreements giving contractual status to ground transit of Germans between Federal Germany and Berlin, ensuring access to the GDR for millions of residents of Federal Germany and West Berlin, and enabling the in-gathering of hundreds of thousands of ethnic Germans from the Soviet Union and Eastern Europe.

The new German Eastern policy—continued after Helmut Schmidt replaced Brandt as chancellor in 1974—was a genuine and decisive breakthrough. Over the years, Federal Germany's exclusively pro-Western policy had been a source of growing frustration and dissatisfaction for Federal Germans. The new policy resolved the increasingly resented dilemma of having to make an exclusive choice between close relations with the NATO allies and modestly improving relations with the East. It combined both elements, relying on the Western connection as a base for a more modest policy toward the East. In a sense, "Eastern policy" is a misnomer for this combination; "West-East policy" would come closer to capturing its essential elements. The new policy provided a practical way to help fellow Germans in the GDR, to work toward some long-term solution of the German unity issue, and to promote the in-gathering of ethnic Germans. In the process, it gave Federal Germany a distinctive foreign policy role and an identity that takes account of its history and geopolitical situation.

The extent to which this West-East policy corresponds to Germans' sense of their national role became even more apparent with the election of the Christian Democratic–Free Democratic government of Chancellor Helmut Kohl in 1982. Although the majority of Christian Democrats had voted against the treaties embodying the Social Democratic Eastern policy while in opposition, they took up that policy with alacrity after assuming power. Indeed, more precedent-shattering high-level visits to East Berlin took place in the first six months of the new Kohl government than in any similar period in the history of Federal Germany. These actions of the Kohl government demonstrate the nonpartisan support for the new German West-East role among the public and the major institutions of German society—political parties, churches, trade unions, and public media.

The Federal German government recognizes that the Soviet Union is profoundly opposed to any change in the status of the GDR and fully able to prevent such change through its military power. Nevertheless, the German government takes a position that must be objectively described as revisionist, though not with the usual negative connotations of this term. Federal Germany, hoping for change in the GDR by peaceful means, wishes to keep open the long-term possibility of change in the status of the GDR, especially its internal political system through self-determination—in other words, through free elections at some point. This, in short, is the "German question" in its modern guise. The leaders of the GDR, on the other hand, wish to make permanent the status quo and to consolidate the GDR's position as a separate state controlled by the communist Socialist Unity party of Germany. For the GDR, there is no German question.

The substance of Federal Germany's policy toward the GDR—

what it calls its inner-German policy—is to improve relations with the GDR as much as may be feasible, with the goal of promoting personal contacts on the individual level and drawing the East German government into an increasingly cooperative position. On the East German side, the root of the leadership's motivation for pursuing the inner-German relationship is the desire of its population for increased contact with Federal Germany and the interest of the GDR leadership in maintaining its rule by improving the viability of the GDR system. A probably irreducibly large majority of the East German population regards the Federal German system as far more attractive than the GDR system. The GDR leadership realizes the value of Federal German contacts as a palliative for the discontents of its population, both political and economic. Without Federal German subsidies, it is improbable that the GDR would be able to maintain the highest living standard in the Warsaw Pact. Moreover, if the gap between Federal German and East German living standards were to widen further—the living standard in the GDR is now about 40 percent of that in Federal Republic—it would be a dangerous source of public discontent.

GDR policy toward Federal Germany is not without risks of increased public demand for freedom of movement and access, demands that GDR leaders could not afford to fulfill without serious loss of control over their population. The GDR leadership maintains an intricate balance of control over its population while on the one hand accepting economic benefits from Federal Germany and in return permitting a limited relaxation of police controls over the East German population, allowing them to receive visits, packages, money, and telephone calls from friends and relatives in Federal Germany. As insurance against this policy going wrong, the GDR has an effective and well-trained riot police and, as final insurance, the massive presence of nineteen Soviet divisions in the GDR. Despite the risks, the GDR leadership calculates that the net advantage is on its side. GDR leaders seem well aware that the motivation of Federal Germany's inner-German policy is, as they would put it, to destabilize the GDR. But the reverse is also true, and the GDR calculates to gain the greater long-term advantage in this contest for influence.

The Inner-German Relationship Today

In view of the near total isolation of the two German states from one another in the 1950s, the scope of the relationship that has grown up during the first decade of applying the Federal German policy of political engagement is remarkable. Erich Honecker and Chancellor Kohl run inner-German relations directly from their own offices. The official interaction between the two German governments is increasingly intense. At one point in mid-1983, nine separate negotiations were going on between Bonn and East Berlin with regard to river pollution, radiation and disaster control of nuclear facilities in the border area, air pollution, science and technology, cultural exchange, and further improvement of transport routes.

In addition to the attraction the Federal German system holds for the East German population, Federal Germany's greatest asset in promoting the inner-German relationship is its economic strength, with which it buys, in various forms, improvements in relations between the two states. Federal Germany has guaranteed large private bank loans that have helped to put the GDR on its feet economically, financed the East German trade deficit with Federal Germany on favorable terms, and, early on, successfully pressed for suspension of the European Community's customs duties and restriction on East German goods entering Federal Germany, giving the GDR the hard currency it needs to import manufactured goods. The GDR is also being paid, and paid well, for Federal German access to individual citizens. The Federal German government pays the GDR about 2 billion deutsche marks annually for road, rail, water transport, and communications fees to Berlin and the GDR, and is also buying the freedom of about 1000 prisoners a year from the GDR. Individual Federal Germans visiting the GDR must exchange 25 deutsche marks a day in hard currency, even if they are staying with relatives. Still, at least 5 million Federal Germans and West Berliners visit the GDR and East Berlin each year, and nearly 2 million East Germans, mainly pensioners, visit Federal Germany or West Berlin.

Most of these aspects of the inner-German relationship have a characteristic pattern. Federal Germany seeks to improve access to the population of the GDR, as well as to Berlin, through better roads and postal service and by easing exchange requirements and restrictions governing travel of GDR residents to Federal Germany. The GDR splits up each of these issues into numerous subcomponents and sells each for the maximum Federal German subsidy. There is no doubt about who will continue to be the major economic beneficiary of the inner-German relationship.

These fairly humdrum issues, the lifeblood of the inner-German relationship, do not appear to have the potential to bring about fundamental change in Central Europe no matter how they are resolved. As observers in West and East have projected their worries about the possibility of such change onto the prosaic inner-German relations, they have sometimes been convinced that there is more here than meets the eye.

In searching out the impetus for the ever-growing inner-German relationship, we must therefore discern not only what this unique relationship is but also what it is not. The developing inner-German relationship has elicited nervousness in Federal Germany's allies because it seems to bespeak a goal of a reunified Germany, an outcome that would fundamentally change the political map of Europe. And in view of the more visible indications of neutralist sentiment in Federal Germany, some allies also fear that the Federal German public may endorse neutralism as a route to reunification. It is not surprising, then, that Western observers have a tendency to equate German neutralism with Federal Germany's inner-German policy.

Yet the two are fundamentally different. The neutralist approach would relinquish or dilute Federal German membership in NATO in return for some improvement in the relationship between the two German states negotiated with the Soviet Union. The inner-German policy of the Kohl government and its predecessors, on the other hand, is premised on continued German membership in NATO and a genuinely close alliance relationship as an indispensable requirement for a long-term German effort to influence developments in the GDR.

This policy is not only official lip-service; it is based on the conviction of most Federal Germans in the government and outside it that the close alliance relationship continues essential to their national and personal security and well-being under all conditions foreseeable today. For its part, the GDR's policy toward Federal Germany is also premised on continued East German membership in the Warsaw Pact; the GDR's leaders could not survive without this membership.

As we have commented, Federal German leaders accept as a practical matter that negotiation of a unified Germany with the Soviet Union or solution of the problem through severe internal weakening or collapse of the Soviet system is highly improbable for the foreseeable future, which is indeed the case. Nevertheless, there is some reason for confusion in the West and for the Federal German government's continuing difficulties over the years in presenting a clear picture of its inner-German policy to its allies. Although effective pursuit of the inner-German policy does require a close Federal German relationship with its NATO allies, the problem is that ultimate success of that policy in terms of reunification of the two German states, under all imaginable conditions short of total collapse of the Soviet Union, would logically require Federal German withdrawal from NATO. Successive German governments have tried hard to cope with this paradox, mainly by suggesting that the solution of the division of Germany is very far off and that they cannot at this time foresee any specific solution and certainly no reunification of Germany in isolation from a general settlement of the division of Europe.

In terms of Federal German public opinion, the allies' fears are also well founded in one sense but baseless in a more important one. Most polls over the years do show that a strong minority of about one-third of the Federal German public rather consistently favors neutral status for Federal Germany, independent of the reunification issue. The durability of this attitude reflects disappointment and pessimism over East-West arms control, prompting a desire for a political solution of the underlying problem of East-West political confrontation. Public opinion polls also show that Federal Germans strongly desire a change in the status quo in the GDR, with the majority of respondents agreeing that the reunification issue must be kept open.

These results are in no sense indicative of lack of realism on the part of the Federal German public, however. Polls have repeatedly shown that most Germans do not believe reunification is possible. What the polls show is the continuation of an ideal desire: when Germans are faced by the need to decide on specific East-West issues, these sentiments are suppressed. Federal Germans are not willing to sacrifice the political and economic system of Federal Germany to some reunification scheme, and they are extremely skeptical that the Soviet Union would offer reunification on terms of internal freedom for the GDR as well as Federal Germany. In a December 1984 poll, 88 percent of the sample answered "no" when asked whether they would be prepared to accept German reunification if it meant fewer political freedoms for them.[1] Despite increases in support for neutralism, the great majority of Germans remain too cautious, too security conscious, and too hardheaded to accept mere talk from the Soviets on the German unity issue. They will want specific genuine moves on elimination of the communist system in the GDR, as well as real assurances that the liberties and well-being of the Federal German population are not at risk in any change—actions that the Soviets cannot and will not deliver. And there is a limit to Soviet promises of such relaxation. Even Soviet hints of such actions can risk deadly repercussions in Eastern European opinion.

Another poll of December 1984 got to what appears to be the real nub of the Federal German attitude on the German question: 89 percent said they doubted German reunification would take place, but 73 percent said they nonetheless hoped it would take place.[2] In sum, the desire of both German public and government to keep the German question open represents an uneasy compromise between the German desire to change the status quo and the recognition that this cannot be done on acceptable conditions because of Soviet opposition.

Many Federal Germans are skeptical that Federal Germany is getting GDR concessions commensurate with the large economic benefits it is giving the GDR, and it is reasonable to question how long the Federal German political system will continue to support such a policy. Will practical-minded Germans, having recognized the impossibility of German reunification, cease to hold it as a goal? Some transformation may already be taking place among the young. A 1984 poll showed that 49 percent of Federal German youth between the ages of fourteen and twenty-nine considered the GDR a foreign country as far as Federal Germany is concerned (only about a third of the adult population has this view).[3]

Yet the interest of Germans on both sides of the border in maintaining ties has had great durability during nearly forty years of the division of Germany. Former Chancellor Helmut Schmidt commented in a lecture series in the United States in 1985 that German desires to reunify Germany would persist indefinitely; he compared German attitudes to those of the Poles, who persevered for centuries in the desire to restore the unity of their country.[4] Moreover, it appears likely that pursuit of an improved relationship with the GDR is an integral part of the emerging Federal German identity, an identity that combines strong Atlantic and Western European ties with an enduring interest in the countries to the East.

In the first decade of the inner-German relationship, it seems already to have developed to a point where it cannot easily be broken off by outside pressure, and the odds are that it will continue to intensify. Over 20 percent of Federal Germans have relatives in the GDR, and numerous close contacts among individual Germans across the inner-German border will preserve strong feelings of national unity. Association between the churches, political parties, and trade unions in East and West, as well as contacts between government agencies, will reinforce this. And the past record indicates that even future ups and downs of their own public's overt interest in the unity issue will not stop Federal German officials from pursuing the government's inner-German policy.

Yet neither Federal Germany nor the GDR can permit its inner-German policy to become a serious source of friction with its allies. Indeed the fundamental axiom of the inner-German relationship as it concerns outside states is that this relationship will be supported, or at least tolerated, by the respective allies of the German states as long as those allies do not believe it will have any effect in changing the status quo in Europe—but only for so long. The result is mutual restraint and, in Federal Germany, a tendency to downplay inner-German activities so as not to worry NATO allies, the GDR, or the Soviet Union. In sum, the Federal German government has the tremendously difficult task of convincing its own allies and the Warsaw Pact states that it is doing nothing that is on balance injurious to their interests, while at the same time convincing its own electorate that it is doing something significant for German interests. Its diplomacy has done a brilliant job in this effort.

As far as Federal Germany's NATO allies are concerned, the situation is complex. Militarily, Federal Germany is the most important European member of NATO. Federal Germany's allies realize that the inner-German relationship is important to it and generally approve efforts to encourage evolutionary change in the GDR and elsewhere in Eastern Europe. Federal Germany's allies also recognize that frontal efforts to bring the Federal Germans to relinquish their inner-German interests could create great friction within the alliance. Of Federal Germany's allies, only the United States may have the power to put a stop to Federal German policy toward the GDR, though in practical terms, it is doubtful that any Western ally can any longer do so. Even the Reagan administration, despite its fears of expanding Soviet influence in Europe and elsewhere, officially supports Federal German policy toward the GDR.

Some Western political leaders have seen in the Federal German policy a dangerous edging toward Moscow. Others, less fearful on this account, are nonetheless concerned that Federal German public opinion, with its interest in improving human contacts, will push its leaders into unwise economic relationships with the Soviet Union and the GDR—relationships that may make Federal Germany dependent on the Soviet Union for energy supplies and vulnerable to political pressures.

These Western concerns, however, reflect an unrealistically low opinion of the common sense of the German public and political leadership, as well as an unrealistically high opinion of Soviet capacity to play on German psychology. The Soviet Union could in theory exert pressure on Federal Germany by threatening to cut access of Germans to Berlin or to friends and relatives in the GDR. In fact, it has done just that—without results. Federal Germany has reacted to Soviet pressure tactics in the past by emphasizing its primary concern: security through armed forces and the alliance. In 1983, faced with repeated Soviet and East German threats that a Bundestag vote for U.S. missile deployment would have fatal effects on the inner-German relationship, Federal Germany made the traditional choice: priority for security and the alliance, placing the inner-German relationship second. If the Soviets revert to their 1950s pattern of continual threats, the long-term effect would almost certainly be to reinvigorate German support of NATO and, with it, the possibility of an increase in German and other NATO armed forces, and to end the economic benefits of Federal Germany's Eastern policy. Such an approach would be self-defeating given the Soviet objective of improving relations with Western Europe. It would also elicit resentment from East Germans, both political leaders and the general public, to a degree that could be damaging to long-term stability of Soviet control.

East-West Security: A New Dimension
of Inner-German Relations

The relationship between the two German states has been given new impetus, as well as a new focus on East-West security, by several converging developments. One factor is a broad revival of national feeling in Federal Germany as the passage of time has slowly dissipated the postwar sense of guilt and humiliation for Hitlerism and World War II. Polls by the respected Allensbach Institute show that in the early 1950s, only 2 percent of German respondents considered their period the best epoch of German history; in the 1970s and 1980s, that figure was over 80 percent.[5] A healthy national pride has become respectable in Federal Germany and, with it, the idea that Germany has interests of its own that are not purely NATO interests. The Social Democratic slogan for the March 1983 general election was "In the German Interest." Although the Social Democrats lost the election, their slogan captured the spirit of the times.

Even as Germans' pride in their own society has revived, their respect for the United States and U.S. leadership in international affairs has fallen off. The United States was a model for Germans in the postwar period, but disillusionment set in with the assassination of President Kennedy, the Watergate scandal, failure in Vietnam, and the Iranian hostage crisis. German skepticism about the Soviets is also high and has remained consistently so even during the decade of Eastern policy and détente. But now, with the slipping respect for the United States, there is a strong trend toward seeing the two superpowers in an equally negative light. This is the same tendency seen among adherents of the antinuclear movement in all Western European nations to blame their nuclear worries fairly equally on the two superpowers. Taken together with the fading of feelings of German guilt for World War II and its aftermath, this development has also meant that many Germans no longer consider the continuing division of Germany to be the consequence of earlier German actions or even of Soviet policy alone. Some younger Germans are beginning to consider it the result of the superpower confrontation as such.

Part and parcel of these developments is a widespread feeling in Western Europeans of powerlessness to decide their own political and economic future, which is seen as depending on arbitrary actions of the two world powers. This sentiment, with the resentment and longing for greater autonomy that it entails, is perhaps at its strongest in Federal Germany. Both trends—the tendency to blame both superpowers equally and the tendency to feel powerless in the face of their confrontation—provide further motivation to pursue interests considered purely German, like the inner-German relationship.

In the wake of the peace movement focused on the INF deployment, pursuit of inner-German relations has become identified, for many Germans in both German states, with progress toward peace and security. The mounting feeling of frustrated powerlessness in the face of the great powers has found an outlet in both German states in the idea that there is a special contribution that Germans, and no one else, can make to peace; moreover, that to some extent, Germans can make this contribution independent of the great powers and whether or not the great powers like it. Notably, the Kohl-Honecker collaboration to try to salvage the inner-German relationship and even to intensify it at the time of the missile crisis received overwhelming approval from the public in both German states.

The new Federal German perception of its own role and that of the GDR is seen very clearly in the developing inner-German dialogue on security issues. This dialogue, strongly supported by public opinion in both German states, has the potential to become

an important aspect of the relationship between the two Germanies. In 1985, public statements of the special German responsibility
to maintain peace came from Chancellor Kohl and Erich Honecker,
meeting in Moscow at the Chernenko funeral, and in a joint statement of the Council of German Protestant churches in Federal Germany and the Federation of Evangelical Germans in the GDR. In
Federal Germany, the Social Democrats, in their resolution of February 1985 submitted for the annual Bundestag debate on the State
of the Nation, emphasized the "contribution of both German states
to the consolidation of peace in Europe," calling for new initiatives
for peace, arms control, and disarmament that would transcend
the military blocs.

The first such alliance-transcending initiative has already taken
place. Meetings between the East German Socialist Unity party Pol-
itburo and the Social Democratic leadership culminated in June
1985 in a draft agreement prohibiting storage of chemical weapons
on the territory of Federal Germany, the GDR, and Czechoslovakia. And this initiative, whatever its immediate fate, is likely to be
only the first of a series of similar enterprises. The Social Democrats and the Socialist Unity party have already entered on a fol-
low-up discussion on a zone where tactical nuclear weapons would
be prohibited.

An important impetus for the inner-German dialogue on security issues will doubtless be the slow progress of East-West arms
control, which can almost certainly not keep pace with the developing desires of the German public. Both German governments will
continue to put strong pressure on their respective superpower allies for more progress in negotiations. Given the strong public support in both German states for the inner-German discussion of
security issues, the locus of serious initiatives may shift from political parties to a more significant dialogue between the two governments. Although such a dialogue has already begun at Federal
German initiative, it has so far been limited to rather stylized discussion of the arms control position of both sides. Both governments may come under considerable pressure in coming years to
expand this security dialogue and may well be inclined to do so.
Thus over the long run, the inner-German security dialogue may

increasingly appear as a supplement to, or even as a substitute for, a bogged-down East-West arms control process.

The developing inner-German dialogue on security issues is one aspect of the inner-German relationship likely to produce friction between Federal Germany and its allies in the coming decade. The U.S. government has already discouraged Kohl-Honecker discussion of an inner-German commitment on nonuse of force, arguing that an independent German dialogue outside the Stockholm CDE negotiations would weaken the unity of the Western negotiating position. Given the strength of German public support for the idea of a security dialogue, however, continued efforts to suppress it could reinforce anti-NATO trends in Federal Germany.

From the viewpoint of East German and Soviet leaders, on the other hand, inner-German discussion on security issues involves little risk. It gives the GDR leadership an important role and function of its own in the Warsaw Pact, which only it can carry out. Soviet leaders will be interested in the contribution of the inner-German dialogue to long-term Soviet security goals in Western Europe—decreasing the NATO military potential and U.S. influence in Europe, and more active East-West economic collaboration—and in its contribution to the shorter-term Soviet goals of mobilizing peace sentiment in the Federal Republic and causing friction between the United States and its European allies.

Yet despite the Soviet Union's interest in promoting the inner-German relationship in all its aspects, there seems no doubt that in 1984, Erich Honecker's planned visit to Bonn was postponed because of Soviet pressure. The Soviet motive for intervening to stop the Honecker visit appears to have been the fear that the relationship was developing to the point that threatened to destabilize the postwar status quo. The pressures came during the physical decline of Konstantin Chernenko and were uneven and sporadic enough to show the existence of divergent opinions in the Soviet leadership. It seems probable that similar negative pressures will be applied in the future if Soviet leaders become apprehensive that events making for a change of status are in the offing, for Soviet control over the GDR is the keystone of Soviet control over Eastern Europe. Yet such extreme assessments will be infrequent, for the

Soviet leadership has considerable interest in and tolerance for the inner-German relationship.

Defining the Western Interest in the Inner-German Security Dialogue

Although Federal Germany agrees with the United States on the nature of the Soviet system, political opinion in Federal Germany accepts its relationship with the Soviet Union as a difficult, up-and-down one extending into the indefinite future and sees the Soviet Union as a power whose agreement or at least acquiescence is necessary for the furtherance of its inner-German policy. The Federal Republic is the prototypical supporter of the two-track approach of defense and dialogue with the Soviet Union set forth in NATO's 1967 Harmel report, in whose formulation Federal Germany played the central role. Although the United States also follows a declared two-track policy, the practical emphasis of its policy is perceived by most Germans to be more on the track of militant containment than the dialogue track. Both the governing Christian Democrats and Free Democrats, as well as the leadership of the opposition Social Democrats, firmly adhere to the new, broader definition of the German international position that combines close ties to the United States and to the European Community with a sustained effort to achieve a modus vivendi on political issues and arms control with the Soviet Union, the GDR, and the other Warsaw Pact states.

Where in this complex issue does the Western interest lie? The United States and other allies of Federal Germany should recognize that it is to their advantage to maximize the gains of the inner-German relationship and also to minimize the losses from intra-alliance frictions over East-West policy.

Federal Germany's policy toward the GDR has some very solid benefits for the West. It suppresses the East-West tension that would result from continual friction and overt hostility between Federal Germany and the GDR in the area of the world's largest military confrontation. It promotes continued Soviet and East German restraint with regard to West Berlin, an area where East-West frictions have in the past repeatedly threatened conflict. It stabilizes the situation in the GDR while at the same time promoting gradual change there, the one area of Eastern Europe where widespread public unrest could trigger panicky Soviet actions leading to East-West conflict. It is highly useful for the Western alliance that Federal Germany has taken on such a major share of responsibility in attempting on a long-term basis to bring Western influence to bear in the GDR and Eastern Europe. Federal Germany is in a better position than the United States and than most of the other Western European countries to provide the sustained interest and detailed activity that this objective will require for decades to come. The alliance should consider this activity a constructive German contribution to Western policy toward the Warsaw Pact, a kind of political burden sharing.

Taken together, these positive aspects of Federal Germany's inner-German policy mean that this policy is a development that the United States and other NATO countries should seek to further, not stifle. In the coming decades, the inner-German relationship could make a more explicit contribution to reducing the scope and the dangers of the East-West military confrontation if the Western allies can perceive the potential benefits and give the Federal Germans the confidence and encouragement their past record of alliance loyalty and support justifies. Both Germanies, especially Federal Germany, are too apprehensive about the mistrust of their allies to undertake this role without encouragement. Yet the two German states know the rules for their political engagement. They know full well that the NATO and Warsaw Pact alliances will continue. Indeed, each German state identifies its security and survival with continued membership in its alliance.

The two German states have on their territories the majority of foreign troops involved in the East-West confrontation. In consequence, they have a more consistent interest than other members of their alliances to temper and diminish that confrontation. Through their dialogue on the official government-to-government level, they could bring added dimensions to the fragmentary, episodic discussion of the European military confrontation in the CDE, MBFR, and INF forums; they can discuss the confrontation more comprehensively and more consistently. Although the opening phases of this official dialogue have been cautious and hesitant, it could treat issues under formal negotiation in an informal, exploratory way. The two German governments could then turn with the results of the discussion to their respective alliances for further consideration by them. The two German states could also, as the Social Democrats are now doing with the East German communist party, identify aspects of the confrontation that are not being discussed, such as NATO–Warsaw Pact risk reduction centers, reduction of conventional armaments, or limited zones of prohibited armaments, and do some advance exploratory work on them.

Viewed on a long-term basis, the inner-German security dialogue could make an important contribution to making the European confrontation less dangerous. But that contribution will be circumscribed. The chance that the Soviet Union will withdraw from Eastern Europe and let the countries of the area take their own course is nearly excluded. Inner-German relations can mitigate the risks of the East-West confrontation, but they cannot change the political map of Europe.

Notes

1. Published in *Géopolitique*, Paris, Winter 1984–1985, pp. 6–9.
2. Published in *Der Spiegel*, 44/1984, October 29, 1984, p. 43.
3. See chapters by Elisabeth Noelle-Neumann and Anne Koehler in Werner Weidenfeld, ed., *Nachdenken Ueber Deutschland* (Cologne: Verlag Wissenschaft und Politik, 1985), especially pp. 138, 153.
4. Helmut Schmidt, *A Grand Strategy for the West* (New Haven: Yale University Press, 1985), p. 54.
5. Elisabeth Noelle-Neumann, ed. *The Germans: Public Opinion Polls, 1967–1980* (Westport, Connecticut: The Greenwood Press, 1981), p. 103.

Part IV
Conclusion

12
Dismantling the NATO–Warsaw Pact Confrontation

V iewed dispassionately, the huge East-West military confrontation in Europe seems to have passed its high point, politically if not militarily, and to be in decline. A watershed has been reached and passed. Viewed in terms of the fears and antagonisms that characterized its beginnings a generation ago, the confrontation is now on the downward slope.

Several contingent possibilities of Soviet attack on Western Europe continue to exist, all of them remote: miscalculation, fear of Western attack, panicky reaction to widespread revolt in East Germany, or acts of sheer irrationality driven by power struggle inside the Soviet Union. But the possibility of deliberate, aggressive Soviet attack for the sake of conquering and holding Western Europe, however large it may have been in the past, has become so small as to be negligible. While NATO's professional soldiers would not go this far, they do publicly characterize the risk as very low.

Active-duty NATO forces are more evenly matched with Soviet forces than most NATO analysts allow for. For a blitz attack on Western Europe, Soviet forces would be largely on their own; the Warsaw Pact allies of the Soviet Union are increasingly unreliable politically, and militarily of low value. Only those Soviet forces in forward position in East Germany and Czechoslovakia could be used at the outset, possibly with a limited number of East German, Czechoslovak, and Polish divisions. Standing NATO forces deployed in the Federal Republic are a match for these Warsaw Pact forces; in fact, qualitatively they are superior. If properly organized, German reservists and NATO reinforcements could probably cope with Warsaw Pact reinforcement echelons. In effect, Warsaw Pact and NATO forces are sufficiently closely balanced that neither side has been able to gain an enduring, decisive advantage; neither is likely to do so in coming decades. Attack on Europe would entail a high risk of worldwide conventional or nuclear war, which would set at risk the entire Soviet system. Beyond that, Soviet gains from even a successful military occupation of Western Europe are questionable and almost certainly would not exceed the gains of peaceful trade and credits from Western European countries.

The record shows that the second great fear of Western leaders, the Soviet Union's ability to translate its great military power into a source of intimidation and pressure on Western European governments, has not materialized, despite repeated attempts to do so. Soviet threats to use nuclear weapons to burn Western Europe to a cinder have been so frequent as to be a regular occurrence. Not once have European countries made a major concession to the Soviet Union in the face of such pressures. This must be counted a full and important success of the NATO alliance.

NATO's success in repelling these Soviet intimidation efforts has rested primarily on the political cohesion of European NATO countries with their militarily powerful U.S. ally, and this will continue to be the case. Maintaining rough U.S. parity with the Soviet Union in nuclear forces is essential for retaining this capability to deal with Soviet pressures. U.S. nuclear superiority over the Soviet Union has been lost for good, and this has created grave but not insuperable problems of European confidence in the United States. But given the very large number of strategic nuclear weapons deployed by both superpowers, victory through a preemptive first strike is excluded. Knowledge of the catastrophic consequences of strategic nuclear war will, together with the forward deployment of sizable U.S. forces, continue to serve as the ultimate deterrent of war in Europe. The second requirement for alliance political cohesion is maintaining personal relationships between the president of the United States and his chief advisers and European political leaders and maintaining the respect of European public and political opinion for the quality of U.S. leadership in world affairs. Alliance cohesion cannot be achieved by deploying additional U.S. weapons systems in Europe.

Taken together, the success of the NATO alliance in maintaining Western European freedom of decision in relation to the Soviet Union, the low possibility of Soviet attack, and progress in recent years toward achieving a number of arms control agreements of modest scope have created a far different situation in East-West relations than when NATO was established. A huge military confrontation on the downgrade has risks and dangers of its own, one of which is maintaining the alliance cohesion that has brought this success. Clearly it is much easier to maintain the political unity of a military coalition in a situation that participants consider as one of high external threat. A second difficulty is related to the first: as NATO moves into its fourth and fifth decades of peace, it will inevitably become more and more difficult to convince the citizens of the member countries to maintain NATO forces in the face of a threat that has in fact declined.

The Outlook for the Military Confrontation

Despite the generally acceptable situation regarding the East-West military balance, NATO forces in Europe face a number of difficulties. In recent years, Soviet and Warsaw Pact forces have, through introducing improved models, converted their numerical advantage in aircraft, tanks, attack helicopters, and artillery into a more impressive advantage. Moreover, over the next twenty years, the arms competition may well continue in nuclear delivery systems, high-technology conventional weaponry, and missile defenses. Driven by the apprehension of technological advantage on the other side, each side will add to its armaments at great cost, with limited net gain, if any, for its security.

Meanwhile, NATO is short of the supplies of ammunition, motor fuel, and armament replacements to fight the four-week conventional war that would be a reasonable objective for it. NATO is also dangerously short of operational reserves—mobile armored backup forces that could plug holes in NATO front lines if Soviet forces broke through in an attack. Airfields in NATO Europe are too few, too crowded, and too vulnerable. NATO forces continue to be plagued by a lack of interoperability of ammunition and the absence of coordinated production of increasingly expensive major armaments like aircraft and tanks.

Answers to all these problems have been evident for decades: increased specialization among NATO countries, with the United States taking up the slack in naval and air forces in return for an increased number of ground force divisions from European partners; formation of an increased number of combat units from Federal German and other continental reservists; a simple declaration from France that in the event of war, it would place lines of communication and airfield facilities at the disposal of NATO; and greater standardization and coordination of military production between Europe and the United States.

Yet apart from some increase in stocks of ammunition and wartime supplies, none of these actions is likely to be taken to any decisive degree. The reason is quite clear: none of the NATO countries think the situation urgent enough to justify the political and economic dislocation such actions would entail. The reluctance to act decisively to improve defenses evidences an assessment on the part of all the governments involved that Soviet attack on Western Europe is extremely unlikely.

One positive aspect of the wide public opposition in northern Europe to INF deployment is that it has generated a large number of proposals for alternate defense. Many are ingenious, would improve NATO's chances of successfully defending against Soviet attack, and would have the additional advantage that by restructuring NATO forces, they would help to break the cycle of competitive force improvements between Warsaw Pact and NATO forces now structured in a similar tank-heavy way. But few of these schemes will be adopted, mainly for the same reason that they were rejected when first advanced thirty years ago: because most of these schemes involve a forward screen of German light infantry or reservist militia, they have no role for U.S. and other allies in a frontline position that would involve them in conflict from the outset. This outcome is politically unpalatable to German political leaders. Objectively seen, it would weaken the deterrent effect that flows from the presence of allies in the forward position. This difficulty could be overcome by restructuring a portion of the U.S. and other allied forces to operate the forward belt of light infantry and static defenses.

Germans also object to the political connotations of many of these schemes, especially those involving field fortifications and tank barriers, as emphasizing the division of Germany (although if they felt genuinely threatened by Warsaw Pact attack, these objections would fall rather rapidly). Nonetheless, continued dissatisfaction of left-wing opposition parties with the status quo of the NATO–Warsaw Pact confrontation, along with economic and demographic pressures, are likely to bring about the slow adoption of some of these concepts, to the benefit of NATO defenses.

Theoretically the European members of NATO, grouped in something like the Western European Union, which provides a treaty framework for their military cooperation, are capable of mounting adequate conventional defense against Soviet attack without a large U.S. troop presence. But the underlying factors that inhibit all moves toward more effective conventional defense will also slow progress here: the continuing pull of national sovereignty; a low degree of urgency and fear of Soviet attack; a simultaneous desire not to provoke still greater buildup of Soviet forces and a deterioration of East-West political relations; and the fear that an evidently effective European conventional defense of Europe would lead to withdrawal of U.S. conventional forces.

The presence of these U.S. forces is correctly regarded as the most effective deterrent to Soviet conventional or nuclear attack on Western Europe, as well as the most effective insulator against Soviet political pressures based on military power. Beyond that, the presence of the U.S. forces makes possible cooperation within NATO with large and effective German forces, which otherwise would be a source of worry and concern to Western European countries with strong memories of Hitler Germany. Fear of Soviet attack is also insufficient to overcome British and French political resistance to active German participation in decisions to use their own nuclear weapons, which could give the Federal Germans a degree of confidence in French or British nuclear protection. Consequently, despite low fear of outright Soviet attack, the concern of the nonnuclear members of NATO over possible use of Soviet nuclear weapons in extreme situations and over Soviet efforts at political intimidation will remain sufficiently strong to continue nuclear dependence on the United States. This continued dependence, however, is likely to become increasingly chafing to large segments of the populations of the nonnuclear countries, especially Federal Germany and the countries of northern Europe—and to their national leaders. Deep reductions in Soviet and U.S. strategic weapons and in INF and tactical nuclear weapons would provide some answer to this frustrating dilemma, but such developments do not appear probable in the next decade.

The Prospects for Arms Control

A modest degree of reduction and relaxation of the East-West confrontation through arms control appears possible in that time period. A first agreement in the Stockholm CDE conference appears likely in 1986 or soon after; it will result in detailed measures for preannouncement of larger out-of-garrison movements of ground forces and for the presence of foreign military observers at these movements. This outcome is nearly certain to be followed by further CDE negotiations to place constraints on the duration, frequency, and location of ground force movements, as well as the type of activities that can be included in exercises, such as loading up with live ammunition. Results here will be slower and more difficult to achieve than in CDE phase 1, but the confluence of strong, continuing Western European, Eastern European, and Soviet interests appears likely to ensure some further outcome. Future phases of CDE, however, are not likely to succeed in devising an acceptable formula for extensive force reductions, partly because they cover a large part of Soviet territory without any compensation with regard to U.S. forces. The logical answer here would be to include a portion of the U.S. home territory under the coverage of future agreements.

After nearly a decade of marching in place, the Vienna force reduction negotiations, the MBFR talks, have at last reached the point where a real test can be applied as to Soviet willingness to make a small, initial negotiated reduction of Soviet and U.S. ground force personnel in the center of Europe. The main issue has been narrowed to Soviet willingness to accept on-site inspection, more easily acceptable in MBFR than in CDE because it would take place outside the Soviet Union. NATO requirements for on-site inspections to verify force levels on the ground are excessive in number but justified in their character by the nature of the problem: how to test compliance with manpower ceilings when it is physically impossible to inspect a large force at one given time. The answer to this problem is sampling inspections by each alliance of the other's forces on the basis of detailed information on manpower submitted by each alliance.

For some years, the Soviet leadership has been indicating increasing readiness to accept on-site inspection, as emphasized even further by General Secretary Gorbachev. There is some chance of a first agreement in Vienna reducing 5000–6000 U.S. personnel in return for about twice that number of Soviet personnel. Although a first MBFR agreement would reawaken European interest in the process of reducing conventional forces, the prospects for further, more sizable reductions are not very good. NATO has lost the taste for force reductions and limitations in the face of possible requirements for increased manpower from force modernization and after long difficulties with MBFR. And the continuing need for a large Soviet military presence to bolster the shaky communist governments of Eastern Europe means that large Soviet forces will remain in Eastern Europe and will receive high priority in allocations of military resources and new equipment, generating pressures for further improvements in NATO forces.

Since for these reasons, large manpower reductions appear unlikely for some time, the MBFR talks should be used to negotiate a 50–100 kilometer zone on the line of confrontation in which mobile weapons that could be used for attack, such as tanks, self-propelled artillery, and attack helicopters, as well as long-range nuclear-capable and conventional missiles and aircraft, would be prohibited. Although there would be a ceiling on ground force personnel in the MBFR reduction area, there would be no personnel limit within the border zone, and light field fortifications would be permitted. This approach might oblige some restructuring of tank-heavy forces of both sides and should make palatable to Federal German opinion the field fortifications and tank obstacles that would improve its defensive position.

The INF negotiations, where reductions in nuclear weapons deployed in Europe and the Soviet Union are being negotiated, also appear to hold the possibility of a first agreement with modest reductions in the intermediate-range missiles of both sides, although the obstacles to agreement are greater than in MBFR. The obstacles include some resolution of the issue of British and French forces and Soviet willingness to make at least a modest reduction in SS-20s deployed in the Far East, as well as U.S. restraint in pressing for deep Soviet cuts in the first agreement.

A partial solution to the first problem might be possible if the United States and the United Kingdom agreed to include in the U.S. total of strategic armaments British nuclear weapons that are assigned to SACEUR. French nuclear weapons, which are not so assigned, would not be included, and the Soviets would have to accept half a loaf in this compromise solution. As in MBFR, after a first INF reduction, agreement on further reductions may be difficult for a considerable time. European worries about the effects of U.S.-Soviet nuclear arms control agreements on their own situation are likely to continue unless the United States at some later date is willing to adopt the principle that all nuclear weapons capable of striking a target on the territory of the other alliance are to be considered strategic.

Not covered by active East-West negotiation at present are a possible NATO–Warsaw Pact risk reduction center, preferably in the MBFR context, negotiation on chemical weapons in the specific European context, and reduction of both conventional and tactical nuclear armaments. It may be possible to deal with reductions of conventional armaments to a modest extent by specifying that the armaments of personnel reduced by agreement should be taken out of active-duty units and turned over to the reserves in both Central Europe and the Soviet Union. Presumably a first INF agreement would freeze nuclear delivery systems of ranges below INF systems—1000 kilometer range or below—at their present level, including those that could be equipped with conventional or chemical warheads. Once frozen, some might be withdrawn unilaterally, perhaps others by later agreement. It may become feasible to negotiate in either MBFR or CDE certain mutual constraints on how tactical nuclear weapons are deployed, such as limitations on dispersal of launchers from garrison, taking nuclear-capable aircraft off quick reaction alert, separating delivery systems from storage sites for nuclear warheads, and subjecting storage sites to inspection by sensors and by military personnel of the opposing alliance.

These are some partial steps that might be considered in the future; more dramatic steps appear unlikely. Reorganization of the CDE, INF, and MBFR negotiating forums to get more impact and direction does not appear readily feasible, although more thought on this possibility is needed. The Soviet proposal of April 1986 to reduce conventional and tactical nuclear armaments in the area from the Atlantic to the Urals may in the long term create an opening for lowering force levels if a suitable reduction fomula can be devised. Yet the proposal's immediate effects are to undermine the MBFR talks and to postpone any force reductions. Given the limited capacity of all these existing negotiations to make deep cuts in existing forces, arms control does not have great capacity to do what is logical in the circumstances: to move forward toward dismantling the East-West military confrontation in Europe. After its cautious beginnings in four-power discussions of the German question forty years ago, arms control in Europe has taken just enough form to be on the verge of limited agreements for confidence-building and limited reductions. It is in an experimental stage, about where U.S.-Soviet dialogue on strategic nuclear weapons was fifteen years ago. Although a few modest successes would increase support for continuing efforts, opinion in East and West on the arms control process is too divided and mutual distrust too high to move arms control beyond this experimental stage for a considerable time to come.

The Contribution of Political Change

These limited prospects for arms control might be easier to accept if there were some prospect that political change in East-West relations could improve prospects for some more substantial reduction of the European confrontation in the foreseeable future, whether by negotiation or not.

Nearly everyone in the West dreams at one time or another that the Soviet Union would someday permit the countries of the

Warsaw Pact to become increasingly autonomous in their domestic political and economic affairs, contenting itself with maintaining a defensive glacis. This might take the form of continued membership of the Eastern European countries in the Warsaw Pact or of an obligatory Austrian-style neutrality, accompanied by deep reductions of Soviet forces in Eastern Europe or even their complete withdrawal, a condition sometimes called the Finlandization of Eastern Europe. This situation would, of course, represent a vast improvement over the status quo and would entail the possibility of far-reaching steps toward dismantling the East-West military confrontation. But there is little, if any, chance of achieving it by peaceful means within the next decades.

As demonstrated by a long series of events—the East German riots of 1953, the Hungarian uprising of 1956, and Polish trade union unrest of the 1950s, the Prague Spring of 1968, and the rise of the Solidarity movement in Poland, events that almost certainly will have their counterparts in the future—there is little or no chance that the governments of the Eastern European countries will become self-sustaining in the next decades. Without Soviet troops in their countries or within hailing distance on their borders, the communist regimes of these countries would collapse, some sooner and some later.

Slow economic progress through cautious, hesitant experimentation can be expected in all the Eastern European countries in the coming period, but there is little prospect that their economies would become so successful, especially in comparison with the highly visible economies of Western Europe, that their governments could cease to rely on force and on the ultimate threat of force by Soviet troops to make themselves self-sustaining. If these Eastern European regimes did become self-sustaining, what would happen with their large, well-equipped armed forces, whose loyalty to the Soviet Union is already in question? This problem for the Soviets would surely worsen.

Nor would the Soviet leadership content itself with a mere cordon sanitaire in Eastern Europe, allowing the Eastern European states to cast off their communist governments. Soviet residual fear of a united Germany remains too high. Equally important, the elimination of Marxist-Leninist governments in Eastern Europe would be a shattering and unacceptable blow to the legitimacy of the

Soviet system itself, an impermissible admission that in countries where the forces of history have brought Marxist-Leninist systems to power, it can die out. If such a reversal could happen in Eastern Europe, it could happen in the Soviet Union itself. Consequently it would require radical internal change within the Soviet Union itself before such massive amputation became acceptable to the Soviet leadership—a radical transformation of the main tenets of their own beliefs. Of this there is no sign.

What of the negotiated resolution of the European confrontation that European neutralists have hoped for from the Soviet Union for a generation and that European conservatives have feared for an equal period—a negotiated solution that would bring withdrawal of both U.S. and Soviet forces from Europe and take the two German states or a united Germany out of their respective alliances into a state of enforced neutrality? The United States and Western European governments would reject this outcome because they believe it would make Western Europe indefensible against Soviet pressures, and both Western and Eastern European countries would oppose the prospect of a united Germany in any guise. The Federal German population too would refuse any scheme that would jeopardize their own economic status and political freedoms and did not give East Germans these same rights. But giving East Germans these same rights would mean the end of the communist regime in East Germany, which in turn is not acceptable to the Soviet Union. For good or ill, there is no prospect of success for such schemes, however often they are raised. Both German states will remain loyal members of their respective alliances, for the governments of both consider that their survival is dependent on that membership.

The inner-German policy of the Brandt and Schmidt governments in the 1970s made an important if insufficiently recognized contribution to Western security. It suppressed friction in the day-to-day relationship of the two German states as a source of continuing friction between the two alliances. Economic rewards from Federal Germany to East Germany have secured the continued compliance of the Soviet Union and East Germany with the 1971 Quadripartite Agreement, which in practical terms eliminated major East-West friction over Berlin, a cause of serious U.S.-Soviet confrontation for two decades. By making possible contacts between the inhabitants of East Germany and fellow Germans in the Federal Republic and by contributing significantly to the economic well-being of East Germans, Federal Germany has, while promoting change in the East German government, contributed to avoidance of widespread unrest in the East German population, which through panicky Soviet reaction could be a source of devastating East-West conflict. Of all countries in Eastern Europe, East Germany is the one where the West should want peaceful evolution.

The inner-German treaties provide for consultation between the two governments on security issues. As yet, the content of this dialogue has been purely formal, and the more active dialogue on East-West security issues has been between the opposition Social Democrats in Federal Germany and the East German Socialist Unity party on creating zones free of chemical and tactical nuclear weapons in Central Europe. There does not seem much prospect for the next several years that NATO governments, with their heavy reliance on deterrence through U.S. chemical and nuclear weapons, will seriously investigate these specific possibilities developed in the channel of inner-German security dialogue. But the Social Democrats, who may well come to power in the next five to eight years, will keep pushing these ideas.

Potentially the government-to-government channel between the two German states has more promise than the interparty dialogue. Taking a long-term view of developments over the next two decades, if the allies of the two German states trust them sufficiently— and it is a big if—the two Germanies could contribute a good deal to exploring possibilities of making the East-West military confrontation, which is centered on their territories, less dangerous. But that contribution is in practice likely to remain limited because of the apprehension of the two German governments that their motives will be misunderstood by their allies and by the failure of these allies to overcome their own suspicions and recognize the opportunities of this channel.

Dismantling the Confrontation in Europe

The conclusion must be that although the East-West military confrontation has passed its peak and is on the downgrade, it is likely to continue for many decades to come. No single, decisive approach to speeding the process of dismantling the confrontation is evident. In Chancellor Schmidt's London speech of 1977, he said that Western Europe could deal with the problem of Soviet military power either by significantly increasing its own forces or significantly reducing Soviet and Warsaw Pact forces; neither development seems likely to occur in the next two decades in decisive measure. The prospects of force improvements that would bring significant change in the East-West force balance in favor of NATO are slight, while the contribution of arms control in the foreseeable future is likely to be circumscribed.

Because force modernization will continue on both sides, it is likely to remain unclear for some time whether the level of the confrontation is going down or up. Probably it will take a decade or more to discern a clear trend out of this indeterminate zone. The vested interests in the status quo in East and West remain stronger than the forces making for change. In the West, these vested interests include the ingrained dependence of the NATO states on the United States for conventional and nuclear protection, less against the possibility of outright Soviet attack than to counterbalance the political weight the Soviet Union draws from its military power. In the East, the vested interest is the realization of Eastern European governments and of the Soviet leadership that these governments cannot survive unless propped up by Soviet military forces. Even where there is some realization on the part of the NATO and Warsaw Pact governments that the European confrontation is winding down, this would be the last point they would make explicitly to their own publics, for then how could they confidently rely on continuing support for the defense budgets that will still be necessary?

Nonetheless, despite the strong psychological, political, and economic forces in East and West supporting continuation of the status quo in Europe, there will also be continuing pressures for dismantling a confrontation regarded by many Europeans as increasingly nonfunctional and obsolete. The continued absence of conflict between the two alliances in Europe, an absence that is highly probable, will feed these pressures.

It would appear, then, that no single approach to dismantling the confrontation has much chance of decisive impact. Instead, over the next two decades, it is probable that the military confrontation in Europe will be further reduced not by a single rational policy but by a disorderly, uncoordinated, intermittent, gradual process of attrition, taking place through a combination of confidence-building, arms control, and political measures—both reciprocated and unreciprocated measures on both sides. One continual pressure on both alliances, despite large differences in costing practices, will be the increasing cost of major armaments. In the West, steps of force rationalization and economy are likely to be the source of considerable shrinkage in active-duty forces. Some shift in NATO from active-duty to reserve units manned by a cadre of active-duty personnel is desirable on both economic and demographic grounds, but it is limited by scant prospects of large-scale withdrawal of Soviet forces from Eastern Europe. Nevertheless, to diminish Soviet capacity to reinforce Soviet troops in Eastern Europe through reducing the readiness level of Soviet forces in the western Soviet Union by negotiation might be feasible. Since the bulk of Soviet forces in Eastern Europe will probably remain there, however, the problem then becomes one of devising means of bringing the Soviet Union either to restructure these forces, by unilateral or reciprocal steps, to reduce their forward mobility, or to reduce their manning level progressively so they are no longer readily usable for blitz attack but could still be used to maintain East European governments and for self-defense.

The problem of bringing about some sort of reciprocal, if not matching, action by the Soviets to Western moves of force reduction will be a task of extreme difficulty. Perhaps it will be impossible to achieve. The Soviet Union will have to be pressed continually to translate its stated desires for arms reduction and improvement of East-West relations into specific actions. NATO states will have to insist on either parallel or similar unilateral measures or on negotiated ones.

New Trials for Western Leadership

It may be possible over coming decades to slowly reduce the level of forces in both NATO and the Warsaw Pact while maintaining adequate equilibrium. With a clear vision of the objective and a mix of measures of confidence building, arms control, and self-restraint, the East-West military confrontation can be deliberately moved past its military as well as its political peak, out of the indeterminate phase combining build-down with buildup, and into a definite process of build-down.

But the task of building down the confrontation increases the requirement for farsighted leadership in Western Europe and the United States and in the Soviet Union as well. It will be a severe test of the common sense of Western publics and national leadership to maintain defenses in a period of decreasing danger. It will be even more difficult to do this while using every available leverage to move toward mutual lowering of forces with the Warsaw Pact. Building down forces and guiding the European confrontation through a period of routinization and gradual dismantling is a far more difficult and divisive task than building up the confrontation.

It is a task that will place even greater strain than previously on U.S.-European relations on issues of defense and East-West relations. The perception that the European confrontation is in decline is bound to continue stronger in Western Europe than in the United States, given the global U.S. objective of countering the Soviet Union's efforts to increase its influence in Third World countries. Again and again in the past, the key factor for the defense of Europe has been cohesion between the United States and its allies. For at least a decade, the United States has not done well in this regard, compounding the problem through overlooking its foundation in psychological factors and personal relations and seeking to resolve it through deploying new weapons.

The main future risk is the intensification of existing intra-alliance difficulties. There is a continuing strong trend in European public opinion toward willingness to take unilateral European action of arms reduction, especially in the nuclear field. There is an even stronger trend in Britain and Federal Germany, the two most important countries for the future of the U.S.-European relationship in NATO, toward a position of blaming the United States and Soviet Union equally for U.S.-Soviet tensions. The Soviet Union is having some success in creating the appearance of being more con-

ciliatory than the United States in arms control matters—for example, in its position on cessation of nuclear testing—and in making
the case that the United States is to blame for lack of progress in
arms control. In the coming several years, the Soviet Union may
follow a deliberate policy of concluding modest agreements on arms
control in Europe while pointing to the difficulties of reaching
agreement with U.S. administrations on reduction of space and
strategic weapons. Over the longer period of the next two decades,
it is quite possible that governments espousing steps of unilateral
nuclear disarmament will come to power in one or more Western
European countries. The result—whether or not U.S. nuclear
weapons are actually forced out of, say, Great Britain—would be
deep intensification of U.S.-European frictions and, depending on
the wisdom and maturity of the U.S. reaction, withdrawal of some
or many U.S. forces from Europe.

This is a description of a worst-case situation; it is by no means
automatic that such intense differences need arise. Possibly U.S.
and European leaders can develop a closer common understanding
of long-term trends in the East-West confrontation—a common
realization of the direction they want to go in and the vision to
guide the countries of the NATO coalition safely toward a new
East-West equilibrium at a lower level of forces. But it appears
improbable that such a vision of the future, even if it becomes more
influential in Western Europe, can succeed in gaining more than
suspicious, grudging acceptance from future U.S. administrations
unless it fits into a different U.S. vision of the U.S.-Soviet relationship than the one that has long prevailed in Washington.

The underlying difficulty of the U.S. approach is that many
Americans are still looking for a definitive, comprehensive solution
to the difficult problem of the U.S.-Soviet relationship, some approach that will deal with this problem once and for all. The exceptionally successful history of the American society in dealing
with its major problems accounts for a characteristic American
belief that all problems have some full, rapid solution if enough
resources are applied. Successive U.S. administrations have in-
dulged this tendency with regard to the problem of U.S.-Soviet
relations with a series of approaches to the issue: containment until
the Soviet system mellows; massive retaliation for acts of Soviet
expansionism; rollback of the Soviets from Eastern Europe; the

superior magnetism of the Western system; collapse of the Soviet system through its own internal contradictions; creation of a restraining web of mutual interests; bringing U.S.-Soviet relations to a new plateau of mutual understanding and détente; spending the Soviet system into collapse; or establishing military or technological superiority over the Soviet Union. All of these approaches have failed and will continue to fail because they posit full resolution of the problem, in most cases through elimination or radical transformation of the Soviet Union. The fact of the matter is that despite the numerous defects of the Soviet system, the Soviet Union is physically the world's largest country, with an enormous supply of raw materials and an increasingly better-educated population. The Soviet system has many weaknesses but shows no signs of collapse. The real problem in U.S. policy toward the Soviet Union is the inability of the United States to admit to itself the continuing existence of the Soviet Union as a co-equal in power, and to draw the logical consequences from that admission.

What Americans need from their government is not further theories on how to get rid of the problem of U.S. relations with the Soviet Union, but ideas on how to live with that problem more safely. We must accept that U.S.-Soviet competition will continue indefinitely and that the task is not to eliminate the competition, which is impossible, but instead to make it safer by limiting and regulating it, especially its military aspects—seeking step by step to move toward demilitarizing it to the extent possible.

Through no special virtue of their own but rather from being victims of their own tragic history of wars, victories, and defeats, Europeans have learned one key lesson of international life Americans too need to learn: some international and domestic problems cannot be resolved in an acceptable way; we just have to learn to accept their existence and learn to live with them. This is the European attitude toward the Soviet Union: a difficult and dangerous neighbor that will not go away. As the Germans did with regard to the division of Germany and the existence of two German states in the early 1970s, Americans have to accept the status quo in order to improve it. The United States has to accept as a fact of life the continuing existence of the Soviet Union and its political system and go on from there.

When the United States has moved to a policy of accepting

continuing competition with the Soviet Union while attempting to reduce its military component, it will have a policy framework compatible with an objective of dismantling the East-West military confrontation in Europe and therefore the basis of close and continuing association with European allies that can ensure a safe transition to reducing the level of the confrontation. This approach to the U.S.-Soviet relationship would also make it possible to engage the Western European allies in closer cooperation with the United States in political and economic programs of limiting Soviet influence in the developing countries. It would also reduce present European apprehensions over militant U.S. confrontation with the Soviets in these countries, with the resultant tendency to dissociate Europe from U.S. policy and actions.

But whether or not the United States moves toward a new vision of Western policy toward the Soviet Union that can be subscribed to by its European allies, on one matter we should be clear. In the absence of total reversal of Soviet policy toward Western Europe, Western European members of NATO are likely to continue their effort to improve relations with the Soviet Union and the countries of Eastern Europe and the Federal Germans to continue their policy of seeking to intensify inner-German relations even if there is friction with the United States over these policies.

In its forty years of existence, the East-West military confrontation has entailed high costs and risks. Yet it has not prevented hundreds of millions of people in both alliances from leading useful, "normal" lives. The major forces are moving in the right direction. The European confrontation is so huge and deeply rooted that it is beyond the scope of specific programs to eliminate it. It has to be resolved at the slow pace of generational social change in East and West. At the end of the next two decades, although NATO and the Warsaw Pact will endure, although billions may be spent on new weapons systems, and although Europe will continue to be divided by a line going through Germany, it is likely that Europe will be a safer place, both for itself and as a factor in world politics.

Index